Praise for *Come Forth*

"James Martin—arguably our greatest writer priest—has penned a genius meditation on the Raising of Lazarus. It's a travel story and a spiritual manual to renewing one's faith. Destined to be read and reread forever. Bravo!"

—Mary Karr, author of *The Liars' Club* and *Lit: A Memoir*

"This is as soul-nourishing a book as I have read in a long time. Highly recommended."

—Ben Witherington III, Amos Professor of New Testament of Doctoral Studies, Asbury Theological Seminary

"God calls each of us into a new life, inviting us to leave behind whatever is dead. But how? James Martin's magnificent new book on the Raising of Lazarus shows us! *Come Forth* is a spiritual masterpiece."

—Richard Rohr, OFM, author of *The Universal Christ*

"James Martin has written an expansive meditative exposition on the narrative of the raising of Lazarus from the dead, Jesus's "greatest miracle." Beyond the complexity of critical study and the obscurity of historical data, this book is a pastoral summons into a world of grace-filled honesty."

—Walter Brueggemann, author of *The Prophetic Imagination*

"James Martin's *Come Forth* is a significant example of an honest and healthy interpretation of a biblical text. A must read for all searching for examples of the ongoing relevance of the Word of God in contemporary Christian life and practice."

—Francis J. Moloney, SDB, author of the *Sacra Pagina* commentary on the Gospel of John

"From historical investigation to literary and artistic imaginings, Martin guides readers from despair to hope and from shame to acceptance. A magnificent, moving spiritual journey."

—Amy-Jill Levine, Professor of New Testament Studies Emerita, Vanderbilt University author of *The Misunderstood Jew*

"*Come Forth* is a marvel: deeply researched, judicious in its analysis and opinions, and yet friendly and highly personal. We read the Gospels for illumination, consolation, direction, and inspiration, and in James Martin's fascinating study of Lazarus we find them all."

—Ron Hansen, author of *Mariette in Ecstasy*

"Reading *Come Forth* is like being led by a guide who takes you through the art, the history, the Scripture, until you arrive at the place he had in mind: the understanding that the story of Lazarus reveals Jesus the God/Man: the God who raised from the dead, the man who weeps with and for his friends."

—Mary Gordon, author of *Final Payments* and *Joan of Arc*

"One of life's joys is to read a compelling book, a "page turner," as they say. Those who have the pleasure of reading Father James Martin's book *Come Forth* will discover one of life's joys! Happy page turning as you read this spiritual gem!"

—Archbishop John C. Wester, Archbishop of Santa Fe

"James Martin has drawn from the story told in John 11 a wealth of reflections of a spiritual and pastoral nature."

—Brendan Byrne, SJ, Emeritus Professor of
New Testament, University of Divinity,
Melbourne, Australia

"*Come Forth* reflects on the grief, compassion, and glory that surround Jesus's suffering and action in the face of the death of his beloved friend Lazarus. Probing the profound spiritual and emotional dimensions of Christ's experience at this pivotal moment of the Gospel, Father James Martin brings profound insight to the themes of faith, betrayal, wonder, misunderstanding, and questioning that touch us all in our journeys here on this earth."

—Cardinal Robert McElroy, Bishop of San Diego

COME
FORTH

THE PROMISE OF JESUS'S
GREATEST MIRACLE

JAMES
MARTIN, SJ

HarperOne
An Imprint of HarperCollins*Publishers*

Imprimi Potest: Very Rev. Joseph M. O'Keefe, SJ

HarperCollins books may be purchased for educational, business, or sales promotional use. For information, please email the Special Markets Department at SPsales@harpercollins.com.

FIRST EDITION

Designed by Nancy Singer

Library of Congress Cataloging-in-Publication Data is available upon request.

ISBN 978-0-06-269438-6

23 24 25 26 27 LBC 5 4 3 2 1

For my mother,
Eleanor Spano Martin

Contents

CONTENTS

CONTENTS

The Raising of Lazarus

The Gospel of John (11:1–44)

(New Revised Standard Version)

[1]Now a certain man was ill, Lazarus of Bethany, the village of Mary and her sister Martha. [2]Mary was the one who anointed the Lord with perfume and wiped his feet with her hair; her brother Lazarus was ill. [3]So the sisters sent a message to Jesus, "Lord, he whom you love is ill." [4]But when Jesus heard it, he said, "This illness does not lead to death; rather it is for God's glory, so that the Son of God may be glorified through it." [5]Accordingly, though Jesus loved Martha and her sister and Lazarus, [6]after having heard that Lazarus was ill, he stayed two days longer in the place where he was.

[7]Then after this he said to the disciples, "Let us go to Judea again." [8]The disciples said to him, "Rabbi, the Jews were just now trying to stone you, and are you going there again?" [9]Jesus answered, "Are there not twelve hours of daylight? Those who walk during the day do not stumble, because they see the light of this world. [10]But those who walk at night stumble, because the light is not in them." [11]After saying this, he told them, "Our friend Lazarus has fallen asleep, but I am going there to awaken him." [12]The disciples said to him, "Lord, if he has fallen asleep, he will be all right." [13]Jesus, however, had been speaking about his death, but they thought that he was referring merely to sleep. [14]Then Jesus told them plainly, "Lazarus is dead. [15]For your sake I am glad I was not there, so that you may believe. But let us go to him." [16]Thomas, who was called the Twin, said to his fellow disciples, "Let us also go, that we may die with him."

[17]When Jesus arrived, he found that Lazarus had already been in the tomb four days. [18]Now Bethany was near Jerusalem, some two miles away, [19]and many of the Jews had come to Martha and Mary to console them about their brother. [20]When Martha heard that Jesus was coming, she went and met him, while Mary stayed at home. [21]Martha said to Jesus, "Lord, if you had been here, my brother would not have died. [22]But even now I

know that God will give you whatever you ask of him." [23]Jesus said to her, "Your brother will rise again." [24]Martha said to him, "I know that he will rise again in the resurrection on the last day." [25]Jesus said to her, "I am the resurrection and the life. Those who believe in me, even though they die, will live, [26]and everyone who lives and believes in me will never die. Do you believe this?" [27]She said to him, "Yes, Lord, I believe that you are the Messiah, the Son of God, the one coming into the world."

[28]When she had said this, she went back and called her sister Mary, and told her privately, "The Teacher is here and is calling for you." [29]And when she heard it, she got up quickly and went to him. [30]Now Jesus had not yet come to the village, but was still at the place where Martha had met him. [31]The Jews who were with her in the house, consoling her, saw Mary get up quickly and go out. They followed her because they thought that she was going to the tomb to weep there. [32]When Mary came where Jesus was and saw him, she knelt at his feet and said to him, "Lord, if you had been here, my brother would not have died." [33]When Jesus saw her weeping, and the Jews who came with her also weeping, he was greatly disturbed in spirit and deeply moved. [34]He said, "Where have you laid him?" They said to him, "Lord, come and see." [35]Jesus began to weep. [36]So the Jews said, "See how he loved him!" [37]But some of them said, "Could not he who opened the eyes of the blind man have kept this man from dying?"

[38]Then Jesus, again greatly disturbed, came to the tomb. It was a cave, and a stone was lying against it. [39]Jesus said, "Take away the stone." Martha, the sister of the dead man, said to him, "Lord, already there is a stench because he has been dead for four days." [40]Jesus said to her, "Did I not tell you that if you believed, you would see the glory of God?" [41]So they took away the stone. And Jesus looked upwards and said, "Father, I thank you for having heard me. [42]I knew that you always hear me, but I have said this for the sake of the crowd standing here, so that they may believe that you sent me." [43]When he had said this, he cried with a loud voice, "Lazarus, come out!" [44]The dead man came out, his hands and feet bound with strips of cloth, and his face wrapped in a cloth. Jesus said to them, "Unbind him, and let him go."

1

Al Eizariya

An Introduction

Today the town is known by its Arabic name, which is variously transliterated as El Azariyeh, Al Eizariya, El Azariya, or simply Azariya. They mean the same thing: "the Place of Lazarus." In Jesus's time, the town, now in Palestinian territory outside Jerusalem, was called in Greek *Bēthania*; in English, it is known as Bethany.

It is the site of the Gospel story known as the Raising of Lazarus, in which Jesus raises from the dead a man named Lazarus, who had been shut away in his tomb for several days. Before his death, the

Pilgrims wait outside the Tomb of Lazarus, Al Eizariya, Israel.
COURTESY OF THE AUTHOR

man had lived with his two sisters, Martha and Mary, in their house in Bethany, where Jesus would find respite from his busy public ministry in nearby Jerusalem. Lazarus's story—which is also his sisters' story and Jesus's story—is the reason that, more than two thousand years later, pilgrims still visit Al Eizariya. It is also the reason for this book.

The etymology of the town's original name is complicated. It could mean "House of Affliction" or even "House of Figs" (or dates). Aramaic-speaking tour guides in Israel sometime opt for Beth'anya, "House of the Poor." An almshouse may have been in the town, or the town may have been where sick people and their families lived.

Some scholars have posited that Bethany, perched on a limestone ridge on the Mount of Olives, was one of the three villages located east of Jerusalem that are mentioned in the Temple Scroll, one of the ancient Dead Sea Scrolls found at the archaeological site at Qumran.[1] According to the Temple Scroll, these villages had to be three thousand cubits from the Temple. Evidently, they served as places for the ritually impure (including those with leprosy and other skin ailments) to wait until they attained ritual purity and could participate in the Temple ceremonies. Thus, the translation as "House of Affliction."

Reaching Al Eizariya from Jerusalem is more difficult today than in past decades, owing to the twenty-foot-high wall that the Israeli government erected around the Palestinian territories in 2002. The Israelis call it the "security wall," the Palestinians, the "separation wall."

In the past one could walk directly from Al Eizariya to the Old City, the walled enclosure in Jerusalem that is composed of four quarters that reflect ancient history and current tensions: Jewish, Muslim, Christian, and Armenian. One could begin at Al Eizariya, clamber down the steep Mount of Olives, linger at the Garden of Gethsemane, where centuries-old olive trees still bloom, descend into the Kidron Valley, ascend again, and pass through the imposing Lion's Gate in the Old City walls, thus retracing the route Jesus would have taken on Palm Sunday.

But today the path is blocked. To reach Lazarus's tomb you must take a bus that boards at the Damascus Gate, wends around the wall, and threads through the narrow streets of Al Eizariya, a trip of some thirty minutes.

Like many other towns in Palestinian territory, Al Eizariya boasts few amenities and, thanks to ongoing political conflicts with the State of Israel, has neither trash collection nor a working police force. Consequently, trash clots the streets, which nonetheless abound with busy residents visiting the modest shops—butchers, hair-dressing salons, convenience stores—that line the streets.

I was once with a group of pilgrims that entered Al Eizariya by bus. After hearing about the lack of police, one of the pilgrims asked our Palestinian Christian guide, a friendly and savvy man named Maher, what would happen in the event of a car accident. He shrugged his shoulders eloquently. "They have to work it out," he said.

Near the highest point in the town is the Church of St. Lazarus, a twentieth-century structure of Jerusalem stone, the material from which nearly all buildings in Jerusalem are constructed. The creamy white limestone gleams in the bright sunlight, making the city shine on both sunny and cloudy days.

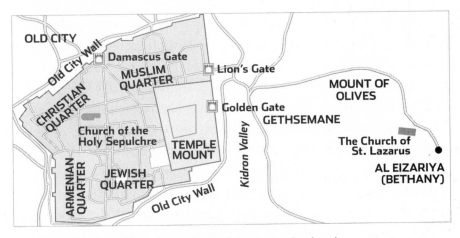

Map of Jerusalem and Al Eizariya (Bethany).
ALLISON HAMILTON AND SHAWN TRIPOLI

The church was designed by Antonio Barluzzi, an Italian architect and favorite of Benito Mussolini who built several structures in the Holy Land, including the Church of the Beatitudes by the Sea of Galilee, the spot where tradition claims Jesus preached the Sermon on the Mount; and the Church of All Nations near the Garden of Gethsemane, where Jesus prayed on the evening before his crucifixion. (The term "Holy Land" refers to the area of Christian pilgrimage that includes the modern State of Israel, the Palestinian territories, western Jordan, as well as parts of southern Lebanon and southwestern Syria.)

The squarish interior of the Church of St. Lazarus, largely unadorned, is filled with hard, straight-backed, wooden pews. Its remarkable acoustics mean that even poorly sung hymns resonate. Every time I've been inside, even on the warmest days, it's been cold. I'm not sure that the interior ever gets warm.

Over the altar is a brightly colored semicircular mosaic depicting the Gospel passage that recounts what happened here more than two thousand years ago. Mary and Martha, two of Jesus's closest friends, send word to Jesus that their brother is ill. After receiving news of his friend's illness, Jesus waits several days before coming to their town. In the interim, Lazarus dies.

In dazzling colors, the mosaic shows the moment when Jesus arrived in Bethany. One sister, wearing a sky-blue robe over a red tunic, falls to her knees, hands outstretched, in awe of their friend, who wears a white tunic and a yellow cloak, his body surrounded by a golden halo. The other sister, in a yellow robe and pale green veil, stands with hands clasped in prayer. On either side, disciples in oranges, pinks, and greens gesture to the central figure of the mosaic: Jesus.

As John's Gospel recounts the story, Martha initially scolds Jesus about his delay: "Lord, if you had been here," she says, "my brother would not have died." In response, Jesus asks Martha if she believes in the resurrection. Yes, she says. She knows that people will be raised up "on the last day," a commonly held Jewish belief at the time.

Jesus's answer is written, in Latin, at the bottom of the mosaic in gold letters:

EGO SUM RESURRECTIO ET VITA
I am the Resurrection and the Life.

In a modest stone courtyard outside the church, pilgrims from around the world gather to listen to explanations from tour guides about this Gospel passage, the church, and the town. Small signs describe the long history of the place. Cats prowl around.

Crowds here are smaller than those at other Holy Land sites such as the Church of the Nativity (celebrating where Christians believe Jesus was born) or the Church of the Holy Sepulchre (celebrating where they believe Jesus died), where pilgrims sometimes stand shoulder to shoulder for hours waiting to enter the holy sites. But here, there is often no one in either the church or the courtyard. The church's location, in Palestinian territory, makes access more difficult and, some pilgrims think, more dangerous. When I ask people who have been pilgrims to the Holy Land if they visited the Tomb of Lazarus, they often say, "Our tour guides said it was too dangerous," or, most commonly, with some surprise, "You can visit Lazarus's Tomb? It's still there?"

Mosaic of Jesus's arrival in Bethany, Church of St. Lazarus, Al Eizariya.
COURTESY OF CATHOLIC TRAVEL CENTRE

A few feet away, at the top of a gentle incline, is a pocket-size garden with succulents and bird-of-paradise plants, enclosed by a gate. Outside the gate are broad steps leading up a hill. The low stone steps enable less nimble tourists to ascend the incline, which leads from the church all the way up to the separation wall.

Near the top of the steps, on the left-hand side, is a stone structure with a door. Atop the stone structure is the prayer tower of a mosque, whose origins date back to the fifteenth century. In the sixteenth century, the Ottomans built the larger al-Uzair mosque, named after Lazarus. Access to the lower level is through a passage cut into the side of the mosque. A weathered orange metal sign affixed to the building points to a small doorway and says in blocky black letters, in Hebrew, Arabic, and apostrophe-less English, "Lazarus Tomb."

Ascending the steps to the Tomb of Lazarus.
COURTESY OF THE AUTHOR

Why Lazarus?

My first visit to Al Eizariya was ten years ago. I had gone to Israel for pilgrimage and research, for a spiritual journey and for preparation for a book on the life of Jesus Christ. A Jesuit friend named George was my travel companion for two weeks. We visited the usual sites that Christian pilgrims have frequented for two millennia, places that even the most lapsed of Christians have heard of: Bethlehem, Nazareth, Jerusalem, the Sea of Galilee.

Initially, I hadn't planned on going to the Holy Land at all. Why travel so far to a place that I had (wrongly) suspected would feel dangerous? Besides, as a Jesuit, I had read about, prayed over, and studied the Gospels for decades. What more could a single trip teach me? Moreover, I didn't want my mental images of these sites "ruined" by the real-life places, which I assumed (wrongly in most cases) would prove too touristy.

But Drew Christiansen, a Jesuit scholar and the editor in chief of *America* magazine at the time, urged me. Drew was an expert on Jewish-Christian relations and had been to Israel many times. "You can't write a book on the life of Christ and not know something about where he lived," said Drew. There is a reason, he said, that the Holy Land is often called the "Fifth Gospel," the Gospel that "opens up" the stories in Matthew, Mark, Luke, and John.

So I went, and the easiest way to explain what happened was that the difference between my expectation and my experience was vast. My expectation? That it would be "interesting" and that I would "learn a lot." That's what I told everyone who asked. My experience? That it was life changing to stand where Jesus stood, walk where Jesus walked, and see what Jesus saw.

You might raise an eyebrow at that last statement. How could anyone know where Jesus walked or what he saw? Well, we don't know the precise locations of many of the Gospel stories. Where did he cure the "woman with the hemorrhage"? Who knows? Somewhere near the shoreline of the Sea of Galilee, but we don't know the exact spot. Where did he preach the Sermon on the Mount? Today you can visit the Mount of Beatitudes, also by the Sea of Galilee, but it could just as easily have been another hillside.

But for other stories, we do know the spot. Jerusalem has always been in the same location. So when you're "going up" to Jerusalem, as the psalms say, you know that you're ascending the same incline that Jesus and his disciples ascended on their journeys there. There is even a series of stone steps leading from the Mount of Olives to the Old City, dating from the time of Jesus, which he and the disciples most likely used. Ditto for Nazareth: it's still there, nestled in the same valley as it was when Jesus lived there as a boy and young adult. The Sea of Galilee: still there. It's the same body of water (a lake, really, not a "sea"), and Jesus saw it. Sailed on it and walked on it, too. There are myriad places in the Holy Land where we can say with complete certainty, "Jesus was here."

Another place that Jesus surely visited was Bethany, high on the list of sites I wanted to visit. I had long been transfixed by the story of Lazarus. But why?

My mother asked me that question when I told her what my next book would be about: "Why Lazarus?" So did many friends, Christians and Catholics, as well as my Jesuit brothers. "Lazarus? Really?" A look on their faces seemed to say, "I know the story and I like it well enough, but a whole book?"

It's best to answer that question straightaway. The story of the Raising of Lazarus, traditionally called Jesus's "greatest miracle" (which is unintentionally risible—as if there were a contest among his miracles), has always exerted a tremendous hold on me.

I can't remember when I first heard the tale of the sisters sending word to Jesus about their dying brother, about Jesus's seemingly inexplicable delay in coming, about their falling at his feet (either rebuking him or pleading with him), about his prayer at the tomb, and about his restoration to life of the man who is called, mysteriously, "he whom you love."

As a boy in suburban Philadelphia who went to Mass most Sundays, I surely heard the passage, which comes midway through the Gospel of John, proclaimed from the pulpit. The Raising of Lazarus occupies an exalted place in the church's calendar of readings: it is heard in churches around the world on the final Sunday of the Lenten season, before Palm Sunday. As far as I can remember, though, hearing it did not make much of an impression on me.

But seeing it did.

Meeting Lazarus on TV

As an adolescent, I was transfixed by a six-hour miniseries called *Jesus of Nazareth*, directed by Franco Zeffirelli, which premiered on television in 1977 and was shown every year around Easter for the next decade or so. Sometimes it popped up around Christmas, too. This visual interpretation of the Gospels shaped my understanding of Jesus in a way that nothing else had. I didn't go to Catholic schools, was a desultory Sunday school student, and took no courses on religion (much less on the Bible) in college. So, for a while Zeffirelli's story of Jesus was the story of Jesus that lived in my imagination. Long before I studied theology, it was my "Introduction to the New Testament."

And for me, the scene depicting the Raising of Lazarus was the movie's undisputed highlight, greater even than the Resurrection in its influence on my sixteen-year-old imagination.

I would later discover that the Italian director had worked closely with several prominent New Testament scholars, including William Barclay, a Church of Scotland minister and author of *The New Daily Study Bible*, a superb biblical commentary, to get the story right—though unaccountably, Mary Magdalene is incorrectly portrayed as a prostitute. The boy Jesus is also, absurdly, blond-haired and blue-eyed. Overall, though, many lines come verbatim from the Gospels. Some scenes subtly mimic classic works of art as well. In the scene depicting the Visitation, where a pregnant Mary visits her cousin Elizabeth in the "hill country of Judea," the women are framed by two graceful arches, mirroring paintings by Fra Angelico of the Annunciation.

In Zeffirelli's rich interpretation of the story of Lazarus, a man on horseback races to find Jesus and, upon meeting him, announces that Lazarus is "near death." Jesus promises that he will come. There is a cut to the next scene, in which Martha rushes to greet Jesus and then throws her arms around him tightly. "Lord, Lord," she says, as the disciples look on. "If you had been with us, my brother would not have died." Then she professes her faith in him and takes him to the tomb.

At the tomb, her sister Mary rebukes him for his absence. "I prayed and prayed for you to arrive!" she says. "You could have kept Lazarus from dying!" Jesus says, "Take away the stone," as the music builds.

Jesus walks to the tomb, depicted as a cave in the desert. (Much of the film was shot in Tunisia and Morocco, so the cinematic Judean landscape looks suitably dry and barren.)

Now seen from inside the tomb, Jesus stands outside, as the crowd watches him intently from the ridge of a cliff. His disciples stand a few feet away as he kneels. Suddenly Jesus looks up and begins to pray, almost in a whisper.

Then Jesus stands, extends his arms, and shouts, "Lazarus, come *forth!*"

A wide shot shows Jesus in front of the tomb as a tiny figure emerges from the inky darkness. As the music swells, the crowd goes mad. Then comes a close shot of Lazarus bound tightly in long strips of cloth.

Jesus says, "He that believes in me, but he were dead, yet shall he live."

I'm not sure what it was that so captivated me as a sixteen-year-old who knew almost nothing about the New Testament, watching in my family's recreation room in suburban Philadelphia. Perhaps it was Jesus's calm in the face of death, his assurance in his own power and ability to change lives with just a few words. As a young person, searching for certainty and cures for what seemed like in-surmountable problems (I was a teenager, remember), I loved the idea of a Jesus who could do *anything*. And that scene raised so many questions, ones that stayed with me for decades: Why did he wait to go to Bethany? Who were these two women who spoke to Jesus so bluntly? What would it have been like to have been in his presence? And who was Lazarus anyway?

Whenever I picture the scene, it is this interpretation that I return to, which was engraved into my memory as a teenager. Sometimes I even hear the music.

My love for the story, my fascination with it, deepened over time. The themes are almost too rich: the universality of grief, the difficulty of belief, and the power of Jesus in the face of both. In terms of drama, I find it unmatched in the Gospels. In terms of storytelling, I think it is a masterpiece. In terms of faith, I believe it to be essential. I have prayed with it during retreats, have listened to (and preached) countless homilies about it, and have read many books about it ever since I saw Zeffirelli's film.

So I had to go to Bethany.

The Site

In his superb book *The Holy Land*, a tour guide cum history book, the New Testament scholar and archaeologist Jerome Murphy-O'Connor examines all the sites of interest to Christian pilgrims. His book was a boon for George and me on my first trip, and I carried it everywhere we went, along with a copy of the New Testament. Other than the Bible itself, Murphy-O'Connor's *Holy Land* was our bible.

Father Murphy-O'Connor, a Dominican priest, is refreshingly blunt about which sites have no basis in fact, which ones are doubtful, and which are authentic. About Al Eizariya, he writes simply, "There is no problem about its identification." Then he lays out the evidence: "A village on the main Jericho Road fits the distance from Jerusalem given in John 11:18, and its Arabic name el-Azariyeh

Al Eizariya, with the Church of St. Lazarus in the foreground.
COURTESY OF CATHOLIC TRAVEL CENTRE

preserves the Greek *Lazarion,* 'the place of Lazarus,' by which it was known to Eusebius (330) and all subsequent Byzantine and medieval pilgrims."[2] Moreover, in the area was a cemetery, and tombs have been found north of the current-day church. Today's Al Eizariya, we can be certain, is Jesus's Bethany.

The first evidence of this site as a place of worship dates from the fourth century, in the writings of both Eusebius of Caesarea, an early church historian, and the anonymous "Pilgrim of Bordeaux," whose *Itinerarium Burdigalense* ("Bordeaux Itinerary") is one of the earliest known records of a Christian pilgrimage. Both Eusebius and the Pilgrim of Bordeaux locate the crypt where Lazarus was laid to rest on this spot on the Mount of Olives.

Between roughly 330 and 387, the first church was built, a structure mentioned by St. Jerome, an early church theologian who lived and worked in Bethlehem at the time. The first church was destroyed by an earthquake, according to Murphy-O'Connor. Mosaics from that church, however, still survive.

A second church was built in the sixth century, roughly over the location of the original church, though the apse was moved some forty-three feet to the east. The extra space was needed, according to Egeria, a fourth-century pilgrim who kept a record for women in her spiritual community, because "so many people have collected that they fill not only the Lazarium itself [the church], but all the fields around."[3] In 680, a bishop named Arculf described a large basilica with a monastery attached. (Some of the most important historical documents about the Holy Land in those days are pilgrims' journals.)

In the Byzantine era, Bethany remained an important "liturgical center," as one plaque at the site notes, especially after Palm Sunday processions began there in the ninth and tenth centuries. Between 1106 and 1107, a Russian abbot named Daniel visited the site, calling Bethany a "little country town situated in a valley." He provided a detailed description of the site of Lazarus's burial:

> On entering the gate of the town one sees to the right a cavern, in which is the tomb of Lazarus; there was also the cell where he fell ill and died. There is a large high church in the middle of this town which was richly ornamented with paintings. . . . The sepulchre of Lazarus . . . is west of the church, while the church itself is toward the east.[4]

In 1143 Queen Melisende of Jerusalem (a woman of Frankish descent) completed the construction of an abbey at the site for a community of Benedictine nuns. Her sister Iveta became abbess in 1157. These ruins are also visible today.

By the end of the fourteenth century, according to Murphy-O'Connor, the church and monastery were in ruins, and the original entrance to the tomb was part of a mosque.

Between 1566 and 1575 the Franciscans cut the present entrance to the tomb. In the fourteenth century, the Vatican had given the Franciscan Order authority over all the Catholic holy sites in the general region known as the Holy Land. Their presence is officially known as the "Custody of the Holy Land," and the director of this ministry is the "Custos," or Custodian.

The Franciscans trace their own presence in the area to 1217, the year that the first "General Chapter," or general assembly, of the Franciscans took place near Assisi, Italy. At that meeting St. Francis of Assisi was inspired to send his friars around the globe and entrusted the Holy Land to the care of his fellow friar, Brother Elias. Two years later, St. Francis himself visited the Holy Land; in the following centuries the Franciscans established communities in both Jerusalem and Bethlehem. Today the brown Franciscan habit is a familiar sight to pilgrims, appearing at almost every Catholic church and holy site.

In 1863 the Custody of the Holy Land began archaeological excavations in Bethany, which brought to light several of the ancient structures just mentioned. In 1952 they invited Antonio Barluzzi to build the church that pilgrims see today.

The Tomb of Lazarus, just up the incline from the church, carved out of the soft rock of the Mount of Olives, is cared for by a Muslim man. This is no surprise because this is a Muslim city in Palestinian territory. He runs a jam-packed souvenir shop on the small concrete plaza by the tomb, which stocks all manner of beautiful icons, scarves, holy cards, sculptures, and even umbrellas.

A few years ago, I escorted about a dozen pilgrims into his shop. They purchased so many souvenirs that the shop owner gave me,

The Church of St. Lazarus, Al Eizariya,
with mosaics of Lazarus and his sisters Martha and Mary.
COURTESY OF DANIEL CUESTA, SJ

despite my protests, a small icon of the Raising of Lazarus, complete with a tiny glass bubble containing dirt from the Holy Land, which now hangs over my desk in my bedroom.

It is the traditional depiction of the scene in Eastern icons, set in a rocky, almost mountainous setting, the tomb to the right, the buildings of Jerusalem in the background. Lazarus's sisters, clad in black, kneel at Jesus's feet. One kisses his feet. Behind Jesus are the disciples. On one side, a man covers his mouth with a cloth, because of the stench from the open tomb. Lazarus, still bound in his white burial cloths, looks stunned. Above the scene in red lettering is the Greek inscription: *He Egersis tou Lazarou*, the Raising of Lazarus.

Today a heavy metal door covers the tomb's entrance, which is unlocked by a key in the care of the shopkeeper. The door opens onto a long, narrow, curving stone staircase leading to the dark subterranean cavity that is the tomb.

A painting by James Tissot, a French artist who spent years in the Holy Land in the late nineteenth century, depicts the tomb as it appears today. A flight of steps leads down to a vestibule (where early pilgrims believed Jesus stood). Three more steps connect the vestibule to the inner square chamber, which originally contained three funeral niches for bodies. Early traditions linked the niche on the right, the northern side, with that of Lazarus.

In Tissot's painting, Martha and Mary have descended the staircase with Jesus, who has just raised Lazarus. He climbs out, like a butterfly emerging from its chrysalis, into the small antechamber. In fact, the tomb may have been closer to ground level; its current subterranean location is likely the result of structures built atop one another over the centuries. Still, Tissot's representation—the stairs, the colors, the complex layout of the tomb—is amazingly accurate.

No matter what time of year, or how wet or dry it is outside, the stone steps leading down to the tomb are always slippery. Curved, uneven, unstable in places, they bring pilgrims to the place where Lazarus, dead after several days of suffering, was laid by his sisters,

The Resurrection of Lazarus, by James Tissot (Brooklyn Museum). Tissot's painting shows with remarkable accuracy the current-day layout of the tomb in Al Eizariya.
WIKICOMMONS

and where he heard Jesus offering him the promise of new life. Metal guardrails bolted into the stone walls offer a modicum of support. Because of the treacherous steps, you must descend slowly.

Visiting for the First Time

I first visited Al Eizariya during my initial pilgrimage, when George and I stayed at the Pontifical Biblical Institute, a Jesuit community and school in Jerusalem. (Its headquarters are in Rome.) One morning we decided to split up: he went to Yad Vashem, the World Holocaust Remembrance Center, and I went to Bethany.

Along with a German Jesuit named Stefan and a Portuguese diocesan priest named Domingo, who were visiting the PBI that week, I took the bus from the Damascus Gate, one of the main gates in the walls that surround the Old City. The bus stop was only a few minutes from our Jesuit community.

We quickly passed from the relative wealth of Jerusalem to the poverty of Al Eizariya. The rattletrap bus was packed with Palestinians chatting merrily—women in hijabs, men in keffiyehs—as the wheels bumped over the city streets. We exited the bus some distance away from the church and the tomb and made our way through streets with shuttered shops, men sitting on old stools, chatting and smoking, and children running around, playing.

Stefan, Domingo, and I caught sight of the Church of St. Lazarus easily enough, and we made our way up the broad steps to the tomb. Here's how I described my first visit in *Jesus: A Pilgrimage*. (Better to rely on memory closer to that time.)

I peered into the dimly lit tomb and tentatively started my climb down the stairs. When I imagined this pilgrimage, I had expected that the Tomb of Lazarus, the site of Jesus's greatest miracle, would be one of the most crowded of sites. But I was alone.

Even lit, the narrow stone stairwell was dim. As I descended, my footsteps echoed against the damp walls. In a few seconds I was in a small chamber, where there was barely enough room to stand. Perhaps, I thought, this was the tomb. But on one side of the room, cut into the wall was a small opening near the ground, perhaps three feet wide by four feet high. This opening led into another chamber: the tomb. To enter I had to get down on my hands and knees and crawl through the tight space.

Standing up in the small, dark, grayish-green stone tomb, I wondered what it was like for Lazarus to hear Jesus's voice. What must it have meant to decide to "come out"? Lazarus could have stayed behind. And who could blame him? How frightening it must have been to die after his illness, knowing he would leave behind two unmarried sisters, crushed that his good friend Jesus had not visited. And frightening to live again. Change of any kind can be frightening.

I knelt down again in the tomb and prayed out loud. No need to be embarrassed now. Who would hear me except God? I asked

God to take away everything that kept me from becoming the person God wanted me to be. And I asked God for new life.

My voice echoed in the dim stone chamber.

Then I left the tomb.

My first visit was fast, moving, and fascinating, leaving me hungry to know even more about what happened here.

Our Journey

This book is a meditation on what happened two thousand years ago in Al Eizariya. I hope to lead you through the story of the Raising of Lazarus, as recounted in John's Gospel (the only Gospel in which it appears), and reflect on what it might say to us today—about love, friendship, family, faith, prayer, sadness, frustration, fear, anger, freedom, joy, hope, death, and life.

Overall, I believe that the story of Lazarus can help us to let go of whatever prevents our coming closer to God, to experience fresh ways of living, and, most of all, to experience new life. His story can help us reflect more deeply on the ways that Jesus frees us from all that keeps us bound, from all that keeps us unfree, from all that keeps us from walking into the sunlight. Lazarus's story helps us understand what it means to hear God say to us, "Come forth!"

My aim is to combine analysis of the biblical text, spiritual insights drawn from each passage, facts about the historical setting of the story, and appearances of Lazarus in the larger culture with reflections on experiences from my own life to help you enter more deeply into this story and, most of all, to help you encounter God there. It is an invitation into Lazarus's life, into his tomb, and into new life.

We will move through the story passage by passage, pausing on specific words, phrases, and themes to help you understand its message better. It is the longest continuous narrative in the Gospel of John outside the Passion narrative and, as we'll soon see, is told with what the biblical scholar C. H. Dodd calls an "unusual elaboration of detail."[5] As we journey through the story, I'll refer to Bible commentaries and include insights from some contemporary New Testament scholars, and even use some Greek from time to time. But you don't need to be a scholar to follow along.

Why unpack the story passage by passage, sometimes sentence by sentence? Because a "close read," as scholars say, of Jesus's greatest miracle can help us see things that we might otherwise miss if we simply focus on the overall message of the passage. If you hear this reading preached about during a funeral service (where it is a go-to reading for obvious reasons), you'll hear about Jesus's power over death and, if you're lucky, the sisters' ability to be honest with Jesus about their frustration and their faith.

But the narrative has much more to offer. Buried (no pun intended) in this story are insights on friendship and love, on work and prayer, on hope and despair, as well as on more specific topics like the tragic history of anti-Semitism and anti-Judaism and the role of women in the early church. A "close read" will also reveal some surprises about this otherwise familiar Gospel passage, especially regarding who Lazarus really was.

To be clear: I'll talk about what happened to Lazarus and his sisters from the vantage point of faith. I take Jesus at his word and believe that he is the "Resurrection and the Life." But you don't need to be a devout Christian to join me in this journey. You need only open yourself to this transformative story and trust that God can use it to free you from whatever keeps you bound, just as God has used it to free me and countless other Christians.

We'll use the insights of contemporary biblical scholarship, but I'll also invite you to see things from a more "spiritual" point of view. As with my earlier book, *Jesus: A Pilgrimage*, each chapter will include some Bible study, some spiritual reflections, and some travel narrative.

The primary goal of this book is not to turn you into a New Testament scholar or an expert in the topography of Al Eizariya.

It is to help you encounter God, who wishes to give you new life, in this case through this Gospel passage. The Bible is often described as the "Living Word," and we are invited to encounter God whenever we read, hear, or meditate on the Bible. At the end of each chapter, reflection questions will help point out and invite you to explore the spiritual import of what we have been discussing.

Lazarus's place in Christian culture around the world will also be part of our journey. We'll look at the various legends about what happened after Lazarus was raised from the dead (was he assassinated in Judea? or did he go to France with his sisters? or Cyprus?), the cathedrals that purport to have his relics, the liturgical celebrations in the Eastern churches called Lazarus Saturday (with some unusual Lazarus-themed baked goods), and a religious order dedicated to him with a fascinating history.

We'll also reflect on what the various artistic representations of the man—in fine art, literature, and poetry, as well as in novels, plays, and films—can tell us about his enduring appeal. Lazarus, at some point, died after he had been raised from the dead (more about that later), but in a sense he's been kept alive all these years in religious and popular culture.

I also invite you to think of reading this book as responding to a call. That may sound strange, but something within you made you want to read a book about Lazarus. You may have picked up this book (or downloaded it) for several reasons. Maybe you've read the story of Lazarus before and found that it held some attraction for you, perhaps an appeal that you don't understand. Maybe someone close to you has died and you've been thinking about what it would be like to have that person back in your life. Maybe in some way you long for "new life." Or maybe you've read some of my other books and wondered, "Why is he focusing on Lazarus?" Or maybe you just liked the image on the cover!

Whatever the reasons, within you is a longing to know more about Lazarus's story. I invite you to see in that not simple curiosity but a way that God is at work in you. I encourage you to trust that your desire to know more about Lazarus, and to experience new life, is an invitation from God, a call. For how else would God call you to experience new life other than by planting this desire within you? Your desire to know more about Lazarus and to experience new life is God's desire within you. As you read this book, then, be aware of the ways that God is calling you. Notice what you find interesting, what appeals to you, and what surprises or even repels you. What is God asking you to notice? To reflect on? To act upon, based on what you have discovered? See the reading of this book not only as a conversation between you and me, but far more importantly between you and God.

Into the Tomb

Each year on the pilgrimage to the Holy Land run by America Media, the visit to the Tomb of Lazarus, which comes on the first day of our stay in Jerusalem, proves a powerful moment for many pilgrims. Before we arrive, we invite the pilgrims to think about what they would most like to "leave behind" in the tomb. What grudge, resentment, or painful memory would they like to "let die" there? Where do they most want to hear Jesus say "Come forth!" and invite them into the light? Where do they most need to experience new life?

Pilgrims are often unsettled, challenged, and inspired by the convergence of these factors: the drama of the Gospel story; the setting in unfamiliar Palestinian territory; the physical challenge of descending the slippery staircase; the fear of entering a dark, ancient, unknown space; and the near-universal desire to leave behind something painful. Often pilgrims are frightened to go down. But usually they stay there longer than they expected. Some emerge in tears.

A few years ago, I stood at the doorway with a few others to help people out of the tomb, offering them a hand to steady them as they navigated their way up the final few steps and crossed the threshold. You must duck your head to exit the doorway.

One man grabbed my hand as he emerged.

"Leaving the tomb is hard!" he said. "But so is going in!"

The stairs descending into the Tomb of Lazarus.
COURTESY OF CATHOLIC TRAVEL CENTRE

Journeying into the place of letting go can be difficult. With this book I hope to be your guide down that staircase, into the tomb, and then back out into the light.

For Your Reflection

1. What prompted you to read this book?
2. What's your own favorite Bible story? Why?
3. When you hear the name "Lazarus," what comes to mind? Before we begin our journey, who is Lazarus for you? Be attentive to how he changes for you throughout the book.
4. At this point, what would you most like to "leave behind" in the tomb?
5. As you begin this book, can you ask God for the grace to be open to whatever God wants to reveal to you?

2

A Certain Man

Did Lazarus Exist?

Now a certain man was ill, Lazarus of Bethany,
the village of Mary and her sister Martha.

I'm not alone in my fascination with Lazarus. Thousands of Christian pilgrims visit the tomb in Al Eizariya every year. Moreover, the story of Jesus's supreme miracle has been the subject of countless paintings, sculptures, mosaics, books (both fiction and nonfiction), plays, poems, sermons, songs, and movies. And no wonder. Visually, it is one of the most dramatic of the Gospel miracles: the dead man emerging into the sunlight from the dark tomb, still bound in his burial cloths, to the shock of his sisters, the disciples, and the crowd. You can almost hear the orchestra swell and the crowd erupt in shouts as he comes out blinking.

The earliest known pictorial depiction of Lazarus, in the fourth-century Catacombs of the Giordani in Rome, shows a beardless youth standing in his tomb before Jesus, who holds a stick or a wand, a common depiction of a miracle worker at the time. Over time, iconographic representations in the East solidified into a common design, as seen in the small icon that I received from the shopkeeper in Al Eizariya: a bandaged Lazarus emerging from a tomb in a craggy hillside on the right, with Jesus and the stunned apostles on the left (see page 279). Since then, he has been the subject of countless other paintings. Giotto, in the early 1300s, shows him pallid and cadaverous, emerging from the tomb, bound tightly, immovable in his grave cloths. Martha and Mary prostrate themselves before Jesus, who stands erect, placid, his hand raised in blessing over the entire scene. The painting now hangs in the Scrovegni Chapel in Padua, Italy (see page 286).

In Juan de Flandes's sixteenth-century painting, now hanging in the Prado, the scene has been moved to just outside a cathedral, somewhere in a nearby garden. Under an arch, men in then-contemporary dress watch as Lazarus emerges from the ground, his skin gray, but his frizzy hair still red. Jesus, clad in a deep blue robe, blesses him as he stands over a skull. The formerly dead man's sister (either Martha or Mary) kneels in a sumptuously brocaded gold dress, her white veil caught in the breeze or perhaps blown back by the presence of Jesus.

Resurrection of Lazarus, Giordani Catacombs,
circa fourth century AD, Rome.
COURTESY OF AKG IMAGES

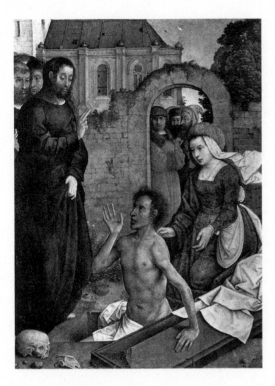

The Raising of Lazarus,
by Juan de Flandes
(Museo del Prado).
WIKICOMMONS

When Sebastiano del Piombo was painting his monumental altarpiece for the cathedral in Narbonne, France, in the 1500s, he turned to his friend Michelangelo to help him with the central figure in the painting, besides Jesus. (This is the image on the cover of this book.) Michelangelo was keen to help Sebastiano on the project because their mutual rival, Raphael, had been commissioned to do another painting for the same church. Now in the British Museum, Michelangelo's red chalk drawing shows a grimacing, bearded man sitting on the lip of his open coffin as two people help him out of the tomb and remove his grave cloths. It is one of the rare portrayals where Lazarus, depicted in a characteristically twisty Michelangelo pose, looks fully alive.

Lazarus would remain a figure of fascination for later painters like Rembrandt, who portrays Jesus standing with a hand raised in a dark setting that vaguely resembles the tomb in Bethany. A sword

The Raising of Lazarus, by Sebastiano del Piombo (National Gallery, London). Michelangelo is responsible for the figure of Lazarus to the right, still wearing his "grave cloths."
WIKICOMMONS

hangs improbably on the wall, and one of the sisters, kneeling at Jesus's feet, looks at her brother as a bright light, its source unknown, illuminates her face. Van Gogh, who called his painting "The Raising of Lazarus (After Rembrandt)," painted the scene in brighter colors, with Lazarus emerging from the tomb into a landscape dominated by a swirling sun, which suffuses the scene with a yellowish green tint. And Henry Ossawa Tanner, in an 1896 painting at the Musée d'Orsay in Paris, places him inside a dark cavity supported by rough-hewn wooden beams. In Tanner's hands Lazarus emerges from a tomb in the ground, as another figure holds his barely conscious head in his hands and a crowd huddles to the side in sepulchral tones of brown and black.

The story of Lazarus, both before and after his raising, is catnip not just for painters but for novelists and playwrights as well. In the Russian writer Leonid Andreyev's harrowing 1906 short story "Lazarus," the raised man appears half-dead, with a bloated, partially decomposed body and a haunted face. Under his eyes lay a "deep and cadaverous blueness," writes Andreyev. Sullen and taciturn, Lazarus is shunned by his neighbors, and rather than representing new life he is seen as a harbinger of death. At the time of the story, his sisters have fled from Bethany. In time, he is summoned by the Divine Augustus, where his countenance strikes terror into the emperor.

In his lengthy poem "Lazarus," from 1920, Edwin Arlington Robinson imagines an extended conversation between the raised man and his sister Mary, who is eager to know what the underworld is like. Brother and sister grapple with the meaning of being brought back from death, and Lazarus asks why Jesus raised him. Was it because he loved him or because he wanted to show a great sign? He wonders about Jesus's feelings toward him: "I heard them saying, Mary, that he wept / Before I woke."

In Kahlil Gibran's only play, *Lazarus and His Beloved*, Lazarus

The Raising of Lazarus, by Henry Ossawa Tanner (Musée d'Orsay, Paris).
WIKICOMMONS

regrets having been raised from the dead. He misses God, "the one my soul loved before time began." He asks: "Why—why—why did you call me from the living heart of eternity to this living death?" (Gibran's play, probably written in the 1920s, was published post-humously in 1973.)

Lazarus makes the same point in William Butler Yeats's short play *Calvary*, from 1921; here he complains of being brought back, apparently against his will:

> But now you will blind with light the solitude
> That death has made; you will disturb that corner
> Where I had thought I might lie safe forever.[1]

Eugene O'Neill, in a seldom-performed 1925 play, *Lazarus Laughed*, also has him visiting an emperor, this time Tiberias, in his villa in Capri. In this allegorical drama, Lazarus laughs when emerging from the tomb and afterward attracts disciples by proclaiming "Death is dead." The conceit of the rather strange play, complete with Greek choruses, is that Lazarus's knowledge of the end of death has freed him from worldly cares, which prompts him to laugh at nearly everything and, as the play progresses, causes him to grow younger and younger. Perhaps the most powerful moment in the drama is Lazarus's first word when emerging from the tomb: "Yes!"

Lazarus makes cameo appearances in many contemporary works. In T. S. Eliot's "The Love Song of J. Alfred Prufrock," one of the most influential modern poems, published in 1915, the nar-rator, a lost and aimless man, uses a variety of classical and biblical references. At one point in "Prufrock," the narrator says:

> Would it have been worth while
>
> . . .
>
> To say: "I am Lazarus, come from the dead,
> Come back to tell you all, I shall tell you all"—

• • •

Prufrock, a quintessentially modern man, adrift and almost deadened by his indecisiveness and impotence, struggles with the question: Is life worth it? Should Lazarus have come back at all? And after he did, could anyone understand him?

A few decades later, Sylvia Plath titled one of her best-known poems "Lady Lazarus," cramming it with allusions to life, death, and resurrection and ending with a description of her own unique resurrection power:

> Out of the ash
> I rise with my red hair
> And I eat men like air.

The raised man makes an appearance, or seems to, in *A Canticle for Lebowitz*, the postapocalyptic science fiction novel by Walter M. Miller Jr. published in 1959. Set in a monastery in the Utah desert, the novel features an enigmatic Hebrew-speaking man who asks to be called "Lazarus" and is on a quest for the man who once shouted to him, "Come forth!" The novel is concerned, perhaps not surprisingly, with rebirth—in this case, of humanity.[2]

More recently, the English novelist Richard Beard's *Lazarus Is Dead* and the American writer Richard Zimler's *The Gospel According to Lazarus* cleverly fill in the gaps of Lazarus's life, death, and raising, with both novels vividly depicting the world of first-century Bethany. In Beard's hands Lazarus is a mournful figure, never fully freed from the experience of death. In Zimler's book he is more high-spirited but still grapples with the magnitude of what Jesus has done for him. In both tales, Lazarus and Jesus knew one another from their youth.

Recently, I asked Beard what made Lazarus such an appealing character for him. "I liked the idea of second chances," he answered, "and then the more I speculated the more I realized that the second chance might not be as uncomplicated as it seemed. In that sense the plight of Lazarus seemed very human." (Speaking of second chances, a relatively new Catholic group based in France brings together young people in community with formerly homeless people. It's called "Lazare.")

Lazarus is a central figure in another contemporary novel by one of my favorite writers, the Irish author Colm Tóibín, *The Testament of Mary*, a finely wrought fictional memoir by Jesus's mother. As in Beard's and Zimler's novels, the families of Jesus and Lazarus are known to one another; here, the two men are relatives. Tóibín's Mary describes Lazarus's rising in vivid detail, often using words taken directly from the Gospels. After emerging from the tomb, Lazarus weeps. For the rest of the novel, he remains largely mute, recovering from his unique ordeal, the object of intense curiosity from others but in most situations "utterly isolated."

The image of Lazarus is commonplace enough to be included in songs meant to appeal to wide audiences, not simply Christian ones. In 2010, the popular British folk-rock band Mumford & Sons

The Healing of the Blind Man and the Raising of Lazarus, twelfth-century fresco from the Church of St. Baudelio de Berlanga in Spain (The Met Cloisters).
WIKICOMMONS

had a hit with "Roll Away Your Stone" and didn't need to explain the title's provenance. ("Roll away your stone I will roll away mine / Together we can see what we will find.") And one of David Bowie's final songs, written as he was nearing death and released in 2016, was entitled "Lazarus." The accompanying video shows the pale, emaciated singer lying in bed, his head swathed in a bandage. ("Look up here, I'm in heaven / I've got scars that can't be seen.")

The story has also exerted a powerful hold on filmmakers, who, like Zeffirelli, grasp the story's importance and its obvious visual power. In Martin Scorsese's *The Last Temptation of Christ*, released in 1988, Willem Dafoe, as Jesus, goes to the tomb in Bethany and pauses after his prayer. His words to the dead man are slightly embellished from the Gospels: "Lazarus, in the name of the prophets, in the name of Jeremiah and my Father, in the name of the Most Holy God, I call you here." Then he begins to whisper almost inaudibly, "Lazarus, Lazarus, Lazarus."

From the darkness a bandaged, decaying hand is suddenly thrust out of the tomb. Jesus grips the hand and yanks Lazarus into the sunlight.

Jesus (Willem Dafoe) embraces the newly raised Lazarus in Martin Scorsese's *The Last Temptation of Christ*. COURTESY OF UNIVERSAL STUDIOS

The film is based on Nikos Kazantzakis's novel, which describes the raised Lazarus in terms almost always related to death: his limbs yellow, his head green, his body smelling of soil. A threat to the Temple authorities in Jerusalem, the resurrected man is murdered by Barabbas, the criminal whom the Gospels describe as being released by Pontius Pilate in lieu of Jesus.

Other filmmakers have approached the story more obliquely. In the 2018 film *Lazzaro Felice* (released in English as *Happy as Lazzaro*), which won plaudits at the Cannes Film Festival, the film-maker Alice Rohrwacher tells a parable-like story about a remote Italian farm in modern times. Bound by a landowner in an arrange-ment close to slavery, a group of sharecroppers eke out a living. Among them is the sweet-natured Lazzaro, perhaps in his twenties. When the illegal arrangement and exploitation of the sharecroppers is discovered by police, the estate is suddenly evacuated. Lazzaro flees and, distracted by a police helicopter, falls into a ravine and is left there, unconscious. Many years later, Lazzaro awakes, not having aged, and returns to the area of the estate, where the townsfolk seem only mildly surprised by his resurrected presence.

Overall, the films that attract me most are those that, like *Jesus of Nazareth* and *The Last Temptation of Christ*, portray Lazarus's story as told in John's Gospel.

But before we go any further, let's ask a basic question: Who was Lazarus? And what can we know about the subject of all these paint-ings, poems, novels, and films? Who was the recipient of "Jesus's greatest miracle"?

"A Certain Man"

In Hebrew his name was El'āzār (Eleazar), which means "God has helped." It was a common name in Jesus's time. In the Greek of the New Testament, the name was translated as *Lazaros*. Today that "certain man" who "was ill" is known as Lazarus.[3]

Lazarus, by James Tissot (Brooklyn Museum). Tissot made several trips to the Holy Land in the late nineteenth century to help with his illustrations of biblical stories and characters.
WIKICOMMONS

Here are the facts of Lazarus's life that can be gleaned from the Gospel of John, the only place he appears in the Bible. He lived in the first century in the town of Bethany, near Jerusalem, with his sisters, Mary and Martha, whose house seemed to be a place of rest for Jesus. Lazarus was a man of indeterminate age who was loved deeply by Jesus, who cared enough for him and his sisters to risk stoning to visit his tomb. After having been dead for several days, Lazarus was raised from the dead by Jesus, to the amazement of his sisters and a large crowd. After his raising, some people wanted to kill Lazarus, most likely because he was a tangible sign of Jesus's power. Later, Lazarus reclined at table during a dinner with Jesus in Bethany. His raising from the dead also helped to set in motion Jesus's arrest and death.

That's all John tells us.

Is there more we can know about this "certain man" beyond those few tantalizing facts? Some important clues about Lazarus may lie in plain sight in the Gospels. We begin with some basics to help us understand the person at the center of this story.

The Significance of Knowing a Name

When a person is named in the Gospels, the naming indicates something significant. Often when Jesus interacts with someone in his public ministry, the person remains unnamed, even if he or she is the recipient of a miracle or some important teaching. Jesus heals people described in the Gospels as "a man with a withered hand" or "a paralyzed man" or "a woman suffering from hemorrhages."

Despite the importance of these stories and the drama surrounding these miraculous cures, most of these people remain anonymous. This is true even for some of Jesus's most dramatic encounters, when one might expect a name to be given—for example, the long Gospel narrative of the "possessed man" in the "country of the Gerasenes." That person is known to us not by his name but simply as "the Gerasene demoniac."[4]

Why? Probably because, after their encounter with Jesus, these people receded into anonymity, known perhaps only to their friends and family and a few disciples with good memories. Or, as Jesus went about his itinerant public ministry, their names were not asked. Perhaps even Jesus didn't know their names.[5] Or, most likely, as the New Testament scholar Amy-Jill Levine told me, "The Gospel writers wanted to keep the focus on the symptoms and thus on the miraculous removal of the symptoms. The focus for the Gospels is always on Jesus."[6]

These healing stories, as well as Jesus's dialogues with "a young man," "a leader of the synagogue," or a "Samaritan woman," were important to the early church. But since the names of the people Jesus encountered may have been unknown to Jesus and the disciples, they were not passed on to the early Christians or the writers of the Gospels.

The Rev. Msgr. John Meier was a Catholic biblical scholar and author of one of the most extensive treatments of the "Historical Jesus," the focus of a scholarly project that aims to understand as much as we can about the life and times of Jesus of Nazareth. His multivolume series of books on the topic is called *A Marginal Jew: Rethinking the Historical Jesus.* In that series, Meier points out something about John's Gospel: "[W]ith the exception of Jesus's immediate disciples, miracle stories belonging to the public ministry almost never name the beneficiary or the petitioner. This holds true even in cases where we would have expected a name"—for example, the blind man in John's Gospel who calls out to Jesus for help and is healed. As Meier writes, "If any miracle story cries out for a name, it is the story of the man born blind."[7]

Imagine all the people Jesus met during his public ministry, not only those whose names we don't know but whose life stories we don't know. Remember that only a small part of Jesus's life is recorded in the Gospels even though, by some estimates, Jesus may have spent upward of three years preaching and healing throughout Galilee and Judea. We would do well to think about the men, women, and children who weren't the recipients of any healings but whose lives were nonetheless changed by their encounters with Jesus. What happened in those interactions? What was it like to engage in a conversation with Jesus? Whose life did he change not with a miracle but with a word of hope, comfort, or encouragement? Whose life did he alter with a word of critique?

We might also think about all the conversations Jesus had with his disciples that go unrecorded in the Gospels, conversations about what they believed, about their former lives, or even about the political situation at the time. What was it like to be in his company and relax with Jesus?

There is in fact an entire period of Jesus's life that we know almost nothing about, what is often called his "Hidden Life," the period between the ages of twelve, when he is "lost" in the Temple in Jerusalem, and around thirty, when he begins his public ministry. During that time Jesus lived what John Meier calls an "insufferably ordinary" life, spending most of it as a *tektōn*, a Greek word usually translated as "carpenter" but probably more accurately as "construction worker." Or perhaps, as Amy-Jill Levine says, a "builder." The biblical scholar Ben Witherington points out that the houses at the time would have been made from limestone, so "carpenter" isn't quite right; but "stonemason" is too specific because doors, tables, and chairs would have been made from wood. So perhaps "artisan" would be best.

Imagine the many people with whom Jesus worked, for whom he built chairs, tables, and doors. All these unnamed people were part of Jesus's life, and yet they remain anonymous to us. During his public ministry, even the recipients of his greatest miracles, or the subjects of important Gospel passages, often go unnamed.

But sometimes we *do* hear a person's name. We meet not "a tax collector," but Zacchaeus. Not "a blind man," but Bartimaeus. Likewise, we meet not "a woman who stood by the cross," but "Joanna, the wife of Herod's steward Chuza."

What accounts for our knowing their names? Scholars say this is most likely because these people were known to the early church, the Christian community that came into being after Jesus's resurrection. We know their names because *they* knew their names.

How the Gospels Were Written (or, More Accurately, Edited)

To understand more about the significance of names—and pretty much everything else we will discuss in this book—it helps to know something about the construction of the Gospels. This explanation may come as a surprise to people who imagine that each Gospel writer was an eyewitness to all the events that occurred during the public ministry of Jesus, and all they needed to do was write down the details. The truth is more complex.

There were three stages in the writing of the Gospels.

The first stage was during Jesus's public ministry, from roughly AD 30 to AD 33. Those dates are slippery, and Jesus wasn't born precisely in year 1 of the Gregorian calendar; we're not sure exactly how old he was when he was crucified, and the Gospels differ on how long his public ministry lasted. But we can safely assume that his public ministry was centered somewhere around AD 30. During these years, there was no need, or at least no perceived need, to write anything down because Jesus was still around. Consider how we don't begin writing down details of family history until we realize that our grandparents may not be with us much longer.

Next came the period after Jesus's time on earth had ended, when his followers would have passed along the stories about Jesus orally, from roughly AD 30 to AD 65. There was also no perceived need to write it down because (1) the milieu in which the story was told was an oral culture; (2) many eyewitnesses were still alive and could tell the tale themselves; and (3) many of the early Christians thought Jesus was returning soon, as he seemed to have indicated.

Finally came the third stage, when it became clear that Jesus wasn't coming again soon and when many eyewitnesses were dying. Moreover, the church wanted his story to become more widely disseminated. This brings us to the writing of the Gospels by the "evangelists," whom we know today as Matthew, Mark, Luke, and John.

Each evangelist wrote in Greek, the *lingua franca* of the day. That's one reason why sometimes we will turn to the Greek in this book, to try to understand the original meaning of what they wrote.

Mark was the earliest evangelist, writing around AD 65; then came Luke and Matthew, around AD 85. Matthew, Mark, and Luke in many ways parallel one another and so are called the "Synoptic Gospels" or "Synoptics" because they can be "seen with one eye" (*synoptikos*, "seen all together"). John's Gospel, however, differs in terms of his stories, characters, language, themes, and tone. As depicted in Matthew, Mark, and Luke, Jesus is often the purveyor of pithy stories, more in line with a homespun carpenter from the tiny town of Nazareth. In John, he is in control, almost as if he were already the Risen One, sometimes speaking in long, oracular statements. But in all four Gospels, of course, Jesus is a majestic leader, inspiring loyalty from his disciples but often arousing resistance from some religious leaders.

The differences should not surprise us. Although each evangelist was telling the same story—the life, death, and resurrection of

Page from the Gospel of John, Papyrus 66 (P66) manuscript,
roughly third century AD.
COURTESY OF FONDATION MARTIN BODMER

Jesus—they were also four different people telling the story for four different communities at (roughly) four different times. Each writer (or, more accurately, each editor, since they were gathering stories together) highlighted different parts of the story, adding a word or phrase here, rearranging the sequence of events there.

As for the writing of John's Gospel, the only place where the Raising of Lazarus appears, the Rev. Raymond Brown, an esteemed twentieth-century Catholic New Testament scholar, posits its construction in two stages: first, with the reminiscences of the person from Jesus's circle known as the "Beloved Disciple" (more about him later), and second, with the refinement of these stories by an editor. Brown dates John's Gospel to around AD 90 to AD 110.[8]

Did Lazarus Really Exist?

Let's return to the significance of named characters. Presumably when these stories were first told orally and someone mentioned a person known to the community—Zacchaeus, Bartimaeus, Mary Magdalene—the storytellers would have included their name, perhaps to avoid listeners breaking in with comments like, "That's Nicodemus you're talking about!" These names were passed along and written down by the evangelists and are preserved in the Gospels today.

So when we meet people who are named, we can assume that these were historical individuals. These include Martha, Mary, and Lazarus. We can presume that Lazarus existed, and that he was known to the early church. This can give us more confidence in what scholars call the "historicity" of the story.

Some scholars debate this, saying that the names could be symbolic. As we have seen, Lazarus means "God has helped." (Names in biblical times were often "sentence names," like Elijah, "Yah[weh] is my God.") Various arguments have been made suggesting that Martha and Mary are also symbolic.[9] We cannot know for certain if

Lazarus of Bethany, by William Hart McNichols.
COURTESY OF THE ARTIST

these names are symbolic ones given to fictional characters or represent people who were known to the early community. But given the strong personalities of both Mary and Martha, which appear not only in John's Gospel but also in Luke's, it seems more likely that these were real people.

One might argue that it doesn't really matter if Lazarus existed or not. What matters instead is that the story was meaningful to the early Christian community, or that there was someone *like* Lazarus who was raised from the dead or who was the recipient of a healing miracle. Thus some theologians see the question "Did he exist?" as beside the point.

To which I say: Baloney. It's natural for believers to want to know whether a story is true, not in an abstract sense ("It communicates a truth") but in a historical sense ("It actually happened"). For my part, I am very interested in whether Lazarus was a real person. So, we have to look at the Gospel stories closely to see what they might tell us about his "historicity."

Before we go any further in our investigation, however, let me anticipate a common reaction among people who have assumed that these stories were written by eyewitnesses, transcribing what Jesus said, word for word.

First, although many eyewitness accounts are included among the Gospel narratives, we should think of Matthew, Mark, Luke, and John more as editors, who are pulling stories together. As a result, it would not be surprising for them to change or delete names of individuals to suit the needs of their varied audiences. A good example here is the story of Jesus encountering a blind beggar in the town of Jericho. As Jesus is passing by, the man cries out for healing. His name is Bartimaeus. At least that's the story in Mark. In Luke, however, Jesus heals a "blind beggar" who goes unnamed. In Matthew, he heals two blind men, again unnamed.

But even if there are differences among the Gospels, sometimes confusing differences, and it can be hard to get to the "original story," considering the historicity of these narratives is an important task for not only the historian, but also the believer.

Now let's return to the historicity of Lazarus. In his series *A Marginal Jew*, Msgr. Meier includes an extensive chapter on Lazarus in which he offers another argument in favor of his historicity. Meier notes that one of the most compelling arguments for the authenticity of a particular Gospel story is what New Testament scholars call "multiple attestation," that is, the same story or type of stories appearing elsewhere in the Gospels. For example, the fact that the story of Jesus feeding a large crowd of people with a few loaves and fishes appears in all four Gospels is an example of "multiple attestation," giving the story greater claim to being a historic event.

And while the stories of Jesus's raising the dead are "relatively rare," they are spread over the Gospels instead of being contained in just one. Meier concludes that the criterion of multiple attestation, at least for Jesus's having been known in his time as someone who raised people from the dead, is adequately proved. In fact, he writes, "Many a word or deed of Jesus in the Four Gospels lack attestation this widely based."[10]

To be fair, not every New Testament scholar supports the criterion of multiple attestation, with some arguing that we can't know for sure the literary connections and relationships between the Gospels. For me, however, it remains persuasive, another argument in favor of Lazarus's historicity.

But what Meier and other Historical Jesus scholars look at is not whether it happened. This, they say, is the realm of theology, as Meier puts it, "beyond what any historian working purely by the rules of historical research could ever establish." Rather, scholars of the Historical Jesus ask "whether some of the Gospel miracle stories are not simply creations of the early church but actually go back to various events in the life of Jesus, however those events can be evaluated and however much they may have been reinterpreted."[11]

If these events are judged, through the tools of historical research, to go back to events in the life of Jesus (rather than having been created by the evangelists), then it is more probable that the *belief* that Jesus raised the dead "already existed among his disciples during his lifetime."[12]

But if we're looking at the historicity of the Raising of Lazarus, we have to confront a problem: it doesn't appear anywhere in the Gospels of Matthew, Mark, and Luke. This will not be the only problem we encounter with the story.

Why Doesn't the Story Appear in the Other Gospels?

One of the most baffling aspects of "Jesus's greatest miracle" is why it is recounted only in the Gospel of John. Some have used its absence from the Synoptics to argue *against* its historicity. If Jesus had truly raised Lazarus from the dead, then Matthew, Mark, and Luke surely would have mentioned it. Thus, some conclude, it probably didn't happen.

Frankly, this part of the story used to trouble me, and I often wondered whether the story was created out of whole cloth by the writer of John's Gospel. How could it not be in *any* of the Synoptics? Wouldn't each evangelist want to give center stage to this earth-shattering event, just as John does? How could something so extraordinary, "Jesus's greatest miracle," be ignored?

Brendan Byrne, SJ, at the time a professor of New Testament at Jesuit Theological College in Melbourne, Australia, in a masterful monograph on the Raising of Lazarus, offers several responses to these questions.[13] His analysis is worth reviewing before we go any further. So is John Meier's extensive treatment of the question in *A Marginal Jew*. Let's look at what both scholars have to say.

Using the tools of contemporary biblical scholarship, Byrne examines the pieces of the narrative that don't seem to fit or that may be later additions to the original story by the evangelist. "When one looks closely," he writes, "not-so-well disguised stitching and patching start to appear."[14] This is a common practice for New Testament scholars: trying to discern which parts of the story were later additions and which were original. It is more art than science, but these efforts are still worthwhile. Remember, the evangelists would naturally edit the story as anyone would, adding links and explanations, for their intended audiences. And there are places in our story where Byrne sees evidence of "stitching and patching."

Meier agrees, saying that the "various signs of awkwardness or confusion in the text," including what he calls the "sutures or seams," suggest that the writer of the Gospel is "grappling with and reworking" with a tradition not of his own making.[15]

Let's look at where both scholars see signs of this stitching.

At the beginning of the story, we are told Lazarus was from "the village of Mary and her sister Martha," with the reference to Martha seeming like an afterthought. Oddly, the situation is reversed when we later read "Jesus loved Martha and her sister and Lazarus," with Mary not even mentioned by name. After a careful analysis, Byrne suggests that the passages where Martha is prominent "give the impression of being somewhat intrusive." None of these characters, by the way, have been mentioned in the Gospel of John before this, immediately lending them—assuming that John does not expect his readers to know the sisters from Luke's Gospel—an air of some mystery.

Byrne notes that other "inconsistencies and repetitions seem to betray a process of composition." Of course all the Gospels are to some degree "composed" (that is, the evangelists took stories and consciously arranged them in a certain way), but New Testament scholars are often able to see where the evangelist may have added to the original tales.

Curiously, Mary is referred to here as the "one who anointed the Lord with oil," though the story of that anointing has not yet been told at this point in John's Gospel. (Other scholars argue that the story was already known in John's community, so this is less problematic.) Mary's words to Jesus when he arrives in Bethany also repeat, word for word, what Martha says earlier, "Lord, if you had been here my brother would not have died." This too may indicate some editorial stitching.

I don't mean to suggest that the story was "made up." Quite the contrary. Rather, we see evidence of a more ancient story that was reworked by the writer of John's Gospel. "Features such as the unevenness of the text and especially the treatment of Martha do indeed suggest that the evangelist has taken up and embellished a pre-existing written source," writes Byrne.[16]

With that in mind, let's return to why the story does not appear in the Synoptic Gospels. Here Byrne is especially helpful, pointing out overlooked links to Matthew, Mark, and Luke.

First, the village of Bethany appears in both Mark and Matthew as the locus for the tale of a woman who anoints Jesus in the days before his death. In these two Gospels, an anonymous woman anoints Jesus in the house of a man called "Simon the leper," closely paralleling the tradition of Jesus's anointing by Mary in Bethany in John's Gospel.[17] In Luke, Jesus is anointed in the house of a Pharisee named Simon. In both Luke and John, the woman anoints his feet and wipes them with her hair.

"Clearly, then," says Byrne, "there was a tradition, later emerging in both the synoptic and Johannine tradition, that a woman publicly anointed Jesus before his death at a meal. The location at Bethany may also have belonged to an earlier stage of this tradition."

John's Gospel identifies this woman as Mary, the sister of Lazarus.

The second and most obvious connection between the Lazarus story and the Synoptic Gospels is the strong presence of Martha and Mary—again, figures who would have been known to the early church.

One of the most well-known of these stories is Luke's recounting of Jesus's visit to the home of Martha and Mary. It is usually described as a meal, but there is no mention of food. The two may simply be offering Jesus some hospitality. Martha complains to Jesus that she's doing all the work (*diakonia*), while her sister sits at Jesus's feet. Martha says, bluntly, "Tell her then to help me." Jesus gently responds, "Martha, Martha, you are worried and distracted by many things; there is need of only one thing. Mary has chosen the better part, which will not be taken away from her."[18]

For our purposes, what is important is not only Luke's naming Martha and Mary, but the coherence of the individual personalities and activities of the women in both Gospels. As in Luke's story of Jesus's visit, John depicts Martha as the more "active" sister, rushing out to meet Jesus to confront him over her brother's death, with Mary the more "passive" one, remaining in the house until Martha calls her.

Moreover, at a subsequent meal in John, after the raising of their brother, Martha again serves the meal, while Mary is at Jesus's feet, anointing them. This again parallels Luke's description of the two women during Jesus's visit to their house. Byrne notes that "there is clearly much congruence between the two traditions."[19]

Another place of congruence is in the Parable of the Rich Man and Lazarus in Luke's Gospel, which tells the story of a poor man named Lazarus who is covered with sores (another way of speaking of leprosy, and therefore a possible, if tenuous, connection to "Simon the leper"). In the parable, this Lazarus lies outside the door of a rich man and begs. After ignoring Lazarus, the rich man dies and goes to the underworld, where he begs Abraham to send Lazarus, who has also died, to warn his brothers of their impending doom if they do not help the poor. Abraham replies that his brothers would not listen to someone even if he rose from the dead.[20]

This is the only one of Jesus's parables in which a character has a proper name—Lazarus. Moreover, the parable points to "a tradition linking the rising from the dead with the name Lazarus."[21] Thus the two Gospels—Luke and John—have a tradition of a Lazarus raised from the dead.

"What is absolutely unparalleled," says Meier, "and demands an explanation is the occurrence of a proper name in a parable."[22] Meier also pokes holes in the theory that the name was created to convey some sort of "meaning." As we've seen, Lazarus (Eleazar), one of the most common names for Jewish men in that area at the time, means "God has helped" in Hebrew. But Meier notes that for this parable many other "symbolic" names could have been chosen: Johanan ("God has been gracious"), Daniel ("God is my judge"), Simeon ("Hear"), and so on.

But could John have simply taken the parable from Luke and enhanced it with the man in the parable *actually* returning from the dead? That is, did John try to turn a fictional parable into a real-life story? After analyzing the passage, Byrne concludes the opposite: "It is very likely that *it is Luke* who has made the poor man Lazarus and has done so on the basis of a pre-existing tradition about a Lazarus who returned from the dead"[23] (emphasis mine).

None of these links on its own establishes a direct connection between the Lazarus story in John and what is contained in Matthew, Mark, and Luke. "But there is enough evidence," says Byrne, "to make it quite plausible that the Fourth Evangelist could have known traditions closely related to those appearing in the Synoptic Gospels, especially Luke, and worked them up for his own purpose—notably combining a tradition about Jesus's raising a person named Lazarus with the Bethany traditions concerning Martha and Mary and the woman who anointed Jesus's feet."

Meier thinks it's more likely that the story of the Raising of Lazarus circulating in John's community may have helped "confer the name Lazarus on the originally anonymous poor man in the Lucan parable."[24]

The extent of such connections, however, and whether the original source of the story of Lazarus already contained these traditions, is hard to ascertain.

Overall, the work of the two scholars reveals traces of the Lazarus story in Luke's Gospel. But there is a more basic question: What about Jesus raising someone else from the dead? Are there traditions of this in Matthew, Mark, or Luke?

Did Jesus Raise People from the Dead?

The question of whether Jesus raised people besides Lazarus from the dead may be easier to answer. There is no doubt that Jesus was regarded as a miracle worker by those in his time. Even his detractors took note of his miracles. For them, the question was not whether Jesus performed miracles, but what the source of his power was and why he did them on the Sabbath.

If you asked Christians about Jesus's raising people from the dead, most would focus on Lazarus. But two other Gospel stories also recount this type of miracle. The first, in Luke, is the story of the Widow of Nain, in which Jesus encounters a funeral cortege in which a woman is grieving the death of her only son.[25] Jesus touches the bier, and the dead man arises. The location in Nain, a town with no other claim to any historical or biblical significance, is a strong argument for the story's historicity.

The other narrative is the Raising of Jairus's Daughter, contained in all three Synoptic Gospels.[26] In this story, Jesus raises from the dead the daughter of a synagogue official named Jairus. An important argument for this story's historicity is the presence of an Aramaic phrase that Jesus used—*Talitha, cumi*, or "Little lamb, arise."[27]

When an Aramaic phrase or word is preserved in the original Greek, it most likely goes directly back to Jesus. That is, the word

The Daughter of Jairus, by James Tissot (Brooklyn Museum).

or phrase *itself* made such an impression on the original hearers that it was passed along and recorded in the Gospels. Other examples are Jesus's saying *Ephphatha* ("Be opened") to a deaf and mute man,[28] and his warning his disciples not to call another person *raca* ("empty-headed").[29]

These two Synoptic stories show Jesus raising people from the dead. So, where is the Raising of Lazarus in the Synoptics? Byrne's answer is that since the Synoptics are more concerned with Jesus's Galilean ministry, and the story of Lazarus took place in Judea, the writers of the Synoptics might have thought that Jesus's power to raise the dead was "sufficiently demonstrated" in Capernaum (Jairus's daughter) and in Nain (the widow's son).

Perhaps the strongest argument for Jesus's ability to raise someone from the dead comes from his own lips. When John the Baptist is in prison, he sends some of his own disciples to ask Jesus if he is "the one who is to come."[30] Jesus gives him this answer: "Go and tell John what you hear and see: the blind receive their sight, the lame walk, the lepers are cleansed, the deaf hear, the dead are raised, and the poor have good news brought to them. And blessed is anyone who takes no offense at me."[31]

In both Matthew and Luke, then, Jesus is reminding John the Baptist's disciples what they have already seen and heard (what has already happened and been witnessed), which includes his raising people from the dead. Significantly, this passage comes immediately after the Raising of the Son of the Widow of Nain. Jesus *himself* says that he is raising people from the dead. (In this he would be emulating the Old Testament figures of Elijah and Elisha, both of whom raised someone from the dead.[32])

And as Meier points out, the writers of the Synoptics may not have known the full story of the Raising of Lazarus, especially not the "huge theological masterpiece" it would become in the hands of the writer of the Fourth Gospel.[33] The audiences of Mark, Matthew, and Luke may have known a shortened, more "primitive" version, which may not have seemed any more compelling than the stories of people being raised from the dead that they already had at their disposal. Meier concludes that the silence of the Synoptics about Lazarus says nothing about the historicity of Lazarus.

Byrne's overall conclusion about the historicity of Lazarus is helpful for the doubtful. Admitting that there are always enhancements to the miracle stories, he says this near the end of his study:

> The existence of this early "Lazarus back from the dead" tradition, now reflected in John 11 and Luke 16, is really the last step we can take with any security in the quest for a historical foundation. What the origins of this tradition were remains a matter for speculation. We cannot exclude the possibility that it does go back to a miracle of arising performed by Jesus. Something must have given rise to the existence of such a tradition and the attachment of the name of Lazarus to it.[34]

After a lengthy analysis of the Gospel passage, Meier arrives at the same conclusion. Meier, who is scrupulous about what can be labeled as historical and not historical, is inclined to think that the story of Lazarus "ultimately reflects some incident in the life of the Historical Jesus." He adds, "In other words, the basic idea that Jesus raised Lazarus from the dead does not seem to have been simply created out of thin air by the early church."[35]

Yes, I Believe

This long investigation into the historicity of Lazarus is important before we dive into the story itself. Of course, none of these arguments is an airtight piece of evidence "proving" the story of the Raising of Lazarus. Despite the evidence, the ultimate question of authenticity is left, as it was in the beginning, to those who hear and read the account in John's Gospel.

For the record, I believe the story is true but that there were, as with most Gospel stories, edits from the hand of the editor of the Gospel of John, who highlighted and even added things that he deemed important for his intended audience. But even those edits are important for helping us see the story of Lazarus from the point of view of John's community. It's difficult to do anything other than to speculate about what is added and what is original. In this book we will deal with the text as it has come down to us, in the Gospel of John.

It's also essential to consider the *overall* historicity of John's Gospel. The New Testament scholar Daniel J. Harrington, SJ, points out that in some places where John differs from the Synoptic Gospels, it may be *more* historically accurate. It's more likely that Jesus's public ministry lasted three years, as in John, rather than one year, as in the Synoptics, and that he made several trips to Jerusalem, as in John, rather than only one as in the Synoptics. Jesus also may well have been crucified before Passover, as John details. Also, Harrington points out that John's Gospel shows a great deal of knowledge of the geography of Jerusalem. "There is much sound historical information in this Gospel," he concludes.[36]

But to return to the question, "Did the Raising of Lazarus really happen?," for me, the answer is "yes." And I don't mean that in a vague way as in, "It's in the text that the community believes and I'm part of the community and so I believe it." Or "I believe in the tradition that includes it." Or even "I believe in the community that believed it." I mean it in a straightforward way. I believe that if we were in Bethany on that day, we would have seen more or less what the story recounts: the stone rolled away and Lazarus walking out, bound hand and foot.

From a more theological point of view, if God could create the universe from nothing, then raising a man from the dead seems a simple thing. This goes against the grain of the rational, intellectual, post-Enlightenment view that mitigates against such things as miracles. Meier begins his discussion of the Raising of Lazarus by saying, "Hardly any type of miracle clashes more with the skeptical mind-set of modern Western culture than raising the dead. Even Jesus's exorcisms pale in comparison."[37]

But over and over in his study of the Historical Jesus, Meier reminds readers that few things are as clear as the centrality of the miracles in Jesus's public ministry. And our difficulties with this are reflective of what we wish to see as "reasonable" or "rational" today. Meier writes: "To Jesus's mind these acts—including what he claimed to be acts of raising the dead—both proclaimed and actualized, however imperfectly, the kingdom of God promised by the prophets. To excise these acts from the ministry of the Historical Jesus is to excise a good deal of what he was talking about."[38]

I have no trouble believing that God's power could be manifest in this way. To paraphrase Mary and Martha, "Yes, I believe."

Also, when we encounter Jesus, we encounter the "reign of God," the elusive but essential idea at the heart of Jesus's message. In that reign, as Jesus said, "the blind see, the lame walk, the dead are raised." Thus, to encounter Jesus means to encounter life in the fullest. I believe that too.

I want to affirm my fundamental belief before we begin our exploration of the story in earnest, because at times we use what scholars call the "historical-critical method," where we analyze the historical background of the story (for example, Jewish ideas about the soul's leaving the body), how the story might have been seen by readers of the time (when John's community was separating itself from the larger Jewish community), and what parts of the story might have been changed from the original story by the evangelist's hand (as Brendan Byrne and John Meier have pointed out).

At times it may appear that I'm casting a suspicious eye on the Raising of Lazarus. But that is not the case. Looking at it with a critical (read: intelligent) eye with all the tools of modern biblical scholarship (and even some archaeology) only helps us understand it more fully. And I invite you into that same kind of faith: one rooted in belief in God's power to do anything and firm enough to explore the variety of ways that the writer of John's Gospel may have edited this story.

There is nothing to fear from good biblical scholarship. It doesn't challenge our faith; rather, it helps us see how those who had the same faith in Jesus chose to tell the story. At times, we will even come across areas where today's best New Testament scholars disagree. I'll lay out all the arguments as best I can and then tell you what I think about the story.

With all that in mind, let's now enter more deeply into our story and look at what another key phrase might tell us about the man known to his friends as Eleazar and to us as Lazarus.

For Your Reflection

1. What do you think about the "historical-critical" method of reading the Bible, which tries to account for the way that the Gospels were written?
2. Do all the arguments for Lazarus's "historicity" convince you that he existed? Why or why not?
3. Based on what you now know, does it trouble you that the Raising of Lazarus appears only in John's Gospel?
4. Do you believe that Jesus could raise people from the dead? Why or why not?
5. Have you ever seen God do something "impossible" in your own life or in the lives of others?

He Whom You Love

Jesus, Friendship, and the Beloved Disciple

*Mary was the one who anointed the Lord with
perfume and wiped his feet with her hair; her
brother Lazarus was ill. So the sisters sent a
message to Jesus, "Lord, he whom you love is ill."*

In 2000, an extraordinary discovery was made at a Jesuit retreat house and retirement center in Wernersville, Pennsylvania, not far from the town of Reading: a formerly "lost" painting by the late Renaissance master Jacopo Robusti, more commonly known as Tintoretto. Its subject was the Raising of Lazarus, and its discovery was covered in media around the world. The oil painting was large (forty-two by fifty-eight inches) and dated to around 1556. When found, it was hanging, "unlighted and unlabeled," as an article from the *New York Times* noted, in a hallway across from the entrance to the Jesuit community chapel. After its rediscovery, its authenticity was confirmed by Christie's auction house in New York.[1]

How did it get there? And how was it forgotten?

The grand and imposing Jesuit Novitiate of St. Isaac Jogues (named for a Jesuit who was martyred in upstate New York in the seventeenth century) was built in Wernersville with a bequest from

The Raising of Lazarus, by Tintoretto (Reading Public Museum).
COURTESY OF THE USA EAST PROVINCE OF THE SOCIETY OF JESUS

Mr. and Mrs. Nicholas F. Brady, two wealthy Catholic benefactors. (One of their descendants, also Nicholas F. Brady, would serve as secretary of the treasury under Presidents Ronald Reagan and George H. W. Bush.) Dedicated in 1930, the sprawling brick building served first as a novitiate for the Maryland Province of the Society of Jesus and then, in later years, as a retreat center and retirement community.

Nicholas and Genevieve Brady were part of an elite group that gathered around a circle of clerics in Rome, where they spent their winters. It was there that they first spotted the Tintoretto, purchased it, and later donated it to the Jesuit novitiate, whose construction they had funded. (The retirement center and novitiate have since been closed, but Mr. and Mrs. Brady are still interred there.) At first it was hung in the novitiate library; then it was moved outside the chapel.

After Mr. and Mrs. Brady died in the 1930s, with no direct heirs, the painting was thought to have disappeared—at least in the eyes of some art historians and connoisseurs.

But why was its provenance forgotten among the Jesuits, in whose house it hung? Probably for the same reason that another painting, of even greater value—a depiction by Caravaggio of Judas's betrayal of Jesus called *The Taking of Christ*, which hung in the dining room of a Jesuit residence in Dublin—was also forgotten. Jesuits are not art historians! (Well, a few of us are, but not most of us.) And sometimes, over time, the provenance of the works of art that we are given are forgotten.

After its rediscovery in Wernersville, the painting was loaned to the nearby Reading Public Museum, where it hangs today.

In Tintoretto's painting, Lazarus has just been brought out of his tomb and is being held before Jesus by a man in a pink gown. But as many art critics remarked in 2000, Lazarus is not a decaying corpse but a vigorous young man with the physique of an athlete— even a bodybuilder. Still, the Gospel-reported stench of the body is conveyed by a man in the background, who covers his face with a handkerchief.

As Professor Franco Mormando wrote in *America* at the time, the depiction of Lazarus was a highly popular theme in Christian art, and Tintoretto returned to the theme several times in his career. Mormando notes several reasons for the story's popularity among Christian artists: first, it was traditionally seen as the greatest of Jesus's miracles; second, it was an "inspiring source of hope" for early Christians, living under the threat of persecution and even martyrdom; and third, it illustrated an important theological concept: "actual bodily resurrection."

Even long after the time of early Christian persecutions, says Mormando, the story held enormous appeal. In the eleventh century, "St. Lazarus" took on new life as a patron and protector against attacks of leprosy and the plague. (The connection was to the Lazarus in Luke's Gospel, the man "covered with sores.") And the years in which Tintoretto painted the canvas that eventually found its way into a Jesuit novitiate coincided with an attack of the plague in Venice, where Tintoretto spent most of his life.

Mormando offers a beautiful description of what the painting might have meant to Venetians during a plague, and to those who gazed on it for the first time in 2000:

> Utterly impotent in the face of this repeated scourge, the government and citizens of Venice turned toward heaven, seeking comfort and help from God and from saintly intercessors like Lazarus. As they contemplated stirring works of devotional art like Tintoretto's, depicting the miraculous raising of Lazarus from the dead, the Venetians found hope and strength to persevere in the face of the merciless scourges of life. These paintings reminded them that even if their prayers for immediate release from sickness and death were not answered, there was nonetheless the promise of a greater destiny, of a joyful new life "in the bosom of Abraham," where there would be no more sorrow, tears or death. In this respect, as a poignant, visual reminder of one of the eternal truths of Christianity and in the face of the new merciless and yet unconquered plagues of our own century, such as AIDS, Tintoretto's "The Raising of Lazarus" remains as emotionally alive and as spiritually relevant to us today as it was to the Venetians who first gazed upon it in the 16th century.[2]

Still, it is a highly *unusual* depiction of the miracle, and first-time viewers might be forgiven for not immediately being able to identify the Gospel story that it illustrates. Lazarus has not "come out" of the tomb on his own volition. It's more accurate to describe him as being carried out. Or perhaps we are meant to understand that he has walked out and has had his burial shrouds removed and has collapsed, exhausted by his illness, harrowing death, and raising. Jesus, on the left side of the painting, clad in red and blue, inclines his body toward his friend, with his hand outstretched. The other figures in the painting all incline themselves toward Jesus, "as if by a magnet," as Mormando writes. In the background is an idealized depiction of Jerusalem.

Jesus's face is shown in profile. So it is the faces of the young man carrying Lazarus and of Lazarus's two sisters that show the most emotion. They look imploringly at Jesus, with a mixture of sorrow and relief, as if exhausted by their own journey.

"He Whom You Love"

As their faces show in the Wernersville Tintoretto, the stakes are high for the sisters, which is true from the beginning of the story. Lazarus was seriously ill, near death, and Martha and Mary would have been desperate to get word to their friend Jesus.

As our story begins, Jesus and his disciples are staying in a locale (still unknown) across the Jordan River, having fled Jerusalem after a threat of a stoning by some angry opponents. Brendan Byrne in an email to me noted the importance of geography here, and in the entire narrative:

> When Jesus receives news of his friend's illness, Jesus is for the time being in what for him is "safe country," on the east side of the Jordan River. In the wider story of the Gospel, Judea and above all Jerusalem has become a place of mortal danger for him. Therefore he is putting his own life at risk if he journeys to Judea to come to the assistance of Lazarus, his friend.

As elsewhere in the Gospels, Jesus does not court death. At the end of his earthly life, he accepts crucifixion only when he sees it as his Father's will. Even in Gethsemane, the night before his execution, he initially says, "Remove this cup from me." In other words, "I don't want to die." It's not surprising, then, that before the story of Lazarus begins, we find Jesus across the Jordan, after leaving Jerusalem, where his opponents were about to kill him. The Greek is *exēlthen ek tēs cheiros autōn*: literally, "he went forth from the hand of them."

Mary and Martha need to get word to Jesus that their brother is ill. In doing so, they use a striking expression, one of the most important in the entire story.

To recover the freshness of the narrative, it helps to consider what the people in these stories *didn't* say or do. We may be so used to Gospel stories that describe the words and actions of Jesus and his followers that we think what they do and say are preordained. We forget that these were real-life people, who could have said or done anything. They're not fictional characters in a novel, play, or film, with scripted lines to declaim.

In this case, let's look at how the sisters *don't* describe their brother:

The sisters don't say, "Lazarus, your disciple, is ill."

They don't say, "Lazarus, our brother, is ill."

They don't even say, "Lazarus of Bethany is ill."

Instead, they say something unexpected, identifying their brother in a special way for Jesus. The Greek is *hon phileis asthenei*: "He whom you love is ill."

What does "he whom you love" mean? And what does it mean for us?

Jesus and Friendship

At the simplest level, *hon phileis* means that Jesus loved Lazarus. More precisely, it means that Mary and Martha believed that Jesus loved their brother. Lazarus was an intimate friend of Jesus.

Nearly everyone knows that Jesus chose twelve apostles. Jesus also gathered around him a larger group of disciples (seventy-two, as they are numbered in one passage). More broadly, there were the still larger and more amorphous "crowds" and "followers" who were part of his ministry. But we often forget that Jesus had friends.

The German Catholic New Testament scholar Gerhard Lohfink notes, "Nowhere is it said that Lazarus belonged among Jesus's disciples or followers."[3] Rather, Lazarus was Jesus's friend.

Some have suggested that, based on their apparent celibacy

(i.e., none is described as being married in the Gospels), Mary, Martha, and Lazarus were members of the Essene community, an ascetical sect that flourished around the time of Jesus. (The Essenes are generally agreed to be the source of the Dead Sea Scrolls, a group of writings from that era that were discovered in a cave in Qumran, in the West Bank, in the twentieth century.)[4] But this is debatable.

What is not debatable is that Jesus spent time—perhaps a great deal of time—at the home of Martha, Mary, and Lazarus in Bethany. Most likely, he visited them during trips to Jerusalem, perhaps seeking a place where he could rest, apart from the demands of his public ministry and apart from his disciples, who, according to the Gospels, could feud and quarrel with one another, in addition to failing to understand Jesus. Lohfink calls their house a "support station."[5]

Notice too that in their message to Jesus, the two sisters don't even need to ask him to come to Bethany. St. Augustine, in a homily on Lazarus, notes that the mere *mention* of the illness was sufficient. "It is enough that You know," says Augustine, writing of Jesus's love for Lazarus, "for You are not one that loves and forsakes." Then in a beautiful phrase Augustine refers to the three as "the one sick, the others sad, all of them beloved."[6]

Like Augustine, Byrne also believes that the way the sisters communicate with Jesus shows his affection for his friend. Martha and Mary, he writes, do not ask Jesus specifically to come. They know it is dangerous for him. Instead they simply say, "Lord, he whom you love is ill." They allow the love that they know he has for Lazarus to put pressure on him to come. "This is the first of several indications in the story of Jesus's love for Lazarus."[7]

In his book *You Are Never Alone*, the bestselling Christian spiritual writer Max Lucado offers this preceptive insight about the sisters: "They appealed to the love of Jesus and stated their problem. They did not tell him how to respond. No presumption. No overreaching or underreacting. They simply wrapped their concern in a sentence and left it with Jesus. A lesson for us perhaps?"[8]

Mosaic of Jesus at the home of Martha and Mary,
Church of St. Lazarus, Al Eizariya.
COURTESY OF CATHOLIC TRAVEL CENTRE

Jesus was (and is) fully human and divine, as the Christian tradition proclaims, yet we often overlook the first of what theologians call his two "natures." As a fully human person, Jesus would have needed, desired, and sought friendship. And from the evidence of his visit to the home of Mary, Martha, and Lazarus, and the way that the sisters speak to him, they—in particular, Martha—seem to have been among his closest friends.

As we've seen, when Martha feels that her sister is not pulling her weight in what Luke calls "service" or "ministry" (*diakonia*), she says to Jesus, "Lord, do you not care that my sister has left me to do the work by myself? Tell her then to help me!"[9]

It's a small but telling sign of their intimacy. No one else but a close friend would have spoken to Jesus so bluntly. And in the story of the Raising of Lazarus, the sisters are equally blunt, both saying, "Lord, if you had been here, my brother would not have died." These words are often interpreted as the sisters' profession of faith in Jesus.

Yet they also reveal two sisters expressing disappointment in their friend. These feelings—faith and disappointment—may have been felt side by side. (The expressions on their faces in the Wernersville Tintoretto show a certain relief as well.)

We tend to underestimate Jesus's need for friends. Even when thinking about the twelve apostles, we tend to imagine Jesus calling them for the eminently practical reasons of assisting in his public ministry, and for the efficient running of the future church.

Gerhard Lohfink suggests that the calling of the Twelve was more symbolic in nature, mirroring the number of tribes of Israel. Selecting the Twelve, Lohfink believes, was less about setting up leadership roles in the early church than representing a kind of "gathering." If the Twelve had been significant leaders in the early church, he argues, we would have heard much more about them in the Acts of the Apostles, and the Gospels would at least have agreed on their names. Certain ones—Peter and James among them— exercised leadership roles, but not all of them.[10]

In addition to assisting Jesus and proclaiming his message, the Twelve may have had another role: Jesus needed people to rely on. His public ministry wasn't always public. During private times, he and his disciples would have relaxed in one another's company, told stories, and laughed. (Yes, Jesus laughed. He was human after all.)[11] He easily could have chosen a single "assistant," say, Peter. But he didn't: he called a group of disciples and among them were the Twelve. And when the burden of leading his disciples became too great, he may have sought comfort and solace and fun with friends like Mary and Martha and Lazarus.

Even before his public ministry began—during his years as a boy, an adolescent, and a young adult in Nazareth—Jesus would have had friends: childhood friends with whom he played; adolescent friends with whom he discussed their Jewish beliefs and practices; and young adult friends, perhaps other builders and laborers, with whom he worked constructing and repairing houses.

How could Jesus not have had friends?

Friendship in the Christian Life

Friendship is an overlooked aspect of Jesus's life—and the Christian life in general. Sometimes we envision the ideal Christian life as centering around dramatic acts of charity. Recently a couple at whose wedding I presided quit their high-paying jobs and comfortable lifestyle in the United States to move to Ecuador to care for orphans—a noble act and one that brought them great happiness. But not all of us are called to that kind of service; we tend to overlook simpler, quieter acts of charity, like being a good friend.

Being a friend is one of the most important things we can do, one of the most appreciated and one of the most difficult. Friendship is a real ministry.

A few years ago, I needed to have surgery to remove a small, benign tumor under my jaw. Even though it was benign, I was worried. Fortunately, a Jesuit friend who is also a physician said that he would accompany me to the hospital on the day of the surgery, which allayed my fears. Who better than a friend who is a doctor as your companion during such times?

The night before the surgery my friend injured his foot and told me, regretfully, that he would be unable to accompany me. In desperation, I turned to another friend, Ivan, a married man with three children and a busy job. Earlier in the week Ivan said to me, "If you need anything, just ask." So even though I felt bad about asking someone at the last minute, I texted him, "I may need someone to take me to the hospital tomorrow."

"Don't worry," he wrote back immediately. "I can do it. What time?"

I was stunned by his generosity. I texted, "6 a.m."

He replied, "Don't worry. I can do it. Where?"

The next day Ivan met me at the hospital, stayed with me as I was prepped for surgery, remained throughout the several hours of the operation, and was the first person I saw when I woke up after surgery. A few hours later, after making sure I was in my hospital room, he returned to his office downtown. Then a few hours later again, in the teeth of a raging summer thunderstorm, he returned to the hospital to see how I was doing. I could barely take in his generosity.

Soon after Ivan left, another friend, Kevin, a married man with two young children, texted and asked me, "How are you? Do you need someone to pick you up? If yes, what time?"

Again, I was amazed by his generosity. A Jesuit friend had offered to collect me, but I knew it would be a busy day for him, so I said yes to Kevin. The next day he drove from his house, more than an hour away, arrived at noon, helped me out of bed, took me to the pharmacy, drove me home, gave me a small icon of Mary, and made sure I was settled in my room before he left a few hours later.

This experience revealed to me the overwhelming love of my friends (especially Ivan and Kevin, but others too). It was hard to process, understand, even accept. Their willingness, attentiveness, and care were almost palpable. It's still hard for me to believe how kind they were, and I'm still overwhelmed with gratitude. All because of friendship.

A few years later, I had to have another surgery—this time "minor." (As the joke goes, "minor" surgery is when it happens to someone else!) As an aside, I'm focusing on these medical problems because I think it is in such situations, when we are often at our most vulnerable, when friends are the most helpful.

This time, it was the members of my Jesuit community who blessed me with their companionship. My Jesuit brother Sam got up early in the morning to take me to the hospital, accompanied me during the surgery prep, prayed with me, waited for me until I was out of recovery, drove me home, and got me settled. Then for the next week, Jesuits in my community made runs to the drugstore, did my laundry, prepared my food, prayed for me at Mass, asked after me, and on and on. It was a powerful experience to be so cared for in one's religious community. This was not just about being brother Jesuits but about being friends.

In fact, one of the highest compliments Jesus gives to his disciples is this: "I do not call you servants any longer . . . but I have called you friends."[12]

Jesus valued friendship and his friends. Among those friends were Mary, Martha, and Lazarus. And who knows in what ways they helped him? But we know one dramatic way in which Jesus helped Lazarus.

How Did Jesus Know Lazarus?

As we've seen, *hon phileis* means that Jesus loved Lazarus deeply.

Where did this affection come from? The Gospels are silent on the matter, which means that novelists, poets, and playwrights have had free rein to imagine. In Bill Cain's novel *The Diary of Jesus Christ*, the two are depicted as having worked together. In Father Cain's hands Lazarus is part of a wealthy family that controls "a big part of the building trade," with Jesus traveling to Bethany when there is abundant work for carpenters. The two become close: "We were brothers."[13] In the TV miniseries *The Chosen* (2017), Lazarus is introduced as a friend who tried to get Jesus to join him in business.

Richard Zimler's novel *The Gospel According to Lazarus* casts the two as friends from childhood. In his story, Lazarus's father and Jesus's foster father, Joseph, are fellow craftsmen from Nazareth, working together to rebuild the nearby town of Sepphoris.[14] Archaeologists tell us that the much larger town, only a ninety-minute walk from Nazareth, was being rebuilt by King Herod Antipas, "tetrarch" of Galilee, at the time when Joseph and Jesus were working as carpenters.[15] It's almost a certainty that the two would have traveled there, at least once or twice, to find work.

When the boys are both twelve, Lazarus rescues Jesus (called "Yeshua," his original Aramaic name) from drowning in the Jordan River. In a vivid passage, Lazarus says: "After I dragged Yeshua through the rushes fringing the river into a clearing, he pressed a hand of thanks to my chest, too weak to speak. His long hair was slicked to his neck and brow and he was crying with relief. His eyes shone with an otherworldly light, as though his near death was a sign of God's glory."[16]

Jesus later explains that he had been "lost in fervent prayer in one moment and the next was being carried downstream."[17] Afterward he calls Lazarus *dodee*, "my beloved" in Aramaic. The two are soulmates in the book, and there is even a hint of romantic love that Lazarus feels for Jesus, which is obviously not in the Gospels.

Nikos Kazantzakis's novel *The Last Temptation of Christ* simply has Jesus entering the house of Martha and Mary in Bethany, unannounced, seeking a place to rest. "I'm cold, hungry and sleepy," he says on their threshold. Their brother, Lazarus, who is a follower of John the Baptist, will meet Jesus later. In Colm Tóibín's novel *The Testament of Mary* the two men are related, and Jesus's mother, Mary, recounts her fondness for Lazarus: "I had known him since he was a baby. Of all the children that any of us had, he was, from the day he appeared in the world, the most beautiful. He seemed to smile before he did anything else."[18]

These are the fictional derivations of *hon phileis*: he whom you love. Certainly Lazarus and Jesus were good friends, and backgrounds as boyhood pals, cousins, or fellow laborers are as likely as any explanations. So is the possibility that he met Martha and Mary first and then came to know their brother. We will likely never know the genesis of Jesus's affection for Lazarus. What we do know is that it was deep. He was *hon phileis*, "he whom you love."

For an increasing number of New Testament scholars, however, *hon phileis* means something else.

A Dinner Conversation Takes a Surprising Turn

A few years ago, I was having dinner in New York City with my friend Michael Peppard, who is a theology professor at Fordham University. Michael writes a great deal about the early church and has an interest in archaeology, having produced a fascinating book on what is believed to be the oldest Christian building ever discovered, essentially a church, in Syria. His book *The World's Oldest Church: Bible, Art, and Ritual at Dura-Europos, Syria*, focuses mainly on the unusual wall paintings in the building.

I had thought of Michael primarily as a scholar of early Christianity and had forgotten that he was also a New Testament scholar—though it's not surprising that these two interests would go together. In passing, I mentioned that I hoped that my next book might be about Lazarus. As is my experience with many scholars, Michael casually mentioned something well-known in the academic community that both surprised and delighted me.

"You know that there is a theory that Lazarus is the Beloved Disciple, right?"

What? No I didn't. I was thunderstruck.

The Beloved Disciple, who plays a prominent role in John's Gospel, is a mysterious figure, the source of countless books and articles, whose identity remains the subject of lively debate among biblical scholars.

"What do you mean?" I asked.

Michael laid out the case, step by step, in just a few minutes, like a good instructor. What he said astonished me. For the rest of the dinner, we talked about nothing else, though I'm not sure if Michael wanted to spend our meal in a Lazarus seminar!

The Beloved Disciple, or the "disciple whom Jesus loved," makes his (or her, but most likely his) appearance in six Gospel passages in John. Critically, one passage in John's Gospel says, "This is the disciple who is testifying to these things and has written them." In other words, he, rather than the final editor, is the source of many of the stories contained in John's Gospel. Raymond Brown writes that the Beloved Disciple was the "eyewitness who was responsible for the basic testimony/witness that was incorporated into the Fourth Gospel."[19]

Another person would later edit and shape the Fourth Gospel, but the one whom scholars call the "BD" first witnessed what was recounted there. In John 21:24 the evangelist says of the Beloved Disciple: "We know that his testimony is true."

Obviously, the Beloved Disciple, an eyewitness source for much of what is recounted in John, holds a key place in the New Testament. But his identity has always remained a mystery.

Some of the traditional explanations are laid out by Raymond Brown in his magisterial commentary on the Fourth Gospel. One of the most common is that the Beloved Disciple is "not a real figure but a symbol."[20] In this approach, the BD is the ideal Christian disciple—reclining next to Jesus at the Last Supper, physically and emotionally close to him during the Crucifixion, the first to believe in the Resurrection, and the one who takes Jesus's mother into his home. The reader, then, is encouraged to identify with him.

In that sense each of us can be said to be Jesus's Beloved Disciple. This is one traditional explanation for his identity.

Other theories advanced by Brown (and other scholars) are that the Beloved Disciple is John Mark, who is identified as a friend of Peter's in the Acts of the Apostles; or that he is John, the son of Zebedee, one of the first disciples called by Jesus at the Sea of Galilee.

Scholars have pointed out the difficulties with these two figures: John Mark has been rejected since there is no evidence that John Mark knew Jesus at all. And John, the son of Zebedee, a Galilean, makes little sense as the BD since the Fourth Gospel centers on Jerusalem, not Galilee. Martin Hengel writes that this makes it "extremely improbable" that the Gospel of John was written or even inspired by a Galilean disciple like the man often called "John Zebedee."[21]

The biblical scholar Ben Witherington III noted some other objections to that identification.[22] There are, he pointed out, no "Special Zebedee" stories in the Fourth Gospel, that is, stories centering on James and John, the sons of Zebedee. By contrast, there are many such stories in the Synoptic Gospels: Jesus calling James and John from their nets at the Sea of Galilee, their presence at the Raising of the Daughter of Jairus, their presence at the Transfiguration, their bold request for special places in the reign of God. "If this Gospel was by John Zebedee and is intended to be an eyewitness testimony," Witherington said, "then it makes no sense that none of these unique Zebedee stories are in the Fourth Gospel."

In addition, Witherington noted, Jesus predicts the martyrdom of James and John: they were to receive a "baptism" like his.[23] There is also an ancient papyrus that indicates that John, like his brother, was martyred early on; therefore, he could not have produced a Gospel late in the first century.

So, again, the BD is most likely not John, the son of Zebedee.[24]

Also, it is most likely not Mary Magdalene, as some have suggested—even though she was herself a "beloved disciple." Why not? Because at the foot of the Cross, John's Gospel describes them as two separate people, and John uses a masculine pronoun for the Beloved Disciple: "Meanwhile, standing near the cross of Jesus were his mother, and his mother's sister, Mary the wife of Clopas, and Mary Magdalene. When Jesus saw his mother and the disciple whom he loved standing beside her, he said to his mother, 'Woman, here is your son.' Then he said to the disciple, 'Here is your mother.' And from that hour the disciple took her into his own home."[25]

The Beloved Disciple was apparently a man. And probably a Judean. But who?

Is Lazarus the Beloved Disciple?

During our dinner conversation, Michael Peppard told me that much of the most recent work identifying Lazarus as the Beloved Disciple comes from Ben Witherington III, whose thoughts on John Zebedee we just considered.

An esteemed New Testament scholar at Asbury Theological Seminary, a school in the Methodist tradition in Wilmore, Kentucky, Witherington has set forth several compelling arguments for why he believes the most obvious candidate for the Beloved Disciple is Lazarus. Witherington is probably the highest profile scholar who has taken this position.

With Witherington and other biblical scholars as our guides, let's take a quick tour through the four Gospels, moving beyond the story of the Raising of Lazarus, to investigate the identity of the mysterious Beloved Disciple. Is it Lazarus? Has the BD been lying in plain sight all these years, like the Tintoretto painting in the Jesuit community?

Witherington begins his analysis with the "Judean character" of the Gospel of John. The Gospel is centered on Judea (in the south) rather than Galilee (in the north). For example, none of the exorcisms found in the Synoptic Gospels occur in John, and none of the parables found in the Synoptics appears in John. Instead, the miracles recounted in John happen mainly in and around Jerusalem, that is, in Judea. There is also no emphasis or interest in John about the Twelve, or the Twelve as Galileans. John's Gospel, largely independent of the Synoptics, also has fuller accounts of the Passion and Death of Jesus, including many details about the Temple authorities and Roman administrators in Jerusalem, as well as multiple trips to the Jewish festivals in Jerusalem.

As for the Beloved Disciple, he does not appear at all in the Galilean ministry stories but seems to be involved with, and know personally about, Jesus's ministry in and around Jerusalem.

Thus, says Witherington, it is likely that these stories from the Beloved Disciple originated with someone living in or around Jerusalem. But there were other disciples in the area besides Lazarus. What points to him?

The most obvious of several strong arguments that point to Lazarus as the Beloved Disciple is that he is the only one in the Gospels called *hon phileis*, "he whom you love." Even at Lazarus's tomb people exclaim about Jesus, "See how he loved him!" Recall that Jesus risked stoning to return to Bethany.

In fact, the Beloved Disciple is mentioned only *after* the story of

The Beloved Disciple, by Ruben Ferreira.
COURTESY OF THE ARTIST

the Raising of Lazarus is recounted in John 11, as if that story was the BD's introduction into the narrative.

As the New Testament scholar James H. Charlesworth says in *The Beloved Disciple*, an exhaustive investigation into the BD's identity, the identification of Lazarus as the BD would also explain the "centrality" of the Raising of Lazarus in John's Gospel.[26] In other words, if the BD is Lazarus, and the BD's eyewitness testimony underlies the Fourth Gospel, then it makes sense that the Raising of Lazarus stands at the center of that Gospel. It marks the end of what is often called by scholars the Book of Signs, roughly the first half of the Gospel, which focuses on the seven "signs," or miracles, that Jesus performs. And it is portrayed as Jesus's "greatest miracle." Brendan Byrne describes it as "the climax of the public life of Jesus in the Fourth Gospel."[27]

All these things make more sense if Lazarus is the Beloved Disciple, the privileged eyewitness of John's Gospel.

Witherington also points out what the original hearers of the story would have concluded simply by listening to it. Today, we tend to read these stories in discreet packages, but in an oral culture the passages would have been heard in sequence. He calls this the "internal evidence" in the text.

To that end, he reminds us that in John 12, following the story of the Raising of Lazarus, comes a dinner in Bethany, at Lazarus's home. Then in John 13 comes *another* dinner, also before Passover. This event is best known for Jesus's washing the feet of his disciples. During the meal, the "one whom Jesus loved" (*hon ēgapa*, this time, using another word for "loved") reclines on Jesus's chest. Witherington reminds us how people in an oral culture would have heard the story:

> In John 11 there was a reference to a beloved disciple named Lazarus. In John 12 there was a mention of a meal at the house of Lazarus. If someone was hearing these tales in this order without access to the Synoptic Gospels, it would be natural to conclude that the person reclining with Jesus in John 13 was Lazarus. There is another good reason to do so as well. It was the custom in this sort of dining that the host would recline with or next to the chief guest. The story as we have it told in John 13 likely implies that the Beloved Disciple is the host. But this means he must have a house in the vicinity of Jerusalem. This in turn probably eliminates all the Galilean disciples.[28]

After the Raising of Lazarus, the moniker "Beloved Disciple" appears regularly in the Gospel, alternating with "the other disciple." After surveying the evidence, Witherington believes that the Beloved Disciple was most likely the leader of the disciples in Judea, a counterpart to Peter as the leader of the Galileans.

The identification of the Beloved Disciple as Lazarus helps clear up some mysteries that have bedeviled New Testament scholars. The presence of mourners, for example, who subsequently report the Raising of Lazarus to the Pharisees and Temple authorities, may explain how the Beloved Disciple had access to Caiaphas's house after Jesus is taken prisoner. The "other disciple" is described in the Passion as follows: "Simon Peter and another disciple followed Jesus. Since that disciple was *known to the high priest*, he went with Jesus into the courtyard of the high priest" [emphasis mine].[29] Many scholars have puzzled over this connection to the high priest.

At Lazarus's tomb, however, were several Jewish people, presumably mourning with his family, who later reported the miracle to the Pharisees. This suggests that Lazarus had some relationship with them and perhaps even with Caiaphas.[30] This in turn may explain how the Beloved Disciple had access to the high priest's house. A Galilean fisherman like Peter, for example, would not have had access, nor would he have been known. Likewise for the other Galilean disciples. Lazarus makes more sense.

The Empty Tomb: A Mystery Solved?

The identification of the Beloved Disciple as Lazarus also explains part of the tale of the "Empty Tomb," in this case not Lazarus's but Jesus's.

In John's Gospel, Mary Magdalene is the first to arrive at Jesus's tomb on Easter Sunday. This is not surprising, since she never left his side at the Crucifixion. When she discovers the stone rolled away, her response is confusion. "We do not know where they have laid him," she says to Peter and the Beloved Disciple, who both race to the tomb.[31]

The Beloved Disciple arrives before Peter. This may be a subtle putdown of Peter by John's community in favor of the Beloved Disciple, whose testimony informs John's Gospel. In any event, the Beloved Disciple peers in the tomb but does not enter. Peter then arrives, goes into the tomb, and notices the burial cloths and the head covering. Then, we are told, the Beloved Disciple "saw and believed."[32]

So how do the disciples respond on Easter Sunday in John's Gospel? Mary is confused. About Peter we hear nothing. But the Beloved Disciple believes.

The thesis that the Beloved Disciple is Lazarus helps explain why the BD arrives at the tomb faster. As someone living in Bethany, near Jerusalem, he would be more familiar with the locale and perhaps even knew Joseph of Arimathea, who donated the tomb, or Nicodemus, who helped prepare Jesus's body for burial. He knew the area well. Certainly better than Peter the Galilean would have.

As the theologian Mark W. G. Stibbe points out in his book *John as Storyteller*, the Beloved Disciple's ability to outrun Peter may be because Lazarus has himself already experienced the "resurrection power of God."[33] In other words, having been raised from the dead, he is more certain of what has happened to Jesus. But Lazarus may simply know the way better, thanks to where he lives.

More important, the identification with Lazarus may explain how the Beloved Disciple is *able* to believe. And how he believes in the Resurrection, without having yet seen the Risen Christ, may help us in our own lives as disciples.

How does the Beloved Disciple know instinctively and immediately what has happened? The Gospel writer may intend for us to understand that the closer one is to Jesus, the more one can see, a common theme in John. Or he may intend for us to see the Beloved Disciple as an Everyman or Everywoman character. Thus, the anonymous figure of the BD may be an invitation for all of us to believe, even without being present at the empty tomb, even without seeing. But if the Beloved Disciple is indeed Lazarus, then something else may be at work.

When Lazarus is called out of his tomb to new life by Jesus, just a few days before in Bethany, he emerges bound head and foot. John tells us that he is wearing a *soudarion*, a head covering. That Latin "loanword" (meaning sweat cloth or handkerchief) appears only twice in John's Gospel, once in the Raising of Lazarus and again in the story of the Empty Tomb.[34] And that small piece of cloth may have helped the Beloved Disciple to believe.

When was the last time the Beloved Disciple would have seen a *soudarion*? If he is Lazarus, at his own rising! He looked inside

The Disciples Peter and John Running to the Tomb on the Morning of the Resurrection, by Eugène Burnand (Musée d'Orsay). Here the Beloved Disciple is identified with John.
WIKICOMMONS

Jesus's tomb and believed because he *himself* had experienced a rising from the dead. He saw a sign and believed. Lazarus believed in something extraordinary based on his own experience. It is also fitting that the one who was raised from the dead be the first one to recognize the new life that Jesus now signifies.

"As the Beloved Disciple," the biblical scholar James H. Charlesworth writes, "Lazarus would be the one with experience of the meaning of the grave clothes and 'instantly recognize there in the still-rolled cocoon-like garments the clear proof of a supernatural resurrection.'"[35]

Come to Believe

This part of Lazarus's story can help those who struggle with belief.

All of us have faced confusing, depressing, and even terrifying situations in which it seemed that there was no life. Like Mary, Peter, and the Beloved Disciple, we have looked into empty tombs and tried to understand. What helps many of us may be what helped the Beloved Disciple, maybe Lazarus: signs that have already occurred, instances when God was with us in the past, times when God brought light out of darkness, brought hope out of despair, brought life out of death. These signs help us see the way ahead. Seeing God in the past makes it easier to see God in the present and in the future.

Something similar happens at the beginning of Jesus's life, as well: at the Annunciation, as recounted in Luke's Gospel.[36] When the Angel Gabriel presents Mary with an uncertain future, she too is confused. "How can this be?" she asks. The angel's response is to invite her to consider her cousin Elizabeth's surprising pregnancy. Many New Testament scholars interpret the angel's words to Mary as news: the angel is revealing something to Mary: "And now, your relative Elizabeth in her old age has also conceived a son; and this is the sixth month for her who was said to be barren."[37]

But other scholars suggest that the angel may be reminding Mary of what she already knows. Why wouldn't Mary have known this after six months about someone in her family, even someone who lived far away? The angel may be inviting her to look back. "Remember, Mary," the angel may be saying to her, "Elizabeth is six months pregnant. Look back at what God has already done. Look at this sign. And trust what God will do in the future."

If we look hard enough, we can see signs of God in the past, even if they seem insignificant in the face of future problems.

Confident in the Resurrection, and invited to move ahead even if we're doubtful, we can look for signs in our own lives, in the past and present, which can help us take steps into a future that is fuller, more joyful, and more secure. We can peer into what seems like an empty tomb and know, based on past signs in our lives, that new life always awaits us. And we can be sure that whether we can see him or not, Christ is risen indeed.

The Beloved Disciple believed after merely seeing an empty

tomb—since Lazarus had himself left behind an empty tomb. Looking back enabled him to look forward.

More Evidence

There are other possible indications that Lazarus was the Beloved Disciple. The BD is described as taking Jesus's mother "into his own home" after the Crucifixion.[38] This suggests a home much nearer than Galilee. Also, because the BD shows up in Jerusalem in John 20, and Mary is still there, after the Crucifixion and the Resurrection, a more likely candidate is someone who lived in or around Jerusalem, just as Lazarus did.

When Jesus tells the BD to take his mother into his home, writes James H. Charlesworth, "the house must be nearby since there is insufficient time for a journey with the Sabbath about to begin. No better place is known from the [Gospel of John] except the home of Lazarus, in which Jesus's mother will also receive the support and assistance of both Mary and Martha."[39] (Charlesworth, though he presents compelling arguments in favor of Lazarus, ultimately rejects them in favor of an identification with the Apostle Thomas.)

Finally, the identification of Lazarus as the Beloved Disciple neatly explains a confusing passage at the end of John's Gospel, in which the Risen Christ appears to the disciples on the shore of the Sea of Galilee and asks Peter three times, "Do you love me?" At the close of this highly charged exchange, when one would imagine that Peter would be more concerned with carrying out Jesus's subsequent command to "feed my sheep," Peter suddenly asks Jesus a strange question about the Beloved Disciple, who is apparently standing beside him.

"Lord, what about him?" he asks.

Jesus says, "If it is my will that he remain until I come, what is that to you?"[40]

John then writes, "The rumor spread in the community that this disciple would not die."[41]

Why else would the Gospel (or Peter) ask this strange question, this non sequitur, unless there were something "different" about the Beloved Disciple? It would be natural for Peter to wonder if someone raised from the dead would die again. To me, this is perhaps the most compelling argument in favor of Lazarus.

Mark Stibbe believes this passage effectively rebuts the theory that the Beloved Disciple was John, the son of Zebedee: "Why would such a rumour have sprung up concerning the immortality of a Galilean fisherman?" Or anyone else for that matter. Frankly, *only* Lazarus makes sense in this context.

Stibbe writes: "I can easily envision a scenario in which a group of Christians centred on Lazarus, who had been raised from death, believed in the immortality of their founding father. It is entirely plausible that they came to mistake his temporary resuscitation with a permanent resurrection. When Lazarus, the BD, eventually did die, an explanation was needed and [the editor of the Gospel] sought to provide it."[42]

Finally, Lazarus's identity as the Beloved Disciple would explain, in a stroke, something that even casual readers of the Gospels note: why John's Gospel can seem so different in tone from the Synoptics. As already mentioned, the Jesus we encounter in the Gospel of John often seems different from the Jesus we encounter in the Synoptics. He is no longer the earthy spinner of parables, but an oracular truth-teller, portrayed almost as if he is already risen. Witherington connects this approach to the identity of the Beloved Disciple:

> Our author, the Beloved Disciple, had been raised not merely from death's door, but from being well and truly dead—by Jesus! This was bound to change his worldview, and did so. It became quite impossible for our author to draw up a veiled

Messiah portrait of Jesus like we find in Mark. No, our author wanted and needed to shout from the mountain tops that Jesus was the Resurrection, not merely that he performed resurrections, that he was . . . a God bestriding the stage of history. . . . He is the incarnation of the great I AM.

Stibbe is convinced about the identity of the Beloved Disciple: "He *has* to be Lazarus."[43]

Raymond Brown, however, did not accept this hypothesis. In his Anchor Bible Commentary on John's Gospel, he said he found it "hard to believe" that the same person spoken of anonymously in several chapters is mentioned by name only in two chapters of the Gospel. "Are we to suppose that the final redactor would have left such a glaring inconsistency and would not have introduced the designation of the BD in those chapters as well?"[44]

But Brown also admits that there are other books of the Bible with this feature: Deutero-Isaiah, for example, in which the "Servant" is anonymous and in other chapters is named, as Jacob-Israel.[45] To me, it seems reasonable to believe that the final editor would not identify him in some places but feel obliged to in others. After all, in the story this book centers on, it would be odd for Jesus to shout, "Beloved Disciple, come forth!," especially if witnesses heard Jesus call out the man's name in a *phōnē megalē* (loud voice), something they never would have forgotten.

So, is Lazarus the Beloved Disciple? Did Tintoretto and countless other artists who depicted Lazarus unwittingly paint the mysterious BD?

Some scholars might respond in the way that John Meier does when faced with inconclusive data: *Non liquet*. Not proved. But Ben Witherington, Mark Stibbe, and other scholars have, I believe, made a persuasive case: Lazarus may not have been simply "he whom you love" but the origin of the Gospel of John, the mysterious Beloved Disciple.

. . .

Why does this matter? Why should we care if Lazarus was the Beloved Disciple? Isn't he already an important enough figure in the Gospels?

To begin with, if he is (or was) the Beloved Disciple, his story takes on even greater importance for the church—and for us. Lazarus becomes not simply the relatively passive recipient of Jesus's greatest miracle, someone who utters no words in the Gospel, but an active member of the early church, in fact, the foundation upon which John's Gospel was built.

Also, the healthy discussion about this unsolved mystery reminds us that there is never an end to healthy discussion about the Bible itself. The Bible is always revealing something new, in two ways. First, on a spiritual level, you can return to a Bible passage that you've read countless times and suddenly discover something new. You can be surprised by an insight that you've never considered before, in even the most familiar of passages. This is a sign of God's boundless creativity: "making all things new," to paraphrase Isaiah.[46]

But on what you might call an academic level (not that the spiritual and academic cannot overlap!), scholars are forever discovering new insights, making new connections, and proposing new theories about the Gospels, based on their constant study of the texts. This should be clear from our discussion about the BD. Likewise, archaeologists often discover new "finds" in the Holy Land that shed light on how people in Judea and Galilee lived during the first century, including Jesus and his disciples. Such discoveries help us better understand the Gospels and therefore what Jesus did and said. What could be more exciting—or important—than that?

This is one reason I find the Bible such an exciting topic: both for my spiritual life and my intellectual life. As the discussion on Lazarus and the Beloved Disciple shows us, the Bible is truly "alive" in so many ways.

What Does It Mean to Be a "Beloved Disciple"?

Maybe you're convinced that Lazarus is the mysterious Beloved Disciple. Then again, maybe you're not. Either way, the phrase poses an important question, especially if the BD is meant to stand for all of us: What would it mean for each of us to be a "beloved disciple"?

First, it means knowing that you are beloved! One of the most important lessons from the Dutch spiritual master and Catholic priest Henri Nouwen was his invitation, repeated over and over in his books, essays, and lectures, for people to see themselves as "God's beloved."

Nouwen realized that for many people this is a challenge, even a stumbling block. "The greatest trap in our life is not success, popularity, or power, but self-rejection," he wrote in *Life of the Beloved: Spiritual Living in a Secular World*. "When we have come to believe in the voices that call us worthless and unlovable, then success, popularity, and power are easily perceived as attractive solutions."[47]

Thus, one of the most important first steps in the spiritual life is recognizing that one is beloved by God. But that's hard for people who see themselves as unlovable. With his typical spiritual acuity (aided by his training as a psychologist), Nouwen put his finger on this phenomenon: "My tendencies toward self-rejection and self-deprecation make it hard to hear these words truly and let them descend into the center of my heart."[48]

How can we move from feelings of self-rejection and unworthiness to an awareness of God's love for us? For many of us, accepting our "belovedness" starts by recognizing the gifts God has given us throughout our lives.

This is also a key part of Jesuit spirituality (sometimes known as "Ignatian spirituality," based on the life and teachings of St. Ignatius Loyola and later Jesuits). At the beginning of the Spiritual Exercises of St. Ignatius, a retreat that invites people to meditate on the life of Christ, spiritual directors often ask retreatants to recall how God has blessed them throughout their lives.[49] Usually only then can someone want to respond to God's call, much less look at his or her limitations or sinfulness. First comes love.

It is often a profound experience for people to take an inventory, year by year, sometimes month by month, of what God has done for them: the talents and skills they have been freely given, the people who have been brought into their lives, the opportunities they have had, and especially the love they have received over the years. When people are given ample time to consider these gifts carefully and can truly appreciate the gratuitousness of the gifts, they are often overwhelmed by God's love. In a retreat setting this can take several days. For those of us engaged in normal daily life, this may be an extended period during which we take time every day, meditating on or even listing the ways God has blessed us. And if we are given enough time, such a recognition can sometimes reduce us to tears.

We need not do this inventory in the context of the Spiritual Exercises or a retreat. Casting our minds back gratefully over our lives, and seeing how God has blessed us, is something we can do anywhere. But we need to give ourselves time to do so.

The first step in the Spiritual Exercises, then, is to come to an understanding of ourselves as beloved by God. The equally profound recognition that these gifts are given to us *even as* we are sinful and flawed beings prompts a desire to respond in love—to love God in return, to follow Jesus, or to lead a more loving life.

Only when we are confident of our innate "belovedness" can true discipleship begin. This is one reason why so many who are healed of their illnesses in the Gospels spontaneously ask to follow Jesus. Before, they may have found it hard to see themselves as loved in any way by God. Freed from this doubt, made aware by Jesus of God's love, they are also free to follow. Freedom from shame leads to freedom to follow. This is also Henri Nouwen's insight.

"Once I have received these words [of my belovedness] fully," wrote Nouwen in *Beyond the Mirror*, "I am set free from my compulsion to prove myself to the world and can live in it without belonging to it. Once I have accepted the truth that I am God's beloved child, unconditionally loved, I can be sent into the world to speak and to act as Jesus did."[50]

Only when we're confident in God's love can we also be "sent out," which is what the word "apostle" means. The word comes from the Greek *apo* (from) and *stellein* (send). If we're unsure of the support of the one who sends us, then it is harder to do what we're being asked to do. Children going to school, secure in the knowledge that their parents love them, can face with confidence the challenges of classwork, socializing, perhaps even bullying by other students. It doesn't mean that things are always easy, but the knowledge that they are loved means that they stand on firmer ground.

What about the second word, "disciple"? We may be "God's beloved," as Nouwen says, but what does it mean to be a "beloved disciple"?

The Greek word for disciple is *mathētēs*, which originally meant "student" or "pupil." (The word "mathematics" comes from the same root.) But in the ancient world, including ancient Greece, the disciple was not simply one who took notes, passed tests, or learned instructions; rather, the disciple was one who imitated the teacher. And this is how the word is used in the Gospels.

Remember that there were several concentric circles around Jesus. In the innermost circle were Peter, James, and John. Then came the circle of the apostles, sometimes called the Twelve. The next largest circle was the disciples, which the Gospel of Luke numbers as seventy-two people.[51] The largest circle might have been the "crowds" and "followers," an even more amorphous group.

Complicating matters is that some New Testament passages use the terms "disciples" and "apostles" interchangeably. The letters of Paul and the Acts of the Apostles also use the term "apostles" to refer more broadly to disciples, and not just to the Twelve. Paul refers to himself as an apostle, along with Andronicus and Junia.[52]

Overall, though, the term "apostle" has more to do with a

person's mission (being sent out) while "disciple" is about the person's relationship to the teacher.[53]

What does it mean to be a "disciple"? It means not only to listen to Jesus, but also to put into action his words and deeds. There are multiple examples of Jesus reminding his disciples of this, when he says, sometimes explicitly and sometimes implicitly, "Go and do likewise."[54] Following Jesus is not simply about believing in his message, honoring him, and telling people that you are a Christian. It's about putting that belief into action. Richard Rohr, a Christian spiritual writer and Franciscan priest, often points out that Jesus never says "Worship me." What he does say often is "Follow me."

One of the clearest examples of this occurs during the Last Supper, in John's Gospel, after Jesus has washed the feet of his

Jesus Washing Peter's Feet, by Ford Madox Brown (Tate, London).

disciples. Bluntly he tells them that they must imitate this act of service, something a servant or slave would do. Beyond that, as the Johannine scholar Sandra Schneiders has written, he is inaugurating a community of equals, which seems to unsettle the disciples as much as his act of humble service does when he bends down to wash their feet.[55]

Jesus is clear in what he wants from his disciples: "For I have set you *an example*, that you *also should do as I have done to you*. Very truly, I tell you, servants are not greater than their master, nor are messengers greater than the one who sent them. If you know these things, *you are blessed if you do them*" (emphasis mine).[56] The disciple is the one who listens, learns, and imitates Jesus. In short, the disciple follows.

The Beloved Disciple, then, is the one who follows, confident in God's love. In John's Gospel the enigmatic Beloved Disciple may or may not be Lazarus. In our own lives, the Beloved Disciple is each of us.

For Your Reflection

1. Why do you think Mary and Martha used the term "he whom you love" when describing their brother to Jesus? What do you think the relationship between Lazarus and Jesus was like?

2. What is the place of friendship in your life? Do you think of friendship as a form of charity, service, or discipleship? Or perhaps all three?

3. After sifting through the evidence, do you think Lazarus is the "Beloved Disciple"? Why or why not?

4. How do you feel about the idea that we can always learn something new from, or about, the Bible?

5. In Henri Nouwen's words, you are "God's beloved." As you look back over your life, what enables you to believe this?

6. What might you do to become a better disciple?

4

Jesus Loved Martha and Her Sister

What Can We Know About Mary and Martha?

> *But when Jesus heard it, he said, "This illness does not lead to death; rather it is for God's glory, so that the Son of God may be glorified through it." Accordingly, though Jesus loved Martha and her sister and Lazarus . . .*

They are among the most important women in the Gospels. Perhaps only Mary the mother of Jesus, Mary Magdalene, and the "Woman at the Well" are portrayed with as much sensitivity. That the personalities of Mary and Martha shine through in narratives written more than two thousand years ago means that the early church retained vivid memories of both women.

Their names (usually mentioned together) have also become shorthand in Christian spiritual circles for contemplation and action. This stems from the most well-known story about the two—besides the story about their brother—of a visit Jesus paid to their house. The story has exerted outsize influence, sometimes for ill. It is told in the Gospel of Luke:

> Now as they went on their way, he [Jesus] entered a certain village,
> where a woman named Martha welcomed him into her home. She
> had a sister named Mary, who sat at the Lord's feet and listened to
> what he was saying. But Martha was distracted by her many tasks;
> so she came to him and asked, "Lord, do you not care that my sister
> has left me to do all the work by myself? Tell her then to help me."
> But the Lord answered her, "Martha, Martha, you are worried and
> distracted by many things; there is need of only one thing. Mary has
> chosen the better part, which will not be taken away from her."[1]

This is our first introduction to Martha and Mary, in Luke's Gospel, as evidenced by the wording: "a woman named Martha . . . She had a sister named Mary."

Luke's depiction of Martha and Mary during this episode is mirrored in John's depiction of them in the Raising of Lazarus. Martha is the "active" one, who first rushes out to see Jesus, and Mary is the more "contemplative" person, who stays home.

Interestingly, Amy-Jill Levine mentioned the possibility that John, writing later, might be "cleaning up" certain elements of Luke's presentation. Martha and Mary are portrayed in similar ways in John and Luke, but in John's story of the Raising of Lazarus they speak to one another and work together. In Luke they do not.

Some recent scholars have even questioned whether the Martha of Luke's Gospel belongs in the Lazarus story at all.

One scholar, Elizabeth Schrader, at the time a PhD student at Duke University, noted some surprising and significant "textual variations" in John 11 around Martha.[2] Schrader's suggestions are based on what biblical scholars call "textual criticism," which is concerned with the different "variants" among the earliest physical texts we have of the Gospels. Specifically, she has examined places in ancient manuscripts where it seems that Martha has been *added in*. (This recalls Brendan Byrne's comments about the "stitching and patching" together of the manuscript.)

Schrader pored through hundreds of digitized copies of these ancient manuscripts and discovered what she calls "significant instability" around the character of Martha in John 11. To begin with, if you look carefully at Papyrus 66, one of the most well-preserved copies of the Gospel of John, dating from around AD 200, you will see something unusual in the first verse ("He was from Bethany, the village of Mary and her sister Martha").

The word "Maria" has apparently been altered, with the Greek letter *iota* erased and replaced with a *theta*. The name seems to have been changed from "Maria" to "Martha." Immediately after this, the words "his sister" were changed to "her sister." And two verses later in Papyrus 66, one woman's name was replaced with "the sisters."

In an interview, Schrader summarized her findings: "I'm not arguing that Martha didn't exist—she definitely belongs in the Gospel of Luke. But I do not believe she belongs in the Gospel of John. There's too much manuscript evidence, where problems appear around Martha in nearly every scene in John in which she appears. You have to look at over 200 manuscripts at once to see this trend; only recently have hundreds of transcriptions of the Gospel of John been made available simultaneously online. I believe that's why this evidence was overlooked previously."[3]

Schrader concludes that it is "worthwhile" to question the consensus view that Martha was always present in the Fourth Gospel: "I believe that the changes around Martha in P66 cannot simply be dismissed as scribal mechanical errors, because there are so many strange variants around Martha through the text transmission."[4]

"Maria" altered to "Martha" at John 11:1 in Papyrus 66.
COURTESY OF FONDATION MARTIN BODMER

We cannot ignore Schrader's research (or that of earlier scholars, like John Meier and others, who argued for a more primitive version of the story sans Martha). For the purposes of this book, however, and since she is in the Gospel story that we know today, I'll continue to speak of Martha, the sister of Mary and Lazarus.

Now let's return to that visit of Jesus to their house in Luke's Gospel.

Martha's *Diakonia*

In Jan Vermeer's almost life-size painting of the scene, Martha, clad in white clothes with a dun-colored tunic, leans over Jesus's shoulder in a dimly lit room. Vermeer has portrayed the scene as a

Christ in the House of Martha and Mary, by
Johannes Vermeer (Scottish National Gallery).
WIKICOMMONS

meal, as most artists have, though there is nothing in this Gospel passage that speaks about a meal. Preachers have often followed the lead of artists, speaking about the "meal" at Bethany. But Martha complains that she is doing all the *diakonia*, which means "service" or "ministry."

Diakonia could mean preparing a meal but could also refer to any number of tasks of hospitality or service to a guest. In fact, it's important to note how often this scene has been characterized—in art, literature, and homilies—as a meal rather than *diakonia*, service. The New Testament scholar Amy-Jill Levine pointed out to me that the emphasis on the supposed kitchen duties of Martha may have been a way, conscious or unconscious, of relegating her to a traditional female role, instead of associating this strong woman with *diakonia*, from which we get the English term "deacon."

In Vermeer's painting, Martha places a loaf of presumably fresh-baked bread on a small table next to Jesus. Martha's mouth is slightly open, perhaps in the act of complaining about her sister. Jesus is seated in a chair and wearing a purple tunic and navy cloak. At his feet, on a stool, sits Mary, her right elbow on her knee, head leaning on her hand. She is clad in a ruby shirt and navy dress, in brighter colors than her more "practical" sister. Mary gazes at Jesus, who in turn looks at Martha, while gesturing to Mary with outstretched hand. The obvious implication is of Jesus teaching or lightly scolding Martha, saying, "Mary has chosen the better part, which will not be taken away from her."

Unfortunately, Jesus's praise for Mary, as well as frequent depictions in art like Vermeer's, gave rise to a strain in Christian spirituality that elevates prayer over activity or even condemns the active life. To me, however, this does not seem to be what the story says or what Jesus is saying.

Rather, it seems that Jesus is telling Martha that there is a time and place for everything. To paraphrase Ecclesiastes, there is a time for preparing the house and a time for listening.

"When I am in the house, it is the time for listening," Jesus seems to say, "and this is what Mary is doing." By sitting at his feet, Mary is clearly portrayed in the role of the disciple.

Too often, however, this passage has led to denigration of the active life and active people. Sometimes people cluck their tongues at hardworking men and women and say, "Martha, Martha," knowing that the listener will fill in the blanks: "You're just like Martha, someone who works too hard!" Alongside that is the implication that the person is oblivious or even addicted to overwork. Or that these Marthas are not contemplative enough.

Sometimes such comments are good-natured, but they can also make active people feel needless guilt. That interpretation works against one of the hallmarks of Jesus's public ministry: *action*. After all, this story of Martha's service or ministry at Bethany comes immediately after Jesus tells the Parable of the Good Samaritan. In that story, the hero, who cares for a man who has been beaten and left beside the road, is active: he bandages the man's wounds, puts him on his donkey, takes him to an inn, and pays the innkeeper. He doesn't simply sit by the side of the road and pray for him. He *does something.*

Jesus was prayerful. He led a contemplative life. We are told many times that he felt the need to "withdraw" from the disciples and the crowds to pray. This is especially the case in Luke's Gospel, often called the "Gospel of Prayer." Jesus also encourages others to pray.

But otherwise, the Gospels depict Jesus as "on the go," traveling from one town to another, journeying for days at a time. He walks, he sails, he preaches, he eats meals, he visits people in their houses, he bends down to speak to people, he climbs hills and mountains. He is *active.* In the Gospel of Mark, Jesus is described in almost breathless terms, as if the evangelist is trying to keep up with all his activity, doing things *euthus*, immediately. At one point in Mark, Jesus is interrupted on the way to performing one miracle (the Raising of the Daughter of Jairus) to do *another* one (the healing of the woman with the hemorrhage).

So, to say that Jesus denigrated the active life is to denigrate his own life.

Nor do I think he is denigrating Martha for her *diakonia*. As you look at the Vermeer painting, it's hard not to think, "Is he castigating her while she's setting before him a loaf of bread that she's just baked for him?" Rather, Jesus is encouraging someone he loved (and us) to slow down from time to time, to understand that there is a time for action and a time for contemplation. We need to be both Mary and Martha.

Contemplatives in Action

St. Ignatius Loyola, the founder of the Society of Jesus, wanted his fellow Jesuits to be "contemplatives in action." But that's a goal not only for Jesuits but for all Christians, in fact for all believers. It's an invitation to be like both Martha and Mary. And to be like Jesus, who led a life of action but also a life of prayer.

Who is a contemplative in action? It is the person who maintains a contemplative stance amid a busy life. It is a "monk in the world," to use another popular phrase.

And even monks lead active lives! The first few times I visited monasteries, whether to see friends or to make retreats, I was amazed by how busy the monastic life is. A monastic community's main ministry is prayer, which monks do several times a day in common (how often depends on the individual order). But all monks, except those who are old or infirm, have other jobs within the house, which often keep them busy: the abbot oversees the running of the monastery (including the finances); the sacristan maintains the chapel (setting up for liturgies, as well as maintaining the vestments, altar linens, prayer books, and so on); the infirmarian cares for the sick and elderly monks (including organizing medical visits); the cellarer manages the provisions (making sure there is sufficient food for the monks and their guests); and other monks might manage the kitchen, oversee the farm, or welcome guests. Also, monasteries

Navajo Jesus with Martha and Mary,
by Fr. John B. Giuliani.
USED WITH PERMISSION

depend on some sort of business with the outside world and are well-known for their wares: breads, cakes, eggs, chocolates, and so on. That involves a great deal of active work.

A few years ago, I visited my friend Jim at St. Joseph's Abbey in Spencer, Massachusetts. Jim, a former Jesuit, is a talented artist, and the order tapped him to run the vestment business. He explained how hard he was working: purchasing fabrics; designing the vestments; overseeing the production of albs, stoles, and chasubles; publishing a catalogue; and running the store on the monastery grounds. He said, "I feel like I left the Jesuits and entered Macy's!"

But at the heart of Jim's vocation, the monastic vocation, is a contemplative stance. The monastic world revolves around prayer.

Few of us live in a monastery. Many of us feel that our lives are the opposite of monastic: busy, hectic, even overwhelming. Perhaps Martha felt like that when she complained to Jesus. Who knows what other tasks she had to complete that day? Maybe stress overwhelmed her, and she could no longer keep silent.

What I see as Jesus's gentle response to Martha invites us to ask how we can lead a contemplative life amid an active one. Here are a few suggestions:

First, take time to review where God has been during your day. The Jesuit prayer known as the "examination of conscience," which invites us to look back and review the day, step by step, to see where God has been active, is of great help in leading a contemplative life. Even though God is active everywhere, we sometimes don't notice it. What is often called the "examen" (the Spanish term St. Ignatius used) is usually practiced in five steps, often at the close of the day:

1. Remember that you are in God's presence (essential for any prayer, to remind you that it's not a monologue).
2. Call to mind what you are most grateful for from the past twenty-four hours, savor these memories, and thank God.
3. Review the day, hour by hour, to see where you have encountered God—in people, places, and things. This makes up the bulk of the prayer, which is primarily a prayer of noticing.
4. Ask for forgiveness for any sins you may have committed, think about how to fix what was broken, and look at places where you could have done better.
5. Ask for the grace to find God in the next day.[5]

The examen helps us lead a more contemplative life because it helps us notice where God has been. That, in turn, makes it easier to see where God is. If we're moved by the generosity of our friends in the past twenty-four hours, the next time we encounter our friends—tomorrow, the next week, or even months later—we will recognize them more easily as great gifts. Soon we will see all things in our day as invitations to experience God's presence, the foundation of the contemplative life.

Second, slow down. Sometimes all it takes to center ourselves is to take a deep breath and slow down. This is especially the case when life is stressful or when we feel frightened or panicky. A friend's father likes to say, "Panic is the enemy." The spirit that leads us away from God causes confusion, fear, and anxiety. This happens most often during what psychologists call a "feeling storm," when strong emotions overwhelm our cognitive functions and it's hard to think straight, let alone make good decisions. Don't worry when this happens: it's part of being human. A few deep breaths, a walk around the block, or shutting off your phone—anything we can do to get away from the situation, either physically or psychologically—can move us from a scattered, stressed, and panicky view of life and into one that is more focused on God.

This is something I need to be reminded of often. Something disturbing happens—an unexpected piece of bad news, a troubling medical diagnosis, a friend seemingly angry at me—and I lose focus. Suddenly life has become a crisis and I lose perspective. This is where panic can unsettle us. This is how the "evil spirit" works, by confusing, unsettling, and, most of all, frightening us, usually about something that will not come to pass. Even if things look bleak, there is no reason to panic.

A surefire way to discern God's presence in these situations is to remember this: panic is never coming from God but hope always is. In these situations, it's essential to listen to the voices, interior and exterior, that call us to hope. But sometimes it takes a while to be able to do this. And just slowing down can help. "Breathe!" as one of my retreat directors often says.

God's spirit calms, uplifts, and encourages us. St. Ignatius points this out in his Spiritual Exercises, saying that it is "characteristic" of the good spirit to "stir up" courage and strength, inspiration, and tranquility. God's spirit "makes things easier and eliminates all obstacles, so that the persons may move forward in doing good."[6]

But how do we access that spirit? It can be hard to feel in touch with the good spirit when we are panicked or frightened. Besides taking a break, the most important step is to be aware that we have a *choice*: we can face the new situation with the calm into which God invites us, or we can remain fearful. Once we realize that we have many resources at our disposal, and that we can, as reasonable and rational people, face life's challenges calmly and maturely, we are able to let the "good spirit" flow into us. Breathe!

Third, be aware that God is with us. Often, we are the most stressed when we feel that we must do everything on our own. Think of Martha saying, "Lord, don't you care?" The feeling that we are doing this alone, with no help, exacerbates our stress. No one likes to face their problems alone. Maybe Martha felt quite alone as she saw her sister sitting by Jesus's feet.

Reminding ourselves that we are not alone and that we never face our problems without God's help can enable us to look at things through a more contemplative lens. Our problems become not simply something to "deal with" but something that God is inviting us to face, with God's help. Slowing down can help us realize that we can get through this crisis, as we have gotten through many crises before, often with the unexpected help of friends. Slowing down helps us see these things. God has been with us in the past. Why would God suddenly abandon us?

Nature can help in these situations. The sight of a sunset or the ocean or a tree bending in the wind becomes not just something beautiful but an invitation to see God's hand in creation. At the same time, a troubling situation becomes something to face with God's grace. Life is not a series of tasks but a journey with God.

Martha has typically been portrayed as the more active of the sisters, but in truth, we have no idea if she was. Mary could have worked as hard as Martha did, for all we know. More important, their roles are often separated—the contemplative one and the active one—when they should be seen in tandem. We are called to be both Martha and Mary, sometimes more active, sometimes more contemplative, but always the contemplative in action.

Tell Her!

The exchange between Jesus and Martha at her home in Bethany also reveals how close the two sisters were to Jesus, who "loved Martha and her sister," according to John's narrative.

In Luke's recounting, Jesus is not visiting the sisters' house out of obligation. Nor is it reported that Jesus went there because someone had requested his coming, as often happens in healing stories. Later in John's Gospel, the sisters ask Jesus to come and heal their brother. But on this occasion in Luke, he seems to be with them for relaxation. He is likely at their house mainly because he "loved Martha and her sister." And Lazarus.

They loved him, too. Ironically, the vehemence with which Martha rebukes Jesus over the lack of help that Mary provides is one of many signs of their intimate friendship. Scouring the Gospels, you will find hardly anyone else, save Peter, who speaks to Jesus so directly.

Martha of Bethany,
by William Hart
McNichols.
COURTESY OF THE ARTIST

Probably with growing frustration, Martha watches her sister sitting at Jesus's feet and listening to his words while she, Martha, deals with tasks or other people in the same room or in the court-yard outside. We can imagine Martha not only resentful at having to do the work, but also jealous of her sister spending time with their friend.

We can imagine her thinking, *Why does Mary get to spend so much time with Jesus? What is he saying that I'm not hearing? Look how much work I'm doing while she's just sitting there. And Jesus doesn't seem to care!*

Eventually her frustration boils over in one of the most remark-able utterances made to Jesus recorded in the Gospels: "Lord, do you not care that my sister has left me to do all the work by myself? Tell her then to help me."[7]

Martha's first sentence accuses Jesus, amazingly, of not caring. The most obvious parallel comes during the storm at sea, when a sudden squall whips up the waves on the Sea of Galilee while Jesus is asleep in the boat with the disciples.[8] In Mark, the panicked disciples say, "Teacher, do you not care that we are perishing?"[9] Jesus then awakes and rebukes the wind and the waves.

Writing a few decades after Mark, Matthew seems to find those words so tart that he softens them, so that the disciples don't accuse Jesus of not caring but say, more politely, "Lord, save us! We are perishing!"[10] Matthew turns Mark's accusation into a prayer.

During the storm at sea, the disciples are under enormous stress. Martha, hard at work, would not have felt the same anxiety; it was not a life-threatening situation. Nonetheless, she accuses Jesus of not caring. To be clear, I'm not faulting Martha. We all get frustrated at times. Rather, I want to focus on her rebuke to Jesus—"Do you not care?"—because it can help us better understand their relationship. She is being honest with her friend.

The second sentence is even more remarkable: "Tell her then to help me."

Tell her? Who else speaks to Jesus like this? Again, perhaps the only comparison is to Peter, who contradicts Jesus when he predicts his suffering: "God forbid it, Lord!"[11] Or perhaps when James and John, two of Jesus's First Disciples, ask to be seated in glory, beside him in heaven. (Matthew's Gospel, apparently finding that too difficult to place on the lips of two disciples, has their mother make this request.[12])

Even then, who tells Jesus what to do in such blunt terms? Only Martha.

Who can blame her for her feelings? Most of us know what it's like to be frustrated, even in a holy setting, when you're "supposed" to be at peace.

I discovered that in, of all places, Bethany.

On Pilgrimage

After my book on Jesus was published, the editor of *America* magazine, Matt Malone, asked if I would be willing to lead a pilgrimage to the Holy Land, following in the footsteps of the book.

After agreeing to Matt's request I grew excited about our first pilgrimage, but I also was apprehensive. The only pilgrimages I had participated in previously were ones in which I had been a chaplain, not responsible for any of the logistics and certainly not a leader in any way. This time I was being invited to return to the Holy Land, but as one of the pilgrimage leaders, along with Matt and another Jesuit.

Fortunately, the planning for the trip was handled by members of the *America* magazine staff. Still, we had no idea how the trip would turn out. The logistics alone were a potential nightmare: making sure that forty-five pilgrims, who were mostly middle-aged or elderly, got from Newark to Tel Aviv; had decent hotel rooms; didn't slip or fall as we walked from holy site to holy site (which all seemed to be paved with slick terra cotta tiles); liked the food;

didn't get sick; could hear the tour guides; didn't miss any of the buses; felt included and welcomed; and on top of all that were able to have some sort of spiritual experience.

In the end, the pilgrimages turned out to be a lot of fun, and our unbelievably experienced tour agency, Catholic Travel Centre, helped it all go without a hitch. We visited the Sea of Galilee, the site of Jesus's baptism, Jericho, Jerusalem, and Al Eizariya. We continued those pilgrimages for several years, until the COVID-19 pandemic shut them down for a few years.

One year, when we reached Al Eizariya, it began to drizzle. Soon it became a steady rain; nonetheless, a hundred or so pilgrims, some of whom were elderly, were slowly ascending the steps to Lazarus's tomb. As I approached the doorway, I grew worried that people would slip and fall, especially as the steps down to the tomb were, even on dry days, slick. I issued a warning as we stood under our umbrellas on the pavement in front of the tomb's entrance, across from the souvenir shop: "I would ask those who are unsteady on their feet *not* to go down into the tomb. It's very slippery!" All I could imagine was people falling, hitting their heads, and dying in the tomb.

Then I climbed a few more stairs, beyond the entrance to the tomb, moving higher in the plaza, so I could keep an eye on the pilgrims. To my horror, I spied one of the oldest pilgrims making her way to the entrance. She was a delightful woman, in her eighties, whose joy, energy, and stamina impressed all of us. But now I was terrified that she would injure herself.

From my post at the top of the hill, I made eye contact with our experienced tour guide, Maher, and pointed her out. I was frustrated that my warning seemed not to have had the intended effect. Maher stood near the doorway and gently took the woman's hand, saying, "Mama, it is too slippery." In response, in frustration, she slapped his hand and continued down into the tomb. Maher looked at me and shrugged.

I didn't blame anyone that day for our shared frustration (and, by the way, she navigated those stairs perfectly well, as did everyone else that rainy day). It's not a sin to be frustrated.

In the same way, I am not faulting Martha for her frustration. Rather, I'm focusing on this part of the narrative to highlight how comfortable Martha must have felt around Jesus to say this to him.

Had Martha known Jesus only as a disciple, the request might have come more obliquely. Consider what else she might have said, without accusing him of being uncaring: "Lord, can you see that my sister has left me to do all the work?" But that second line is harder to imagine from the lips of someone who was a starstruck or overawed disciple: "Tell her then to help me."

We speak in that way only to those we know well. We feel free to speak to family or close friends in those terms because we are confident our language and tone won't rupture a longstanding relationship. By contrast, we are embarrassed to speak so bluntly to those we don't know well—especially those whom we consider more "powerful"—fearing that we might offend them.

Entrance to the Tomb of Lazarus, on a sunnier day, in Al Eizariya.
COURTESY OF CATHOLIC TRAVEL CENTRE

Notice how gently Jesus responds to Martha—far gentler than in similar circumstances elsewhere in the Gospels. When Peter challenges Jesus about the need for suffering by saying, "God forbid," it earns him a fierce rebuke: "Get behind me, Satan!"

But Martha's comments prompt a patient response from Jesus. "Martha, Martha," he says, "you are worried and distracted by many things." His kind words are another sign of his love for her. And in the painting by Vermeer, the look on his face is mild, not cross.

Martha's honesty with Jesus also points out the need for honesty in our relationship with God.

Honesty in Prayer

One of the most common barriers to a deeper relationship with God is the inability or unwillingness to share seemingly "difficult" emotions during prayer. Anger or frustration of the kind that Martha expressed can be challenging to share with God.

Some Christians think that it's inappropriate to be angry, sad, or frustrated. Many have been told that the only thing we should express to God is gratitude. After all, God has blessed us abundantly, and many people are worse off than we are. All this is true, but it's also true that anger is a human emotion.

It's also natural to be angry *with God* from time to time. Disappointment with life can lead to anger. So can frustration, as Martha found out. Anger is a sign that we're alive. A bad medical diagnosis, the loss of a job, a terrible financial blow, the rupture of a relationship, even a sister not pulling her weight can make us want to shake our fists at God.

But God can handle our anger, no matter how hot it burns. God has been handling anger as long as humans have been praying, as long as humans have been living. Just read the Book of Job, where the protagonist rails against God for causing his painful situation. Usually Job is seen as a patient man, and at the beginning of that book he is. But eventually even Job loses his patience and begins to curse the day he was born, saying: "I loathe my life; / I will give free utterance to my complaint; / I will speak in the bitterness of my soul."[13]

Anger, sadness, frustration, disappointment, and bitterness in prayer have a long history. Why shouldn't we allow ourselves to express those feelings? The spiritual writer William A. Barry, SJ, frankly acknowledges these situations and counsels, "All I can do is encourage you to speak directly to God if you have questions about God's ways, as one friend to another, even if anger is the only emotion you can voice."[14]

Not expressing difficult emotions in prayer can lead to feeling blocked in our relationship with God. It's sometimes the same in human relationship. If we are unable to express our anger at someone, our relationship may grow cold and distant. Often the same thing happens in prayer. Expressing our honest emotions can "unblock" our prayer.[15] One of the most common experiences in my work as a spiritual director is hearing someone say that God feels distant or absent. Digging deeper, I almost always find that the person is not being honest with God about an aspect of his or her life.

Just recently a woman who had felt stressed out about what she called an "avalanche" of work and the challenges of caring for an aging (and rather difficult) parent told me that she hadn't been praying lately, because she didn't want to speak with God. She was too angry that God didn't seem to "fix things." When I suggested that she might simply try being honest with God, and even sharing her anger at the lack of "fixing," she visibly softened. I suggested that God may simply want to be with her during this time of stress and confusion. "Yes," she said, "I want that so much."

Honesty is the hallmark of healthy adult relationships. The more we can be honest with a friend—even about difficult issues—the deeper the friendship can grow.

Sometimes people object, saying, "God already knows what I'm thinking. Why do I need to share that?" But, as William Barry says, it's not a question of God's knowing but of our trust in God. Sometimes we are afraid that these difficult emotions might be the breaking point with God. That is, it could somehow end the relationship. Barry often told people, "It's not a matter of whether God knows or not, but whether we trust God's friendship enough to be open about it."[16] Why not be honest, even with those hard emotions?

That goes for more pleasant emotions too: joy, relief, enthusiasm. Why not share those with God as well?

Martha was honest with Jesus during their time in Bethany. Later on, when Jesus fails to visit her ill brother, she also expresses frustration: "Lord, if you had been here my brother would not have died." Her sister Mary is also blunt, saying the exact same words to Jesus. Both women clearly are able to be honest with their friend.

If Martha can be honest in her conversation with Jesus about her overwork, can we be honest in our conversations with God about our lives?

Where Is Lazarus?

Luke's story of Jesus's visit to Bethany raises a few more questions. First, where is Lazarus? He's absent in Luke's Gospel and therefore in depictions of the scene, such as the Vermeer painting.

As Ben Witherington points out, it seems odd that, given the prevailing social norms, none of the three—Mary, Martha, and Lazarus—were married. He suggests that it may have been because the three suffered from leprosy, which he connected with "Simon the leper," their possible father. If that is the case, then it is even more unusual in this patriarchal society that the house in Luke's story is referred to not as "Simon's house," or even "Lazarus's house," but as follows: "a woman named Martha welcomed him into her home."[17]

Neither "Simon the leper" nor Lazarus is there, as Luke describes it. Are we meant, then, to understand this to be the home of Martha? The Greek does not specify anyone as owner: Jesus is welcomed *eis tēn oikian*, into "the" home, not "her" home. But, even if they did have leprosy, why is the home not referred to by a man's name? Why is it not the "house of Simon" or the "house of Lazarus" unless it is because the story is centered on Martha and her sister?

Amy-Jill Levine doesn't deem this unusual: "Women owned homes," she told me recently. "Mary the mother of John and Lydia [in the Acts of the Apostles] are two of several examples." She also pointed to Judith, in the Old Testament. "There's nothing weird here," she said.

Today the connection between Lazarus and leprosy exists in the words "lazarium," "lazarette," or "lazaretto," ancient names for a place where those with various skin ailments would be treated. In English they were sometimes called "lazar houses." (The traditions often conflate the brother of Martha and Mary with the Lazarus, the man "covered with sores," in Jesus's parable.)

In Paris you can still find Rue St.-Lazare, which took its name from a lazarette called the Maison St.-Lazare that was once located on the street. (The Congregation of the Mission, a religious order founded by St. Vincent de Paul, is usually called the "Vincentians" but sometimes the "Lazarists," because their first priory was this lazarette in Paris.) It's an open question whether the millions of passengers who pass through one of Paris's largest railway stations know the origin of the name spelled out by the great letters that hang over the doorway of the Gare St.-Lazare.

The Order of St. Lazarus

An even more surprising connection between Lazarus and leprosy can be found in a religious order with a surprising and inspirational background, explored by David Marcombe in his book *Leper Knights*. In the twelfth century the Order of St. Lazarus was founded chiefly to care for those with leprosy in Jerusalem, which may have been the origin of the word "lazarette." Amazingly, the order also included those with leprosy among its members.[18]

At the time of the order's founding around 1100, the disease,

Coat of arms of the Order
of St. Lazarus, a religious
order with a fascinating (and
sometimes obscure) history.
WIKICOMMONS

because of its relationship to Jesus's public ministry, was seen in some places as a special *imitatio Christi* (an imitation of Christ), but in other places it was considered a kind of punishment for sins. At least initially, the order habitually chose for its superiors those who were "among the lepers." The house had two sets of accommodations: one for healthy brothers and one for those who were sick. At the time, little effort was made to heal or cure the sick brothers; rather, the community strove to care for them with healthy food and sanitary accommodations. In time the order also became a home for "leprous knights," that is, men of noble birth who had contracted the disease.

Their hospital lay just outside the city walls, attracting all manner of pilgrims, who were also potential patrons. In 1187, after the fall of Jerusalem, the order moved to Acre.

Gradually, members of the Order of St. Lazarus assumed the more traditional roles of knights, and the order began to be considered a military order, as were many religious orders and communities of the day, charged with the defense of Christian holdings in the area. Thus the idea of the "living dead" fighting for the Holy Land came into being.

In 1253, the rules of the order were changed to allow a "healthy knight" to become superior. They began to emulate the other military orders in the church, like the Knights Templar, Hospitallers, and Teutonic Knights, and engaged in battles. The order's home in Acre was described by one contemporary writer as the "military convent of the Order of St. Lazarus, complete with fortifications." Owing to the weakened state of many of the knights, however, they were largely unsuccessful in battle. In 1291, in a battle in Acre, according to Marcombe, "all the knights of St. Lazarus perished."[19]

As the order spread to Europe, its character changed and it became less tied to the care of people with leprosy. Its headquarters were split between France and Italy, and it soon became, as Marcombe writes, "an order without a purpose." In 1572, it was merged with the Order of St. Maurice. Its history from then until the current day is shadowy, with some arguing that after the French Revolution it ceased to exist at all.

In 1910 the order reemerged as a "redefined and reinvigorated" order and exists today around the world as the Military and Hospitaller Order of St. Lazarus of Jerusalem, its members dedicated to the care of the sick. "Battles are no longer with the sword," says its website, explaining its new mission; "the modern battle is fought in the struggle against disease, poverty, exclusion and intolerance, by promoting and defending the faith."[20]

Mary's Anointing of Jesus

So far, we have looked only at Lazarus's sister Martha in this story. What can we know about Mary? Is she more than just the "contemplative one" of the sisters?

Mary appears in the Gospels in several places: the raising of her brother, the occasion where she sits at Jesus's feet, and another story that we must consider, in which she takes the lead: the Anointing of Jesus.

Immediately after the Raising of Lazarus comes Jesus's visit to their house in Bethany. John's Gospel recounts what happened:

Six days before the Passover Jesus came to Bethany, the home of
Lazarus, whom he had raised from the dead. There they gave a
dinner for him. Martha served, and Lazarus was one of those at the
table with him. Mary took a pound of costly perfume made of pure
nard, anointed Jesus' feet, and wiped them with her hair. The house
was filled with the fragrance of the perfume. But Judas Iscariot, one
of his disciples (the one who was about to betray him), said, "Why
was this perfume not sold for three hundred denarii and the money
given to the poor?" (He said this not because he cared about the
poor, but because he was a thief; he kept the common purse and
used to steal what was put into it.) Jesus said, "Leave her alone.
She bought it so that she might keep it for the day of my burial. You
always have the poor with you, but you do not always have me."[21]

The story has a complicated history: there are three other versions of it in the Synoptics. In the version recounted in the Gospel
of Mark, also set before Passover, an unnamed woman in the house
of "Simon the leper" anoints Jesus on his head with expensive
spikenard ointment—a symbol of royal anointing. Onlookers complain that the money could have been given to the poor, but Jesus

Mary Anoints Jesus's Feet,
from a 1684 Arabic-
language manuscript of the
Gospels, copied in Egypt
by Ilyas Basim Khuri Bazzi
Rahib, who was likely a
Coptic monk (Walters Art
Museum, Baltimore).
WIKICOMMONS

defends her and says, "Wherever the good news is proclaimed in the whole world, what she has done will be told in remembrance of her."[22]

The New Testament scholar Elisabeth Schüssler Fiorenza makes a trenchant point about this passage in her landmark book on women in the Bible: even though Jesus explicitly tells us to remember her, we don't even know her name. Schüssler Fiorenza's book is pointedly titled *In Memory of Her*.[23]

The account in Matthew's Gospel, written a few decades later, closely follows Mark.[24] Also set in the house of "Simon the leper," the story tells of an unnamed woman pouring oil on Jesus's head and earning the disapproval of the disciples. Again, Jesus rebukes them and reminds them that she is preparing him for burial. Afterward, Judas's betrayal of Jesus is recorded, as if to link the selfishness of Judas with the generosity of the unnamed woman.

Luke's version is thought by some to be a different tale, though it seems connected to the versions in Mark and Matthew through the name of the host, Simon, who is here a Pharisee. In Luke, a "woman in the city, who was a sinner," weeps over Jesus, bathes his feet with her tears, dries them with her hair, and then kisses his feet and anoints them with ointment.[25] The link to John's presentation is also clear, through the wiping of the feet with her hair. Simon complains that Jesus has allowed himself to be anointed by a sinful woman. Jesus rebukes him as well. At the end of the tale Jesus says to the woman, "Your sins are forgiven."[26]

In this one episode, then, we may be able to learn something about Mary, who exercises a prophetic role here (assuming that she is the unnamed woman).

But let's focus on the narrative in John's Gospel.

In her beautiful book on John's Gospel, *Written That You May Believe*, Sandra Schneiders looks at the role of women in that Gospel and highlights the significance of Mary's anointing. Schneiders first points out the "eucharistic overtones" of the meal.[27] It is situated six days before Passover, which according to John's chronology falls on a Saturday, and therefore the meal is on a Sunday, the day for the Eucharist in the Johannine community. Martha is also said to be "serving." The word used is *diakonia,* the word Luke uses when Jesus visits her house. Waiting on table was also at the time a "function conferred by the laying on of hands."[28] Also, if any early Christian community included foot washing as part of its celebration of the Eucharist, it would have been John's community, given the prominence he gives that action in Jesus's life. Mary, then, is seen as a full disciple, in a setting "evocative of the Eucharist."

Three other points are important. First, if Mary's wiping Jesus's feet with her hair is meant to anticipate Jesus's washing the feet of his disciples, then she is doubly depicted as a disciple: the disciple would wash the master's feet, and this was the act that Jesus commanded his disciples to do. This conforms with the image of Mary in Luke's Gospel, a disciple sitting at Jesus's feet. She both listens to and puts into action Jesus's words. John also shows the sisters working together, whereas Luke does not. Overall, John is clearly presenting Mary as a full disciple.

Second, we see Jesus rebuking a male disciple for criticizing a woman. Jesus approves of what Schneiders calls her "original religious initiative." Leave her alone, he says to Judas. This may shed light on the treatment of women in John's community, hinting at early attempts by men to control women there. Schneiders notes: "Jesus's opinion of male attempts to control the relationships between his women disciples and himself is so clear in the New Testament that one can only wonder at the institutional church's failure to comprehend it."

Third, this story, like the story of the Raising of Lazarus, foretells Jesus's own death (through the anointing), thus showing Mary and her sister as full participants in his public ministry. They are faithful to Jesus, as were Jesus's mother and Mary Magdalene, even throughout his darkest moments.

Mary is also a highly *active* disciple in this story, taking the initiative to wash the Master's feet, which counterbalances our understanding of her as passive, compared with her more active sister, Martha. It helps us to see, again, that there is a time for action and a time for contemplation and reminds us not to stereotype or limit either woman to a "type."

Mary's "original religious initiative" leaps off the page. She does something unusual and dramatic—spending a great deal of money to anoint Jesus, even at the risk of offending those around her. How often have all of us feared doing the compassionate thing in other settings—to stand up for a group of marginalized people, take the side of the outcast, seek forgiveness during a time of vengeance—because we are afraid of offending?

On a more personal level, how often are we afraid to do something pious because it will look foolish? On my first pilgrimage to the Holy Land I visited the Church of the Holy Sepulchre in Jerusalem, certainly the holiest physical site in the Christian world. I felt so overwhelmed by a sense of the holy that my first reaction was wanting to bow down and press my forehead against the floor as a kind of gesture of humility, in the way that I have seen Muslims pray. But I wondered what people would think. Would I look showy or stupid or even offensive? Then I thought of how ridiculous those fears were. Unless we're hurting someone else, why should we curb a sincere desire to express reverence for God? I found a quiet space and prayed in that way.

Sometimes I wonder whether Mary felt the same: *I'm going to anoint him with the most expensive perfume I have, even if others find it off-putting.* Like her sister, her strong personality shines through in these stories.

Both Martha and Mary, real women whose memories were treasured by the early church, reveal themselves as complex, complicated, and compassionate women, friends of Jesus, and disciples. Together they give us the courage to approach Jesus with honesty and integrity, relating to him as Lord, but also as friend.

Jesus, John, and Women

A beautiful clause in John's Gospel—"Jesus loved Martha and her sister"—illuminates Jesus's relationships with Martha and Mary. But what can we know about his relationship with women in general, at least as recorded in the Gospel of John?

In *Written That You Might Believe,* Sandra Schneiders offers an astute analysis of Jesus's relationship with Martha and Mary. She also offers three important overall observations about women in the Fourth Gospel. Let's consider these insights before we go any further in our story in which Martha and Mary play such important roles.[29]

First, women are shown in an entirely positive light and in intimate relationship with Jesus. Not one woman is shown resisting him, disbelieving him, or betraying him, which stands in sharp contrast to the way many of the men are portrayed: "vain, hypocritical, fickle, obtuse, deliberately unbelieving or thoroughly evil," as Schneiders writes. Even during a difficult moment for Martha, when Jesus responds to her complaints about her seemingly lazy sister, she is presented in a positive light.

Second, John's Gospel portrays women in ways that are neither "one-dimensional nor stereotypical." Schneiders points to the Samaritan woman, who enjoys one of the longest recorded conversations with Jesus in the entire New Testament. The Samaritan woman, who meets Jesus at a well and offers him water, is depicted as negotiating an "incredible range of emotions," in contrast to some male figures—like Lazarus. Indeed, from John's Gospel we get a better sense of the "warm and dominant" Martha and the "strong and contemplative" Mary than we do of the more "shadowy" Lazarus.

Schneiders suggests that the author of the Fourth Gospel "had a remarkably rich understanding of the feminine religious experience." This could be the result of a fertile literary imagination, but she feels it is more a result of "actual experiences of Christian women who played prominent roles in the community of the Fourth Evangelist."

Third, as we've seen with Martha's blunt comments to Jesus and Mary's anointing of his feet over the protests of Judas, women in John's Gospel are often depicted as living out "unconventional" roles. A few examples: the Samaritan woman who has been married five times questioning Jesus and displaying her uncommon theological knowledge; Martha running the public aspects of the funeral for and mourning of her brother; Mary Magdalene walking to a tomb in the early morning and then announcing the news of the Resurrection to the disciples.

Amy-Jill Levine, however, sees nothing unconventional here. "Women," she wrote me, "could speak honestly with their friends (especially rich women, as they clearly are in John). Why would a woman not go to a tomb? Why would a sister not be in charge of her brother's funeral?" She notes that while the Samaritan woman would have been "unconventional" in having five husbands, the larger point is the contrast to Old Testament stories where men and women meet and then marry.

Schneiders also points out that only two women—Mary the wife of Clopas and Mary the mother of Jesus—are presented primarily as mother or wife or are defined in relationship to men. The rest require no identification with male characters: they stand on their own. Schneiders suggests that this shows evidence of strong women active in the community addressed by the Fourth Gospel.

These observations tell us much not only about women in the time of the Fourth Gospel but also about Jesus's approach to women, which often has not been mirrored by Christians in later centuries. It suggests that women were "fully participating and highly valued community members," in Schneiders's words. It also suggests that the writer of the Gospel considered this in accord with the thinking of Jesus, who is never depicted in any way as disapproving of the women.

And, as Levine wrote to me recently, Jesus's relationships with women made "perfect sense in his own Jewish context," where women had numerous social roles. Jesus is not "inventing feminism" over and against a repressive Judaism. Rather, she says, his relationship with women is consistent with his Jewish culture.

This discussion also has implications for women in the church today, specifically the Catholic Church, where women are sometimes seen as mere complements to men, while the men are depicted as having the more essential roles as leaders.

That "men-first" or "men-only" approach is often depicted by Christians as approved by Jesus because, as the argument goes, he chose only men to be part of the Twelve. But the Twelve, as we have seen, were probably mainly a symbolic "gathering" of the twelve tribes of Israel. Not all of them seemed to have exercised leadership roles in the early church. (Again, the four Gospel writers don't even agree on their names.)

Discipleship, therefore, does not begin and end with the Twelve. And it certainly doesn't begin and end with men. To take just two

Last Supper, by Bohdan Piasecki, shows women disciples and children along with the men at the meal.
COURTESY OF WE ARE CHURCH IRELAND

examples, Martha and Mary were "fully participating and highly valued community members," as Schneiders wrote, with important roles of their own, disciples in their own ways, not dependent on either their brother or their father. Their stories have much to teach us about women's roles in the church as fully participating members.

Jesus's open-minded approach to women had dramatic consequences for Mary and Martha, who felt close enough to him to scold him in their home and anoint his feet over the protests of others. Their intimate relationship with him also comes to the fore in the raising of their brother Lazarus.

For Your Reflection

1. How do you respond when Jesus says to Martha, "You are worried about and distracted by so many things"? Do you think it is a rebuke or an invitation? Why?

2. When are you most like Martha? When are you most like Mary? In the story in Luke 10:38–42, do you identify more with Mary, with Martha, or with Jesus?

3. Luke speaks of Martha as engaged in "much ministry" or "much service" (Greek: *diakonia*, whence the English word "deacon"), but many commentators (and artists) tend to limit her to peeling potatoes. What service or ministry might have overwhelmed her?

4. How would you describe the balance between action and contemplation in your own life? Does one or another predominate? Is there more need for balance?

5. In John's Gospel, it is clearly Mary of Bethany who anoints Jesus's feet. In other Gospels her identity is less clear. What does her action and her being unnamed in other Gospels say to you about the role of women in the Gospels? Or about how the Gospels were written?

6. Sandra Schneiders notes that in John's Gospel, women were "fully participating and highly valued" community members. Is the same true today in the church?

Two Days Longer

Why Does Jesus Wait?

*. . . after having heard that Lazarus was ill, he
stayed two days longer in the place where he was.*

I n Richard Zimler's novel *The Gospel According to Lazarus,* the
first important event described in the book, written in the voice
of Lazarus, is what everyone wants to know about: his experience
of being raised from the dead. Zimler does not, as journalists often
say, "bury the lede." The great miracle is told just as Lazarus remembered it—addled in mind, weary of limb, and confused about where
he was—almost immediately after he has emerged from the tomb
in Bethany.

"My shoulders are gripped from behind, and I am pushed into
an upright position," he says. Zimler's Lazarus is in a daze, needing
people to help him reenter the world.

Next, two people unfold a "coarse linen cloth" that had been
wrapped around his chest and legs: his burial cloth. Lazarus is dimly
aware of people bustling about, some shouting, some whispering.
Soon a "slender man" gives him a cooling drink of water from a
wooden ladle.

As Lazarus becomes more conscious, the slender man speaks to
him in his native tongue, a "comfort," says Lazarus.

"*Shalom aleickem, dodee,*" he says. "Peace to you, beloved."

Lazarus describes him: "Stubble coarsens his cheeks, and his shoulder-length brown hair is in a tangle. He shows me a weary but contented smile."

Gradually Lazarus recognizes the man as his dear friend Yeshua, who looks older than Lazarus remembers him. "Could he be ill?" he wonders. The reader is meant to see Jesus as "exhausted by" the effort of raising his friend.

As people minister to their newly raised friend, Yeshua grips Lazarus's hand and kisses it. Soon he places his hand on Lazarus's head and begins to chant. The scene artfully conveys Jesus's affection for "he whom you love." In fact, one of the themes of the book is this extremely close, almost romantic, friendship of the two, which dates from childhood.

Then Yeshua's eyes fill with tears, and he says, "Can you forgive me for coming too late?"

A still-dazed Lazarus wonders, "Too late for what?"[1]

Why Did Jesus Wait?

In Zimler's novel, Jesus's question refers to one of the most confusing passages in the New Testament. Why does Jesus do something that seems heartless, even cruel: ignore the sisters' plaintive request for help and instead remain "in the place where he was," across the Jordan River, for two whole days?

Was Jesus lazy? Hard-hearted? Obstinate? Trying to teach Martha and Mary a lesson? Trying to teach Lazarus a lesson? The disciples? Was he afraid of returning to Jerusalem, where he had been threatened with stoning? Or is there another reason for this apparent callousness?

The traditional explanations for Jesus's "too-late" arrival are as follows:

First, it is possible that some Jews of the time believed that the soul hovered around the body for three days. John's account, then,

On the banks of the Jordan River.
COURTESY OF THE AUTHOR

implies four separate days: the day it took for the message to reach Jesus, the two days that Jesus purposely waits, and the day of travel from across the river to Bethany.

In this interpretation, Jesus understood that his actions might be dismissed or even laughed at if people believed Lazarus was merely asleep. Perhaps, thinking back on the confusion surrounding the Raising of the Daughter of Jairus—when onlookers said the little girl was dead and he countered that she was only asleep—he wanted to ensure that people understood what he was about to do in Bethany. He wanted people to know, as he says to the disciples bluntly, "Lazarus is dead."

This would make Jesus's delay calculated but not cruel. St. John Chrysostom, the theologian and fourth-century bishop of Constantinople, made that point in a homily on Lazarus: "Why did he wait? That Lazarus might breathe his last and be buried; that none might be able to assert that He restored him when not yet dead, saying that it was a lethargy, a fainting, a fit, but not death. On this account He waited so long, that corruption began, and they said, *He now stinks.*"[2]

When we think of Jesus performing his miracles, we can sometimes miss *his* appreciation of what these miracles would mean. It
is not only his disciples and followers, and later Christians, who
would understand their symbolism, but also Jesus himself probably
intended the symbolism involved. A man so deeply steeped in his
faith surely would have understood the rich signs and symbols of
the traditions of his faith.

When Jesus went up a hillside to preach the Sermon on the
Mount, how could he not have been thinking of Moses coming
down from Mount Sinai to communicate God's law? When he was
silent before his accusers during his Passion, how could he not have
remembered the verses about the Suffering Servant in the Book of
Isaiah? This is not to say that Jesus did these things *merely* to act
out symbolic gestures—as if he were simply reenacting certain passages from the Scriptures for the sake of the crowds. His actions
had meaning in themselves. When he feeds a crowd of people, he's
not simply reenacting Moses feeding the crowds in the desert; he
himself is also feeding real people. Christians believe he is also going
beyond what Moses did. Jesus reveals himself not only as the one
who gives food but as the food itself, *the* Bread of Life.

Jesus, profoundly steeped in the Judaism of his day, would un-
doubtedly understand the symbolism of his actions. For a more
contemporary example, we might think of the Rev. Dr. Martin
Luther King Jr. delivering his "I Have a Dream" speech on the steps
of the Lincoln Memorial. The speech itself was important, as was
Dr. King's own prophetic witness. But Dr. King also grasped and
most likely intended the symbolism of speaking before a memorial
to the president who had issued the Emancipation Proclamation.

When pondering his response to Martha and Mary, Jesus may
have remained behind to ensure that no one could misinterpret what
he was about to do: give life and show himself as life. In his judgment
this self-identification may have outweighed the concern that his
delay would upset Mary and Martha. He wanted his actions to carry

the most weight possible, and this would happen only if people knew that Lazarus was truly dead. Only then would it be clear to people that Jesus was indeed the "Resurrection and the Life."

A second possible reason: Jesus waits because he knows that what he will give Lazarus surpasses healing from any earthly illness. "Out of love for Lazarus Jesus did not go to help the sick Lazarus, for he would be of more help to Lazarus when Lazarus was dead," as Raymond Brown puts it in his commentary on John.[3]

St. Peter Chrysologus, the fifth-century bishop of Ravenna, said that for Jesus it was "more important to conquer death than to cure disease." Jesus reveals his love for Lazarus not by healing him as the sisters might have hoped but by calling him out of the grave. "Instead of a remedy for his illness, he offered him the glory of rising from the dead."[4]

Finally, a third possible explanation: In John's Gospel, Jesus is almost always portrayed as being in control. In this interpretation, his delay was another instance of his asserting his freedom and his authority, saying, in a way, "I will go when I go." Jesus decides when and where and to whom to go. Jesus's delay and his earlier words—"This illness does not lead to death; rather it is for God's glory, so that the Son of God may be glorified through it"—is a reminder of the mystery of what the Johannine scholar Francis Moloney terms "God's designs" in the Fourth Gospel.[5]

Or one could look at it as Ben Witherington does. He told me, "Jesus is waiting for his Father to give him the go ahead to go to Bethany." Even though he is requested to come, he is waiting for some sort of indication from the Father—not human beings—that it is time to go. "He waits for the Lord's will to be revealed."

There are several other occasions when Jesus's negative response to a request leads to unexpected consequences that "transcend the intentions of the original request," as Witherington told me. The most obvious is the Wedding Feast at Cana. There, Jesus's mother (she is never called Mary in the Fourth Gospel) tells him that their hosts have run out of wine, and Jesus responds sharply, saying, "What concern is that to you and to me?"[6] But then he changes water into wine, in abundance, a sign of the superabundance of God's power and love.

As Moloney says, "Jesus's response cannot be measured by human standards. He responds to criteria greater than those expected by the reader, necessarily conditioned by human expectation and behavior."[7]

In Colm Tóibín's *The Testament of Mary*, Jesus's mother explains in blunt terms her son's initial refusal to turn water into wine at Cana and his later delay in going to Bethany: "[I]f the time was not right, he would not be disturbed by a merely human voice, or the pleadings of anyone he knew."[8] In Tóibín's novel, as in John's Gospel, Jesus does things on his own initiative and in his own time. In this way he often confounds the expectations of the disciples and the readers of the Gospel.

Overall, Jesus is presented in this Gospel passage as supremely in control, understanding what people would think if he came earlier and knowing that he would be giving Lazarus, his sisters, and those around him his greatest miracle.

Or, more precisely, his greatest "sign." In the Synoptic Gospels, Jesus's miracles are presented as "works of power" (*dynamin* in Greek) that astonish onlookers. In John's Gospel, they are "signs" (*sēmeia*), indications of his divinity that point toward a deeper understanding of who Jesus is and what he has come to accomplish. Especially in John's Gospel they act as powerful symbols for the disciples and other followers. They are meant not as wonders in themselves, designed to astonish, but as invitations for us to believe. Indeed, one of the main complaints of Jesus in the Gospels is that even though people see these "works of power" and "signs," they still do not believe.

John Meier writes that the "signs" (healings, for example, or in the case of Lazarus, new life) are not ends in themselves but only symbols, pointing beyond themselves to the "fullness of divine life that Jesus offers the believer."[9]

And in John's Gospel, the Raising of Lazarus is not merely the climax of the signs; it is an event that precipitates plots to kill Jesus, which leads to his eventual death. In John, the action leads directly to Jesus's arrest, crucifixion, and death. As such it replaces the Cleansing of the Temple in the Synoptic Gospels. John places that event, when Jesus ejects the money changers from the Temple, at the beginning of his public ministry.[10] Even in Bethany, before his Crucifixion, Jesus is ready to "lay down his life" for his friends.

The New Testament scholar Stanley Marrow, SJ, notes: "That the miracle of bringing the dead Lazarus back to life should be chosen to crown the public ministry of Jesus and be the final major event leading to his condemnation and death is, evidently, a most suitable choice in the gospel of 'life.'"[11]

Who Is Jesus in John's Gospel?

Let's return to the idea of Jesus being "in control" in John's Gospel. His dominance over each situation emphasizes an aspect of Jesus that may surprise readers used to thinking of him as gentle or even passive. The confident Jesus we meet in the Fourth Gospel can seem at odds with the doe-eyed Jesus of some paintings and holy cards.

All Christians must grapple with the variety of presentations of Jesus in the Gospels. And questions surrounding why he stayed "two days longer" highlight this challenge.

We've already noted that the Jesus we encounter in John's Gospel sometimes differs from the portrait of Jesus found in the Synoptics. Still, some connections exist between the Synoptics and John. According to Raymond Brown, the "main body" of John's Gospel does not come from the Synoptics or the sources of the Synoptic stories. Yet Brown suggests influences and connections. And unless we posit a kind of "isolated" Christian community, which he does not deem likely, it is hard to believe that John's community would not have become familiar in some way with the Gospel traditions from other communities, "the kind of tradition that eventually found its way into the Synoptic Gospels, particularly into Mark."[12] Amy-Jill Levine told me, "John most likely had access to the Synoptics, as did John's readers."

Mosaic of Christ Pantocrator (Christ All-Powerful) in the
Hagia Sophia Grand Mosque, Istanbul.
WIKICOMMONS

The focus of each Gospel is the same person—Jesus Christ—but his story is told by four different storytellers telling it at (roughly) four different times. Even within the Synoptics the portrayal of Jesus differs, depending upon what each evangelist wanted to stress for his community.

In our Introduction to the New Testament class in graduate school, Daniel J. Harrington, SJ, summarized these perspectives in a remarkable way. Dan, an internationally recognized scholar, was someone who had, as the saying goes, forgotten more about the Gospels than we would ever know. Before his recent death at age seventy-three, he taught generations of students and wrote hundreds of articles and dozens of books. The lighthearted joke circulating at his Funeral Mass was that God called Dan home because Jesus needed someone to explain the Book of Revelation to him!

So, when Dan gave us a simple grid that summarized the presentation of Jesus, the disciples, and the Christian life in each of the Synoptic Gospels, everyone rushed to copy it. It has helped me so much in the years since. Here it is:

FR. HARRINGTON'S SYNOPTIC GRID	MARK	MATTHEW	LUKE
JESUS	Suffering Servant	Old Testament Fulfilled	Prophet and Example (Martyr)
DISCIPLES	Fools and Cowards	People of Little Faith	Twelve Apostles
CHRISTIAN LIFE	Life Under the Cross	God's People in Christ	Spirit-Guided Church

The portrayal of Jesus in Mark's Gospel is as the "Suffering Servant," an image taken from the Book of Isaiah, which focuses on the innocent one who suffers (often for the sake of others). In Matthew he is the "Old Testament Fulfilled," which makes sense considering Dan's belief that Matthew was writing for a largely Jewish audience and took pains to see Jesus's life, death, and resurrection as the fulfillment of all the promises and prophecies in the Old Testament. In Luke he is the "Prophet and Example," who is also martyred, so a person to be "followed" by the early church, giving us a template for the Christian life.

Based on Dan's other writings, I can posit what he might have said about John:

JESUS	Son of God who reveals the Father
DISCIPLES	People who misunderstand
CHRISTIAN LIFE	Belief in Jesus

I asked Sandra Schneiders how she might answer those questions for John's Gospel. Here's her response:

JESUS	Word of God become truly human and dwelling in and among us
DISCIPLES	Women and men, Jews, Samaritans, Gentiles (all humans) who believe in Jesus
CHRISTIAN LIFE	Community of Spirit-filled believers in Jesus, sent to draw all into divine life

Schneiders's summary of Jesus—"Word of God become truly human and dwelling in and among us"—marvelously captures both his divinity and his humanity. But sometimes for readers of John's Gospel his humanity gets lost. Indeed, in some Johannine passages he sounds distinctly unlike the Jesus of the Synoptics. For several weeks after Easter, Christians in many denominations read from Jesus's "Farewell Discourse" to his disciples in John's Gospel, offering instructions on how the disciples are to carry out his movement and insights on Jesus's relationship with the Father. Modern scholars sometimes refer to this speech, delivered before his Passion and Death, as Jesus's testament. His language is not only poetic but also highly mystical, notably different from much of the language of the Synoptics.

Consider this famous parable from Mark:

"Listen! A sower went out to sow. And as he sowed, some seed fell on the path, and the birds came and ate it up. Other seed fell on rocky ground, where it did not have much soil, and it sprang up quickly, since it had no depth of soil. And when the sun rose, it was scorched; and since it had no root, it withered away. Other seed fell among thorns, and the thorns grew up and choked it, and it yielded no grain. Other seed fell into good soil and brought forth grain, growing up and increasing and yielding thirty and sixty and a hundredfold." And he said, "Let anyone with ears to hear listen!"[13]

Compare that with a few lines from the Farewell Discourse in John's Gospel, in which Jesus bids goodbye to the disciples before the Crucifixion:

> As you, Father, are in me and I am in you, may they also be in us, so that the world may believe that you have sent me. The glory that you have given me I have given them, so that they may be one, as we are one, I in them and you in me, that they may become completely one, so that the world may know that you have sent me and have loved them even as you have loved me. Father, I desire that those also, whom you have given me, may be with me where I am, to see my glory, which you have given me because you loved me before the foundation of the world.[14]

As a friend of mine says about the Johannine Jesus: "It's a long way from the carpenter in Nazareth!"

Finally, Ben Witherington told me that he sees the differences as follows: "In the Synoptics, especially in Matthew, Jesus is portrayed as a sage, who uses wisdom speech of the ordinary sort—aphorisms, riddles, parables, and maxims—whereas in John, Jesus is God's wisdom come in person. And so in the Farewell Discourse he speaks accordingly. He does not merely give wisdom; he is wisdom come in person."

The question is not, Which Jesus do you prefer? It is the same person. But rather the question is, Which portrayal of Jesus appeals to you? And can the portrayals that are less appealing to you also challenge you to see Jesus in a new light? Can the mystical language of John, where Jesus speaks in long pronouncements and is in control even during the Passion, deepen your appreciation of the divinity of Jesus? And can the earthiness of Mark's Jesus, often in a hurry, who calls a woman and her daughter "dogs" and whose mother and family travel all the way from Nazareth to the Sea of

Galilee to "restrain him" because they think he is "out of his mind," deepen your appreciation of the humanity of Jesus?[15]

Jesus is human and divine every moment of his life. It's hard to understand—a mystery if ever there was one—but essential to ponder. Some believers, if pressed, might say that while they believe in both of his natures (human and divine), one is more of a challenge. Those who cotton to his divinity find stories of his human behavior off-putting, as when he loses his temper or curses a fig tree. Those who favor the humanity look askance at his being called Son of God and raising people from the dead. The Orthodox scholar Alexander Schmemann wrote about a Jesus who both weeps and raises Lazarus from the dead, "He who weeps is not only man but also God, and he who calls Lazarus out of the grave is not God alone but also man."[16]

Humanity and divinity are both part of Jesus's story. Leave one of his natures out of the picture, and it's not Jesus we're talking about. It's our own creation. And we are created in God's image, not the other way around.

This is not to suggest that the Jesus in John's Gospel is not human. Indeed, the first chapter proclaims that the "Word became flesh and lived among us." The Greek for "dwell" is even earthier: *eskēnōsen*. The word became flesh and "tabernacled" or "pitched its tent" among us. We are meant to think of a person pitching a tent among a nomadic people. Despite the emphasis on his divine control in John's Gospel, Jesus is always human.

Interestingly, he's not participating only in the human condition. The Gospel does not say that the Word became human. John uses a more elemental word in his Prologue: "The word became flesh and lived among us." As the theologian Elizabeth Johnson, CSJ, writes, "The text does not say that the Word became a human being, although there is a perfectly good word for this in Greek (*anthropos*) let alone that the Word became a man (*aner*)." No, she points out, the word used is *sarx*, flesh. God enters "the natural sphere of what is fragile, vulnerable, perishable, the very opposite of divine glory."[17]

God became not just a man, not just human, but *flesh*—which, as the story of Lazarus shows, eventually decomposes and stinks.

John's Jesus is both human and divine, as in the other Gospels. But at times, because of the words and actions recorded, and John's literary style, Jesus's humanity might seem subsumed under his divinity. Passages in the Gospel of John that seem to show him almost as if he were the postresurrection Jesus can sometimes make his actions seem confusing.

His waiting to go to Bethany is one example of this confusing aspect. The Son of God, the Second Person of the Trinity and the Revelation of the Father, will go when he goes.

Jesus is in control. He will go to Lazarus when he goes to Lazarus. And when he goes, he will change history.

Nonetheless, these explanations, even when accepted by Christians, still may not take the sting away from Jesus's two-day delay. We are uncomfortable with a loss of control, especially during difficult situations.

We Cannot Do Everything

One of the earliest examples of that lack of control in my own life came during my Jesuit novitiate. When I entered the Jesuits at age twenty-seven, my parents were separated. Happily, they later reconciled. But during my first few months in the novitiate, while they were still apart, I was tremendously sad, for two reasons: first, over the pain that they were experiencing; second, over my frustration at not being able to fix it.

As a Jesuit, a Catholic and a Christian, and even more so as a son, I felt I should be able to fix it, I needed to fix it, and I was responsible for fixing it. And the inability to do so, despite my best efforts, was deeply troubling.

The desire to fix things, a noble and sincere desire, can spring up in many circumstances. When people are diagnosed with an illness, the first desire of a compassionate friend is to find a doctor to heal them. When people lose their job, the first desire of a compassionate friend is to find them a new one. When someone is going through an emotional crisis, the first desire of a compassionate friend is to help them weather the crisis. I want to stress: the desire to help is a holy desire. But often all we can do is accompany the other person.

As a young novice, I didn't understand that. One day in tears, I told my spiritual director, David, how frustrated I felt by the situation with my parents.

"Jim," he said, "you may have to embrace your own powerlessness here."

I had no idea what David was talking about. Not having grown up in a super-religious family or having had much religious education or read much about spirituality, I initially found David's words a dreadful response. Why would anyone want to be powerless over anything? What's more, why would someone want to embrace it? It was like someone telling me that I was weak and had to accept it— as if I were a child. That's how I heard it, at age twenty-seven.

"What a cruel thing to say!" I said.

Calmly David explained that there are some things in life over which we have no power. We can do our best, but we must leave the rest to God. And the acceptance of that fact brings not only peace, but also a sense of perspective. What's more, it's true.

This does not mean that we are called to be lazy. Or that we throw up our hands and say, "Whatever." In the case of my parents, it meant that I tried to be as open, loving, and useful as possible. But crucially, it also meant accepting that I was not in charge, it was not up to me, and I was not God. We do what we can and leave the rest up to God.

Paradoxically I found that embracing my powerlessness, as David put it, not only placed God squarely in the center of the picture and freed me from my need to "fix it," but also calmed me down and thus enabled me to accompany my parents with more love. Before, every interaction seemed a kind of reproach to me because I hadn't been able to solve the problem. But when I accepted that their initial failure to reconcile wasn't my fault, I was less angry and frustrated when speaking with them. No longer in "fixing" mode, I was more able to listen.

As St. Paul said, "For whenever I am weak, then I am strong."[18] This may be something of what he meant. Here I always think of what has become known as the Romero Prayer, written by Bishop Ken Untener, expressing the spirituality of St. Óscar Romero, the martyred archbishop of El Salvador and champion of the poor. It's my favorite expression of what it means to work hard but recognize that you're not in control. It reads, in part:

> We plant the seeds that one day will grow. We water seeds already planted, knowing that they hold future promise. We lay foundations that will need further development. We provide yeast that produces effects far beyond our capabilities. We cannot do everything, and there is a sense of liberation in realizing that. This enables us to do something, and to do it well. . . . We may never see the end results, but that is the difference between the master builder and the worker. We are workers, not master builders; ministers, not messiahs. We are prophets of a future not our own.[19]

The Romero Prayer reminds us that we may not see the change that we work for, at least in our lifetimes. But we still work for it.

Ultimately, we must leave a great deal up to God and relinquish our need for control. And in relinquishing that need, we can often discover God in new and surprising ways. My cousin Mary Beth had an experience like that in, of all places, Bethany.

Mary Beth in Bethany

Mary Beth is one of my favorite people in the world. She is bright, capable, loving, and hardworking, and she exemplifies the phrase "no-nonsense." She is my cousin on my father's side, and I always love spending time with her, her sister Marguerite, and their brother, Andy.

On the first pilgrimage to the Holy Land sponsored by America Media, I was delighted that Mary Beth and Marguerite decided to come along. I felt the same every day of the pilgrimage. They had a wonderful time and so did I: it was great being around people I knew so well and who had known me all my life—from infant, to toddler, to bratty adolescent, to college student, to corporate wannabe, to Jesuit, to priest. It's hard to describe how happy it made me to be able to be with them in the Holy Land and visit all the sites important to Jesus's life.

Mary Beth was suffering from some arthritis during the trip, which made walking a challenge. But what I admired most was her equanimity in the face of these physical problems, which she could not control.

Because God was in control, Mary Beth's pilgrimage was not what she might have expected, but rather what God had in mind.

Mary Beth and her sister Marguerite at the Mount of
Beatitudes, by the Sea of Galilee.
COURTESY OF THE AUTHOR

This is not to say, "All's for the best." Rather, it is to admit that in many situations we are powerless before the reality we face, and in those times we are invited to trust God—as much as Mary and Martha did when they were waiting for Jesus to arrive in Bethany.

When we visited the Church of the Holy Sepulchre, one of the greatest shrines in Christianity, Mary Beth confronted what all pilgrims see when they enter: the stairway that leads to the top of the chapel at Calvary, the hill on which Jesus was crucified. Essentially the entire church is built *around* this hill and the nearby tomb in which Jesus was buried. When you enter the church you see, to your right, a stone staircase leading to a chapel built on top of the hill.

Mary Beth knew at once that she couldn't climb that staircase and said, "That's okay. I'll just stay here. I don't have to see everything." I found her equanimity impressive.

A few days earlier in Al Eizariya, she had discovered that God had something special in mind for her. And when I look back, I see it as the result of her "embracing her powerlessness," as my spiritual director David would have said.

When Mary Beth trudged to the top of the hill in Al Eizariya and saw the long winding stone staircase that led to the tomb, she knew that she couldn't make it down the steps. I'll let Mary Beth tell the story in her own words:

Because my arthritic knees prevented me from going down into Lazarus's tomb (which had very uneven steps), I decided to sit on a nearby bench while the group explored.

The bench was directly across from a fruit stand, selling oranges, juice, dates. There was a young (perhaps in his mid-twenties) man sitting there and we got to talking. At first the conversation was very general, weather, scenery, etc.

Then I told him about our trip, about your book and how it made me want to take the trip. In return he told me some things about himself. It turned out he was working at the fruit stand, which belonged to his aunt. He earned $4 per day. He had a finance degree but was unable to find a job. Being a Palestinian, he was confined to specific areas in Israel and not allowed to leave the country. He had a girlfriend, but they had no idea when or if they could ever get married, because of his financial situation.

As the group started to finish up, he went to the stand in hopes of making some sales. Before I left, he gave me a glass of fresh-squeezed orange juice for which he would take no money. I felt so bad for him I bought a box of dates—which were delicious.

Hearing his story and having seen eighteen-year-old Israeli soldiers with Uzis in Bethlehem the day before made my perspective on the Israeli/Palestinian conflict take on a definite pro-Palestinian bent. When I asked him if he thought the Israeli/Palestinian conflict would ever be resolved, he said no.

I remember the next day at Mass asking for prayers for him when it came time for the Prayers of the Faithful.

Mary Beth still talks about this moment as one of the highlights of her pilgrimage, affording her a window into the life of a person she never would have met had her knees not troubled her and had she gone into the Tomb of Lazarus. I often use her story with pilgrims and say, "You won't be able to see everything, do everything, or experience everything. And that's okay. Trust that the pilgrimage you have is the pilgrimage that God has in store for you."

On pilgrimage, as in life, God is in control. Mary and Martha discovered that. So did Mary Beth. And over the course of my life, so have I.

The recognition that Jesus is in control, and would come when he wanted to come, troubled Mary and Martha. It must have seemed inconceivable that their compassionate friend would not come immediately upon hearing the news of their brother's death.

This facet of our story—Jesus's waiting—is not simply an issue for two grieving sisters all those years ago in Bethany. It lies at the heart of our spiritual lives today. All of us have waited for God to do something, have questioned why God is so slow in acting, or even questioned why God does not seem to be acting at all. It is the question of at best a silent God, at worst a seemingly indifferent God. It is the question "Why do we suffer?" It is the question "Where is God?" Sometimes it is even the question "Does God exist?"

Yet Mary and Martha are still in relation with that God, even in the middle of their frustration and perhaps anger. They still are willing to trust in a friend whose ways they don't quite fathom—yet. The invitation for them, and for us, is to believe in a God we don't understand.

For Your Reflection

1. Why do you think Jesus waited several days to go to Bethany?
2. From what you know of John's Gospel, does it seem that Jesus is always "in control"? Does that image of Jesus comfort or disturb you?
3. We're often invited to relinquish control. When have you done so, and what was the result? What can you do to let go of the need for control?
4. Have you ever tried to fix something that seemed unfixable, as I tried to do when my parents were separated? What was your experience like? Did you learn anything about yourself or about God?
5. If you were Mary Beth, how would you have responded to the prospect of not being physically able to enter the tomb?

6

Let Us Go to Judea Again

John's Gospel and "the Jews"

Then after this he said to the disciples, "Let us go to Judea again." The disciples said to him, "Rabbi, the Jews were just now trying to stone you, and are you going there again?"

In the early 1960s, Pope (later Saint) John XXIII convened the Second Vatican Council. Cardinals, archbishops, bishops, clergy, lay theologians, and a few Catholic sisters from around the world gathered to, as Pope John said, "open the windows" of the church and decisively enter the modern age. The last ecumenical, or worldwide, gathering, the First Vatican Council, had been held from 1869 to 1870. Vatican II, as it is popularly known, is regularly termed by historians as one of the most important events of the twentieth century.

In 1965, the Council released one of the most influential documents in the history of the Catholic Church. It was called *Nostra Aetate*, or "In Our Age." (Vatican documents are usually referred to by the first two words of their text in Latin.) As a document written by an ecumenical council, *Nostra Aetate* enjoys one of the highest levels of authority in the church—compared with, say, a statement

The opening of the Second Vatican Council.
CATHOLIC PRESS PHOTO: WIKICOMMONS

from a Vatican department, an apostolic letter from the pope, or one of his homilies. As a teaching document it is almost unsurpassed in authority.

Nostra Aetate revolutionized the church's approach to what it called "non-Christian religions." Until a relatively short time before Vatican II, the approach could be fairly summarized by the Latin phrase *Extra ecclesiam nulla salus*: "There is no salvation outside the church." For most of the church's history those words were understood in the most literal sense: no one who was not Catholic could be "saved" by God. The Fourth Lateran Council, an ecumenical council convened by Pope Innocent III, declared in 1251: "There is but one universal Church of the faithful, outside which no one at all is saved." And in case anyone had any doubts about what that meant, two centuries later, the Council of Florence declared, "The most Holy Roman Church firmly believes, professes and preaches that none of those existing outside the Catholic Church, not only pagans, but also Jews and heretics and schismatics, can have a share in life eternal; but that they will go into the 'eternal fire which was prepared for the devil and his angels.'"

Nostra Aetate, however, set forth the belief that other religions respond to longings of the human heart "each in its own manner, by proposing 'ways,' comprising teachings, rules of life, and sacred rites." And in a statement that would have shocked the participants of previous councils, including the First Vatican Council, *Nostra Aetate* declared, "The Catholic Church rejects nothing that is true and holy in these religions." That marked a sea change in church teaching.

One of the most important parts of the document was its approach to Judaism and the Jewish people, which had been one of the most shameful parts of church history. Until it was changed by Pope John XXIII in 1959, for example, one of the prayers read at the church's Good Friday liturgy prayed for the conversion of the "perfidious Jews," who were seen not only as beyond God's reach, but also one of the causes, if not the main cause, of Jesus's death.[1]

Nostra Aetate, which built on decades of work by more open, progressive, and enlightened Catholic theologians, decisively rejected the old approach to the Jewish people and, in the process, rejected centuries of anti-Semitism (against the Jewish people) and anti-Judaism (against the Jewish religion). One of its most important passages deserves to be quoted in full, for it serves as a foundation for what we will discuss in this chapter:

> . . . [W]hat happened in His [Jesus's] passion cannot be charged against all the Jews, without distinction, then alive, nor against the Jews of today. Although the Church is the new people of God, the Jews should not be presented as rejected or accursed by God, as if this followed from the Holy Scriptures. All should see to it, then, that in catechetical work or in the preaching of the word of God they do not teach anything that does not conform to the truth of the Gospel and the spirit of Christ.
>
> Furthermore, in her rejection of every persecution against

any man, the Church, mindful of the patrimony she shares with the Jews and moved not by political reasons but by the Gospel's spiritual love, decries hatred, persecutions, displays of anti-Semitism, directed against Jews at any time and by anyone.[2]

In the wake of *Nostra Aetate*, every pope since John XXIII not only has emphasized the church's rejection of anti-Semitism and labeled it sinful but has also made significant efforts to reach out to the contemporary Jewish community and apologize for the church's legacy of both anti-Semitism and anti-Judaism. In 2000, Pope John Paul II issued a "confession of sins against the Jewish people," addressing God with this prayer:

> [W]e are deeply saddened by the behaviour of those
> who in the course of history
> have caused these children of yours to suffer,
> and asking your forgiveness we wish to commit ourselves
> to genuine brotherhood
> with the people of the Covenant.[3]

But we must ask: How was it that a statement as simple as "Jews should not be presented as rejected or accursed by God" took so long for the church to affirm?[4] More basically: Where did these strains of Christian anti-Semitism and anti-Judaism come from? This is a complicated question about which perhaps thousands of books have been written, especially in the wake of the Holocaust. But one place that was the source of much anti-Semitism and anti-Judaism was the Gospel of John.

John and "the Jews"

It can be shocking to read how John's Gospel so often speaks disparagingly about "the Jews." Over and over, they are presented in harsh terms, opposing Jesus at almost every turn.

The phrase occurs multiple times in the story of the Raising of Lazarus, appearing first in the verse that opens this chapter. "The Jews" are introduced as the ones who wanted to stone Jesus. Even for those who know little about the Bible, the verse will prompt the questions, "Wasn't Jesus Jewish?" and "Weren't his disciples Jewish?" and "Didn't the writer of John's Gospel know this?" So, before we go any further, we need to look at how and why John uses this term, and how and why we must understand it from a fresh perspective.

John's Gospel uses *hoi Ioudaioi* over and over, and almost always negatively. It appears more than seventy times, with "the Jews" usually seen in opposition to Jesus and his disciples.

This is not as much the case in the Synoptic Gospels, where the term occurs only sixteen times in Matthew, Mark, and Luke combined, chiefly during the Passion narratives, where the writers are concerned mainly with who was responsible for the death of Jesus—the Romans or "the Jews." (To answer that question: only the Romans had the authority to put someone to death.) In most narratives in the Synoptics, the use of "the Jews" seems unnecessary,

Papyrus 66 (P66), also known as P. Bodmer 2, an ancient papyrus book containing the Gospel of John in Greek.
COURTESY OF FONDATION MARTIN BODMER

even superfluous, given that everyone around Jesus, including Jesus himself, was a Jew. But not in every passage. In Matthew 28:15, for example, the Gospel writer uses *hoi Ioudaiois* to refer to those who reject the proclamation of the Resurrection and believe the story about the disciples stealing Jesus's body while the soldiers slept.

To begin our discussion about this term in John's Gospel, we need to state an important and perhaps obvious fact: John knows that Jesus was Jewish. When Jesus meets the Samaritan woman, she asks, bluntly, "How is it that you, a Jew, ask a drink of me, a woman of Samaria?"[5] John also knows that Jesus was from Nazareth (a Jewish town) and was an associate of John the Baptist (another Jew).

Understanding the Gospel of John's use of "the Jews" (which most modern biblical scholars put into quotation marks for reasons that will soon become obvious) is essential for understanding the story of Lazarus, where the term appears five times. In addition to the sentence that leads off this chapter, we read these lines that again seem bizarre, given that Martha, Mary, and Lazarus are Jews too:

> [M]any of the Jews had come to Martha and Mary to console them about their brother.

> When Jesus saw her weeping, and the Jews who came with her also weeping, he was greatly disturbed in spirit and deeply moved.

> So the Jews said, "See how he loved him!" But some of them said, "Could not he who opened the eyes of the blind man have kept this man from dying?"

Moreover, we must understand John's use of this term to understand the Gospel as a whole and to prevent the kind of anti-Semitism and anti-Judaism that some of these passages in John's Gospel and in the New Testament in general have caused. Raymond Brown says that contemporary theologians must address this Gospel's "intense hostility" to the Jewish people, as well as "a terminology whereby

[Jesus's] adversaries are 'the Jews' to the extent that one gets the impression that he and his followers are not Jews."[6]

The Misunderstood Jew

An excellent place to start is Amy-Jill Levine's indispensable book *The Misunderstood Jew: The Church and the Scandal of the Jewish Jesus.* The thesis of this brilliant and highly readable book is that even the most thoughtful and educated Christian preachers and scholars tend to repeat the same lazy stereotypes about Jews, Judaism, and Jewish practices from the time of Jesus. For example: The only thing the Pharisees (or Sadducees or scribes) cared about was the observance of every tiny rule; they didn't really care about human beings. So they never really cared about women, or the sick, or the disabled. Only Jesus did, which was why they opposed him. In her book, Levine carefully demolishes these stereotypes and others. She insists that to get Judaism wrong is to get Jesus wrong and that making Jesus look good should not require making Judaism look bad.

Once we are alerted to these stereotypes, we will start to notice them more often. Even the most educated of scholars and experienced of preachers fall into these traps, and reading AJ's book is one of the best ways to combat this. (I call her AJ because we're friends.) And full disclosure: before I read her book, I too assumed that these stereotypes were true (since I had read or heard them many times) and even used them in my preaching. AJ's book aroused me from what Immanuel Kant called "dogmatic slumber."

To begin with, AJ cautions against lumping the following groups together—Pharisees, Sadducees, chief priests, scribes, and so on—as well as drawing sweeping conclusions about Jewish culture based on the limited (and often skewed) presentation of them in the Gospels.[7] After all, the Gospel writers were not especially interested in making any of those groups look good. Their aim was to make Jesus look good. They were, in addition, reflecting their own relationship to Jews who did not accept their proclamation. She also takes aim at the tendency to draw conclusions about "Judaism" or "the Jews" based solely on the depiction of these groups: "In New Testament classes, many students get a single lecture, or half a lecture, on the four major parties of Jews mentioned by the Jewish historian Josephus: Pharisees, Sadducees, Essenes, and Zealots." Then, she says, the class moves on, "confident that they know what there is to know about first-century Judaism."

She continues: "The modern-day analogy would be to think that if one knows a few details about the Knights of Columbus, the Kiwanis Club, the Masons and the Boy Scouts, one understands American society."

How, then, are we to understand the term "the Jews" in John's Gospel?

First, we must understand that there was a great diversity of Jewish beliefs and practices at the time, and so to talk about what "the Jews" believed or did is akin to saying, "the Christians," that is, every single Christian, believe or do this or that today. Second, we must be attentive to the various "overstatements concerning and misperceptions of, and slanders against first-century Judaism," as AJ puts it, that appear over and over in both the classroom and in church, from podiums and from pulpits. In her book, AJ offers seven (which I summarize here):

1. Jewish Law was impossible to follow and a burden that no one could bear.
2. All Jews wanted a "warrior messiah" who would defeat Rome; therefore, "the Jews" rejected Jesus because he was a peacemaker.
3. Jesus was a feminist in a woman-hating Jewish culture. AJ's earlier point regarding my question about Martha and Mary owning homes is an example of this. "There is nothing weird here," she wrote, "other than the insistence of Christian readers that Second Temple Judaism was hopelessly misogynistic."

4. Jews were obsessed with purity laws and distanced themselves from the outsider, unlike Jesus, who swept aside the laws and loved everyone.

5. In Jesus's time, a "Temple domination system" oppressed the poor and women and promoted division between insiders and outcasts.

6. Jews were (or are) "narrow, clannish, particularistic, and xenophobic"—again, unlike Jesus.

7. The Gospels aren't talking about Jews but about "Judeans."

Third, and perhaps most important, we must recover an understanding of the Jewishness of Jesus. This can't be said enough: Jesus was a devout Jew who worshiped in the Temple and knew his Scriptures. Mary and Joseph were Jewish. The apostles were Jewish. The idea that "the Jews" would have been against them would have seemed nonsensical at the time.

So why is John writing so negatively, even antagonistically, about Jesus's own people? Explanations abound, and AJ considers several of them.

First, as she mentioned in No. 7 above, when John uses *hoi Ioudaioi*, some scholars claim that he is not talking about "Jews" but about "Judeans," that is, people from the region of Judea in the south, versus Galilee in the north. But the first readers of John's Gospel would not have heard it that way. They would associate the term not with Judeans but with Jewish people.

Others suggest that John is talking about Jewish leaders. I confess that I have used this interpretation in my preaching to distinguish between "some Jewish leaders" and the entire population of Jewish people at the time. But as AJ says, this ignores the fact that the "vast majority" of Jews chose to follow some of these leaders rather than Jesus, with the Pharisees being the most popular group, and it becomes a "distinction without a difference."

I asked AJ recently about that approach, common to many well-meaning preachers. Here is her answer:

If you must substitute a new word or phrase for "the Jews," then "religious leaders" is not helpful. If you intend to be talking about the chief priests, they do not "lead the religion." Rather, they run the Temple. They do not set practice for other Jews (they are not comparable to the pope or College of Cardinals or even local bishops). Plus, everyone in the pew knows that "Jewish leaders" or "religious leaders" really means "the Jews," especially since people in the pew think that the Jewish leaders are appointed by Jews, in the same way that priests and pastors generally have some sort of ordination and so are appointed by institutional bodies. Priesthood in Judaism is an inherited position; Pharisees are lay leaders who were respected by the Jews and thus were the rivals of the followers of Jesus.[8]

Another common explanation is that it was a time of "intra-family debate," when Jews were fighting against other Jews. This is the approach taken by many mainstream Christian theologians and biblical scholars, including Raymond Brown, who contends that a good part of the relations between Jesus and "the Jews" goes beyond what happened during Jesus's lifetime: "[T]o a considerable degree the description reflects what happened to the Johannine Christians in their interactions with synagogue authorities."[9] John's Gospel, he explains, was written at a time when the Christians were beginning to distance themselves from the synagogue and were even expelled from the synagogue.

But this interpretation, again common, falters because there is no external evidence that Jews across the empire were expelling Christians from the synagogues in the first century. Up to the fourth century, as AJ notes, there were still complaints from Christian writers that Jews welcomed Christians into their synagogues. John's followers, a specific group of Christians, may have been expelled from synagogues, which may explain, in part, some of his antipathy toward "the Jews." John does use a new term, *aposynagogos*, "to be expelled from the synagogue," three times. And yet even in these cases, John lists such expulsion as a threat rather than an actual practice.

Granted, as AJ notes, Jews can still be anti-Jewish in the sense that "insider location does not preclude one being seen as a hater of the internal group." At the very least there was some enmity between the writer of the Gospel of John and "the Jews."

Perhaps it was the writer of John's Gospel who exaggerated the conflict between the synagogue and the disciples of Jesus.[10] After all, "the Jews" come to comfort Mary and Martha after their brother's death, something that John couldn't overlook.

Brown agrees: "John does not give an objective, dispassionate history of all the factors that entered into the picture, especially on the part of the synagogue authorities."[11] This is essential to understand when we read John: for whatever reason, he is opposed to "the Jews," which obviously does not mean that Jesus or his disciples were opposed to every Jew who was not a follower of Jesus.

By the same token, as Ben Witherington wrote to me, we must remember that there were indeed some Jews who "strongly opposed Jesus and critiqued him, and these included the high priest and his family at the time, who surely was responsible for handing Jesus over to Pilate." While we must condemn the anti-Semitism and anti-Judaism spawned by "ignorant and even malicious readings of the Fourth Gospel" and not paint with a broad brush "all Jews in any age," we must also not "minimize the opposition" to Jesus among some Jewish people.

What about "the Jews" in the story of Lazarus?

I asked AJ about the verse we're looking at in this chapter, which describes "the Jews" coming to comfort Mary and Martha. Was this a rare instance of John making "the Jews" look good, or was this simply to set up "the Jews" as comforting the sisters, only to betray them by going to the "Jewish authorities"? Here's her response:

On "the Jews" coming to comfort—it's one of the few places where "the Jews" appear to be doing the right thing. Whether this is a verse to be celebrated, or whether it just makes them even more demonic since they know how to be nice, depends on how you read the text. Here we need literary critics. I am inclined to go in the direction of your second reading (the "they really are nasty after all" reading), but that is not a necessary reading. Moreover, the phrasing even suggests that Mary and Martha are not Jews.

We will have to choose whether we think John is demonizing all Jews and using "the Jews" to indicate opposition to Jesus, or whether we can still redeem John's Gospel from charges of anti-Judaism. The more I look at the Fourth Gospel, the more I sense that John mostly speaks of the Jews as negative. And yet, I can see other approaches as well. Here, we'll need to be led by theologians and ethicists, rather than historical-critical biblical scholars, to help us sort out how to read John's Gospel.

The historical reasons for John's clear antipathy may remain murky. And who the Gospel means by this term—a certain cadre of leaders, some groups of Jewish people at the time, individual Jewish opponents to Jesus—is also unclear. But the real-life results of that phrase *hoi Ioudaioi* have been devastating: centuries of anti-Semitism and anti-Judaism and even well-meaning congregations hearing phrases like "the Jews" with little to no context. This is one reason why *Nostra Aetate* was needed. And, on a more scholarly level, this is why most mainstream scholars will put that term in quotation marks: "the Jews."[12]

In my own mind I often think of a *group* of Pharisees or scribes who opposed Jesus. It's clear that he faced some opposition. What is the best way, then, to approach this in scholarship and in preaching, if we are not to substitute new phrases? I asked AJ recently, and here's her answer. (Like many Jewish scholars, she uses "G-d" out of respect for the divine name.)

> With over seventy instances of *Ioudaioi* in John's Gospel, the reader is to hear the echo, so much so that the *Ioudaioi* are the quintessential opposition to G-d/Jesus. But we have to train our congregations to listen with ears that know the harm that has been done by demonizing "the Jews" or blaming "the Jews" for the death of Jesus. I am not a fan of over-reading the text. I'd rather read what it says, in terms of being as close to the Greek and the literary sense of the text as possible. And then deal with problems in the text. Better to deal with it.

For his part, John Meier believes that in the case of the Raising of Lazarus, the term *hoi Ioudaioi* does not carry the "fiercely hostile" meaning that it often does elsewhere in John, but rather is more "neutral," given that not only do many Jewish people come from Jerusalem to accompany Mary and Martha in their grief, but eventually many of them end up believing in Jesus as a result of the miracle they witness. He suggests that in the original telling of this story the phrase was probably *hoi polloi* ("the many") with the "typical use" of *hoi Ioudaioi* being added at a later stage.[13]

Nonetheless, as we continue to move through the narrative of the Raising of Lazarus and the rest of John's Gospel, readers must beware of the fraught use of that term and be exceedingly careful not to make overstatements, generalize, or lie about "the Jews." Brown is correct here: "Today, therefore, in proclaiming John preachers must be careful to caution hearers that John's passages cannot be used to justify any ongoing hostility to Jewish people. . . . Regarding the Bible as sacred does not mean that everything described therein is laudatory."[14]

For the purposes of our story, we must always keep in the front of our minds the fact that Martha and Mary were Jews. So was their brother Lazarus. And so was the man who raised him from the dead.

"It's So *Jewish*!"

The Jewishness of Jesus himself—as well as that of his mother Mary, her husband Joseph, the rest of Jesus's extended family, and his disciples—is difficult for some modern-day Christians to accept. Many years ago, at a Jesuit parish where I was living, an elderly Catholic woman in a conversation with a Jesuit priest refused to admit that Jesus could be anything but Christian. She was responding to a homily in which the priest had stressed Jesus's Jewishness.

"At the beginning maybe," she said, "but then he became a Christian, right?" After repeated responses from the Jesuit priest ("Jesus was born, lived, and died a Jew"), the woman simply shrugged her shoulders and said, "Well, I guess it's just a mystery." She was unmoved.

More seriously, centuries of virulent and violent anti-Judaism and anti-Semitism mean that Christians have an obligation to be alert not only to the way that the Gospels speak about "the Jews" but also the way that even well-meaning scholars, theologians, and preachers pass on the harmful stereotypes that Amy-Jill Levine and others have brought to the attention of the church.

An awareness of the ways that the Gospels portray "the Jews" is an important part of the spiritual journey of all Christians. To set Jesus in opposition to his own faith is to set him in opposition to himself. Not to see Jesus as a Jew is not to see Jesus at all. More positively, to see Jesus as a Jew is to see Jesus.

A few years ago during a Holy Land pilgrimage, we visited the Church of the Pater Noster on the Mount of Olives in Jerusalem, which is near where, by tradition, Jesus is said to have taught the disciples the Lord's Prayer (or the Our Father prayer). That event might have happened in many places, but it is commemorated today in a small grotto, very near the larger church, which has been venerated since the fourth century. The grotto is a small stone chamber that can fit maybe twenty people and has perfect acoustics.

Our tour guide, Maher, invited us to pray the Our Father in

English first and then in the various languages spoken by members of our group: Spanish, French, German, and Portuguese. Then Maher announced that he would sing the prayer in Aramaic, the language in which Jesus most likely would have taught it to the disciples. Maher's resonant voice filled the grotto, with the distinctive Aramaic sounds, words, and phrases echoing off the stone walls and ceiling.

A woman next to me grabbed my arm hard after the prayer and said forcefully, "It's so *Jewish*!" The Jewishness of Jesus, she told me afterward, had never been so real for her as when she heard Aramaic being sung by a Palestinian Christian. Would that every Christian could have the same experience.

For Your Reflection

1. How do you feel when you see "the Jews" presented so disparagingly in John's Gospel?

2. Consider reading *Nostra Aetate* and meditating on it. (It's a short document.) Afterward, you might ask yourself: What more can Christians and Christian churches do to counteract anti-Semitism and anti-Judaism?

3. *Nostra Aetate* says that the Jewish people as a whole should not be held accountable for the death of Jesus. As many New Testament scholars point out, only the Roman authorities (specifically Pontius Pilate) had the authority to put a person to death. Have you ever heard any homilies, seen any films, read any books, or heard any lectures that seemed to imply otherwise? What was your response?

4. Amy-Jill Levine lists seven misconceptions about the Jewish people that are often held by well-meaning Christians. Why do you think they are so persistent? Do any of them still "make sense" to you? Why? How might these stereotypes have played into a false understanding of Jesus?

5. What aspect of Jesus's life most helps you understand his Jewish identity?

So That You May Believe

Understanding and Misunderstanding Jesus

> *Jesus answered, "Are there not twelve hours of*
> *daylight? Those who walk during the day do not*
> *stumble, because they see the light of this world.*
> *But those who walk at night stumble, because the*
> *light is not in them." After saying this, he told them,*
> *"Our friend Lazarus has fallen asleep, but I am*
> *going there to awaken him." The disciples said to*
> *him, "Lord, if he has fallen asleep, he will be all*
> *right." Jesus, however, had been speaking about his*
> *death, but they thought that he was referring merely*
> *to sleep. Then Jesus told them plainly, "Lazarus is*
> *dead. For your sake I am glad I was not there, so*
> *that you may believe. But let us go to him." Thomas,*
> *who was called the Twin, said to his fellow disciples,*
> *"Let us also go, that we may die with him."*

O ne of the most difficult aspects of the spiritual life is the question of unanswered prayers. What happens when we pray for something good and it doesn't happen? The question is particularly acute for Christians, because Jesus told his disciples, "Ask, and it will

The Galilean Jesus, by William Hart McNichols.
COURTESY OF THE ARTIST

be given to you; search, and you will find; knock, and the door will be opened for you. For everyone who asks receives, and everyone who searches finds, and for everyone who knocks, the door will be opened."[1]

In the same story in Luke, Jesus gives the disciples illustrations about persevering in prayer and speaks about the willingness of God to give good things to believers: "Is there anyone among you who, if your child asks for a fish, will give a snake instead of a fish? Or if the child asks for an egg, will give a scorpion? If you then, who are evil, know how to give good gifts to your children, how much more will the heavenly Father give the Holy Spirit to those who ask him!"[2]

All this seems to indicate that we will always get what we ask for in prayer.

But unless Jesus is talking only about "spiritual gifts," like courage or fortitude to confront a crisis, this is not the case. If we pray for someone who is sick to get better, and that person dies, we did not get what we asked for. Our prayers may have been answered in some other way, but the fact that we did not receive what we asked for is a source of sadness and confusion for many of us. And at some point, we will all face this. I don't know anyone who has said that all their prayers have been answered.

Many explanations are set forth in these cases, none of which can completely satisfy the believer, especially during times of suffering. The first explanation is that God is "testing" us. That may be the case—I can't speak for God—but when I think about a child stricken with cancer, that approach makes God out to be rather monstrous, at odds with the compassionate God embodied by Jesus, who healed people.

Second is the suggestion that God gives us something "better" in answer to our prayers. Again, while sometimes we receive many graces during times of suffering (wisdom, patience, compassion), the idea that God would countenance a child's suffering so that the parents could grow wiser or more patient also seems monstrous.

Finally is the explanation that God does answer our prayers, but the answer is "no." This explanation, however, flies in the face of Jesus's invitation to "ask" so that we can "receive." Or we could say overall that Jesus really wasn't talking about asking for any*thing*, but just spiritual gifts, which may explain the line that the Father will not deny the gift of the Holy Spirit to people.

Let me be clear: I'm not saying that those explanations haven't worked for some people who are suffering; rather, they don't work for everyone. Many believers are left confused about God's ways.

Christians can be comforted by the fact that Jesus participated fully in human life. Though divine, he suffered physically (not only on the cross but also with the usual aches and pains of a human body) and emotionally (not only on the cross but with the inevitable sadness of human life, for example, experiencing illness and death in his extended family). So when we pray to Jesus, we are praying to someone who understands us because he is divine and knows all things but also because he is human and experienced all things.

In the end, the most honest answer to why our prayers aren't always answered—or why there is suffering—is this: we don't know. Saints, theologians, and writers have grappled with this question for millennia, and we still don't have satisfactory answers. In the face of the mystery of suffering, unanswered prayers, and a mysterious God, the question is not, to my mind, "Why are some prayers not answered?" but "Can we believe in a God whom we don't understand?"

The disciples faced this question as well.

Misunderstanding Jesus

At this point in our story, Jesus and his disciples are on the other side of the Jordan River, apparently having just escaped a stoning in Jerusalem. As Paul McCarren, SJ, notes in his book on John's Gospel, it is easy to imagine the disciples as "dispirited" after Jesus's "hasty retreat" from Jerusalem. At the same time, their presence at the Jordan must have seemed confusing to them. What were they going to do there now—start baptizing again?[3]

One of the main themes of the Gospels is how often the disciples (and others) misunderstand Jesus. It's not surprising. Jesus often spoke in hyperbole ("Let the dead bury their own dead"), exaggeration ("You could say to this mulberry tree, 'Be uprooted and planted in the sea,' and it would obey you'"), and in riddle-like parables ("The kingdom of heaven is like treasure hidden in a field, which someone found and hid; then in his joy he goes and sells all that he has and buys that field").[4]

Some of his words and deeds were offensive to the disciples. When Jesus says to Peter that he must suffer and die, Peter says, "God forbid it, Lord!" That earns Peter a rebuke from Jesus: "Get behind me, Satan!" That must have stung poor Peter.

That exchange happens as Jesus and the disciples are traveling to a town called Caesarea Philippi, in northern Galilee. At one point, Jesus asks them, "Who do people say that I am?" I always imagine

Jesus walking ahead of the group and hearing them argue and turning around to confront the question directly. They answer with what was probably a fair summary of what people were thinking at the time: "John the Baptist; and others, Elijah; and still others, one of the prophets." Finally Peter answers correctly, "You are the Messiah."[5]

This passage from Mark occurs when Jesus's ministry is well underway. This means that the disciples have been spending time with him and still don't understand him. And this misunderstanding of Jesus, on the part of the disciples and more broadly his hearers, will continue.

For example, in the beginning of John's Gospel he tells his hearers that he will "raise up" the Temple after it has been destroyed. His hearers scoff, reminding him that it took Herod many years to complete the Temple. But Jesus is speaking of his own body. Later, in his encounter with the Woman at the Well, he identifies himself as the "Living Water," and if a person drinks it, that person will never again be thirsty. The Samaritan woman asks to know the source of that water so that she does not have to fetch water every day. But it is Jesus himself.

This, in a riddle-like way, seems to be what is going on in this part of our story, where Jesus speaks about people who walk in the light and those who walk in the dark: "Those who walk during the day do not stumble, because they see the light of this world. But those who walk at night stumble, because the light is not in them."

Brendan Byrne points out that what is essentially a parable answer works on a few levels.[6] First, it is about Jesus's "hour" (that is, his crucifixion), which has not yet come. So he and his disciples can walk to Jerusalem in the light and not fear their adversaries. At the same time, it may refer to something Jesus says earlier, after he heals the "man born blind": "We must work the works of him who sent me while it is day; night is coming when no one can work. As long as I am in the world, I am the light of the world."[7]

With Jesus's death approaching (represented here by darkness),

Jesus must give Lazarus life now, while it is still possible. Here we must be careful with the use of these metaphors in John's Gospel. A blind woman once told me how frustrating it was to hear spiritual blindness compared to physical blindness; in the same way, many African Americans and people of color have told me how difficult it is for them to hear constant negative references to darkness.

Finally, we can read Jesus's response as an invitation for the disciples to walk with him, the "light of the world," and, no matter what the time, never fear. "Since they will be with him, the Light, they will always be walking by day, no matter what the opposition," says Byrne.

The Rev. John Dear, a Catholic priest and writer, notes that Jesus refers to "our friend Lazarus," not simply "my friend Lazarus." This may be an implicit challenge to the disciples along the lines of, "What are you willing to do for your friends? . . . Are you willing to risk your lives for Lazarus? As I am for humanity?"[8] Will you choose light or dark?

The disciples still seem to misunderstand. In response to their fears of being stoned again (either him or them), Jesus gives them this miniparable about the man who walks in darkness. But they still don't seem to get it.

This "Johannine misunderstanding" is highlighted by their misunderstanding of Lazarus's death. Jesus talks about Lazarus being "asleep," a common way of speaking of death in the early church. John Meier makes the case that when Jesus uses this term before raising another person from the dead—Jairus's daughter—he may be implying that in his presence death will be as "impermanent" as sleep.[9] Ben Witherington pointed out that sleep was also a metaphor or euphemism used in early Judaism for death, "for those who believed that the person would be raised from the dead, like coming back from sleep renewed and refreshed."[10] Nonetheless, the disciples seem to think Jesus means literal sleep, and so he speaks plainly: "Lazarus is dead."

Brendan Byrne notes it is also possible that they were "clutching" at Jesus's pronouncement that Lazarus was sleeping in the hope that they might not have to go: they too were frightened of returning to Judea.[11]

The reader by this point (as well as the disciple) should be used to Jesus knowing something without apparent knowledge of the facts, characteristic of his "divine foreknowledge."

At this point, Thomas offers his allegiance: "Let us also go, that we may die with him." C. H. Dodd links this "as a sort of equivalent" to the saying in the Synoptic Gospels about taking up your cross daily.[12] Yet as we move through the narrative, none of the disciples, including Thomas, is mentioned as having accompanied Jesus to Bethany. Byrne told me that he sees Thomas as "ever the pessimist," saying with a kind of "hopeless resignation" that they will all die. Amy-Jill Levine told me that she wonders whether Thomas is being sarcastic.

Note too that while Jesus says, "Let *us* go to Judea again," the disciples respond, "Are *you* going there again?" (emphasis mine). Overall, the passage is another example of the disciples' misunderstanding and of their having to be corrected by Jesus. Jesus is not inviting them into a suicidal mission, though danger will be involved (to Jesus, not the disciples). The aim of the journey to Bethany is life, not death.

In terms of misunderstanding, there are also some scholarly disputes about which of the two sisters, Martha or Mary, truly understands Jesus in the story of the Raising of Lazarus. Is it Martha, who rushes out to greet him and proclaims him as the "Messiah, the Son of God," which many point to as a profession of faith as important as Peter's? Or does she understand him only in part, not realizing that he is much more than that?—he is "the Resurrection and the Life." Or does Mary understand him better? After all, she falls at his feet when he comes to Bethany to raise her brother, and later, in John 12, Mary anoints his feet at their home. These questions, which we take up later, turn on the question of the understanding and misunderstanding of Jesus.

Did Jesus Want People to Misunderstand Him?

Sometimes in John's Gospel these misunderstandings are meant to highlight who is and who is not "in the know." This is often the case in the Synoptics, where it's clear that some of Jesus's parables are meant to be understood by some and not by others. Here is Jesus in Mark's Gospel:

> "To you it has been given the secret of the kingdom of God, but for those outside, everything comes in parables; in order that
>
> 'they may indeed look, but not perceive,
>
> and may indeed listen, but not understand.'"[13]

Here Jesus is quoting a passage from Isaiah, speaking of those who are "deaf" and "blind" to the word of God. (Once again, we must be alert to how these metaphors are used, especially as they relate to the blind and deaf communities today.) In Mark's Gospel,

Fourth-century (AD 300) sarcophagus showing the Raising of Lazarus, with only one sister present (Vatican Museums).
COURTESY OF DAVID KATEUSZ

Jesus speaks in parables "in order that" (Greek: *hina*) they do not understand.

But in Matthew's Gospel we read: "The reason I speak to them in parables is that 'seeing they do not perceive, and hearing they do not listen, nor do they understand.'"[14] In this passage, Matthew uses the Greek work *hoti*, which means "because." In other words, they don't grasp the parables *because* they are hard-hearted. Ben Witherington noted to me that the overall passage from Isaiah quoted by Jesus makes clear that the people "do not understand because they are alienated from God and need to repent."

Even with these explanations, we are left with a difficult question: Did Jesus *not* want people to understand him?

A few years ago, when I was working on my book *Jesus: A Pilgrimage*, I contacted the New Testament scholar John R. Donahue, SJ, who had written a great deal on the Gospels, especially the parables. Father Donahue is the author of the excellent book *The Gospel in Parable: Metaphor, Narrative, and Theology in the Synoptic Gospels*. I was curious about the many mentions of secrecy and hidden teachings in the Gospels. In Mark, for example, Jesus says that those on the "outside" may hear the parables but not understand. That they may "look, but not perceive," and "listen, but not understand." Finding that odd, I wrote to John and asked, "Did Jesus not want people to understand him?"

In Mark, he said, these misunderstandings are related to what scholars call the Messianic Secret—an example of Jesus teaching the disciples privately about his identity. Also, there was a tradition in the ancient world of a teaching being open only to "insiders." Finally, he said, Jesus shows a kind of restraint, a holding back from fully revealing everything to everyone at every opportunity.

Still, it seemed odd that Jesus wouldn't *want* people to understand him. So I asked Father Donahue more directly, and he said, "Jesus did not *expect* everyone to understand his teaching." He reminded me that the first use of the word "parable" in Mark's Gospel comes in a setting where Jesus's mother and family members are sitting outside his house in Capernaum, and he addresses his words to those inside the house. Here, there is an implied "inside" and "outside."

This is an indication that the parables were meant to be understood by the inner circle. Yet elsewhere the Gospels seem to indicate that Jesus's parables, and his teachings, will be understood by everyone—in due time. It takes time. And remember how many of the parables are about slow and continuous growth, like those about mustard seeds or yeast. In due time, in God's time, all will be revealed. But time is an important ingredient.

That's one way to look at this question of "misunderstanding." Jesus's private teaching to the disciples will be revealed eventually, as a light to everyone. Indeed, why would God hide this indefinitely? The good news is meant to be public.

The Slow Work of Time

Another way of looking at this misunderstanding might be in a commonplace way. God teaches us things that will be understood and brought to light, for the benefit of all, but only *over time*. And I don't mean only things that we learn in school—as important as they are—but spiritual insights we learn in prayer, by reading the Bible, in spiritual direction, during a homily, or on a retreat. Still more broadly: I mean lessons we learn in our relationships, in our families, in the workplace, and especially in difficult times and periods of personal struggle.

Most deep learning, however, happens gradually. It cannot be rushed. I've seen this especially in my work as a spiritual director to many young Jesuits, as they make their way through their training or what we call their "formation." Often I suggest to them that there are two levels to one's formation, which parallel the learning that we all do.

The *visible* level is apparent for all to see: For Jesuits this means undertaking various ministries in the novitiate; pronouncing vows publicly; then taking classes, studying, and passing exams. Next comes more full-time work for a few years, usually in some teaching capacity; then theology studies; and then, for most Jesuits, ordination. A few years after that, for both Jesuit priests and brothers, comes the pronouncing of Final Vows. All these stages of formation, which are planned and expected, included in all the vocational literature for all to see, are important. They are also public. Some of these events, such as vows and ordination, even include invitations for friends and family to attend. And Jesuits learn much from these visible stages: how to pray, how to live and work as a Jesuit, how to understand the Gospels, how to preach, how to do pastoral counseling, and so on.

But there is also an *invisible* level of formation—for all of us, not just Jesuits—that flows underneath it all, like a deep current in a river that runs according to its own timetable. Many things educate us, in hidden ways, in ways that are just as important as our visible education: we have a retreat that helps us see God or ourselves in an entirely new light; we fall in and out of love; we struggle with an old habit in therapy; we have a difficult relationship in community that must be worked out; a parent gets sick or dies; we have a problem with a job; we face a financial crisis; we suffer a professional disappointment. If we are open to God's forming us, we are slowly changed.

Years later, the fruits of that invisible formation are brought to light, often in surprising ways. Unlike the visible formation, in which we are formally "taught" explicit skills (for example, preaching), when it comes to the invisible formation, we may be unaware of what we've "learned" until years later. Maybe we're counseling a young person who is going through the same thing we went through. Or we remember an insight from a conversation we had with someone in community who always bothered us, but who is now a friend.

Or we simply feel more at peace with ourselves, having worked through some problems in therapy or spiritual direction, or on our own. This invisible formation works its way on us, so that at times we are unaware that we are drawing upon it.

The Greeks had two ways of understanding time: *chronos* and *kairos*. The visible formation happens on *chronos* time, the tick-tock, day-to-day, month-to-month time we're familiar with. We know more or less when we'll be finished with college, when our children will come into adolescence, when our hair will go gray. It's calendar time. The invisible formation occurs on *kairos* time, which is more elusive. It's that time of readiness or ripeness, which can come at any time. In other words, it's God's time.

Never doubt that this kind of hidden teaching will eventually be revealed, for the good of others. God does not give us a light and then ask us to hide it under the proverbial bushel basket. Trust that what is happening to us, even what we learn during the painful moments in life—maybe *especially* during the painful moments—is part of God forming us. And this goes for everyone—not just for people who choose the life of a Catholic priest, sister, or brother.

This pattern mirrors, in a way, Jesus's own formation in Nazareth. Of course, he was the Son of God and enjoyed an intimate relationship with the Father, but the seemingly mundane things that happened to him in Nazareth—including his eighteen years or so of hard work—helped prepare him to become, as the Jesuit theologian John Haughey wrote, "the instrument needed for the salvation of the world."[15]

Who knows what kinds of events or conversations or interactions in daily life helped to form Jesus? Confronting illness and death in his family. Seeing how the poor eke out a living. Learning about his faith from Mary and Joseph. Even interactions with friends as a boy, adolescent, and young adult that taught him about friendship and love. Certainly Jesus is fully divine but he is also fully human. And his human experiences would have contributed to his growth as a person. As the Gospel of Luke said about this period, "And Jesus increased in wisdom and in years."[16]

But all this took time. It is the same for us. Our growth takes time.

And even though it is for our good, it can be arduous. Just recently a young Jesuit talked about how God seemed to be inviting him into change, and he referred to the image of the potter and clay, from the Book of Jeremiah. Jeremiah went to the potter's house and saw him reworking a clay pot that had been "spoiled." He made a new one, "as seemed good to him."[17] Jeremiah saw that God was the potter, and Israel was the clay in God's hands. Like the potter, God shapes Israel "as seems good to him."

The young Jesuit said he loved that image. But he also realized that the molding of the pot, even its being broken for its own good, which needs to happen so God can make us "as seems good to him," can be painful. And it can take time. "But I know it's worth it," he said. That trust comes from knowing that, as it says elsewhere in Jeremiah, God has good things in store for us.[18] This is all part of God's forming us.

Never doubt that God is forming us into an instrument needed for the help of those with whom we'll live, work, and minister in the future, in God's good time. And never doubt that the lights that God has given you, even those that seem hidden from others, will be revealed for the benefit of all your friends and family. You may not understand it all right now, as the disciples did not always understand Jesus. This level of our understanding—insight, really—takes time. And in that intermediate stage there is much "misunderstanding," as there was for the disciples.

Their understanding of Jesus took time as well. Perhaps they didn't fully understand him until Easter Sunday. Elizabeth Johnson, CSJ, in her book *Consider Jesus*, wonders if even he fully understood himself or his own identity until that moment, when, in her lovely words, "his ultimate identity burst upon him in all clarity."[19] But it took the disciples a while to begin to "get" him. Just as it takes us a while to "get" God.

We know that we will never truly understand, much less "get" God. God is ever beyond our comprehension, always escaping the boxes that we try to place God in. God is *semper major*, as theologians say, always larger. Or more pointedly, as St. Augustine said, *Si comprehendis, non est Deus*—"If you understand it, it's not God."

Yet we are called to try to understand, in our own limited way, and to enter a relationship with a mysterious God, as the disciples tried to do. One of the reasons that God became human was so that we could understand God's ways more fully. And understand God more fully. In fact, God desired that so much that God was willing to enter this flawed, painful, and tragic, but also beautiful, joyful, and triumphant, human life.

For Your Reflection

1. Have any of your prayers seemed to go unanswered? How did that affect your faith?

2. Are there parts of Jesus's life or public ministry that you don't understand? How does that affect your relationship with him?

3. Do you think Jesus didn't want people to understand him? Or was he simply allowing only those in his inner circle to understand him? Do you think the disciples ever understood him? Can you ever fully understand other people, even loved ones? Do you ever fully understand yourself?

4. Can you be in a relationship with a God whom you don't understand? What allows you to do this with more confidence?

If You Had Been Here

Disappointment in God

When Jesus arrived, he found that Lazarus had already been in the tomb four days. Now Bethany was near Jerusalem, some two miles away, and many of the Jews had come to Martha and Mary to console them about their brother. When Martha heard that Jesus was coming, she went and met him, while Mary stayed at home. Martha said to Jesus, "Lord, if you had been here, my brother would not have died. But even now I know that God will give you whatever you ask of him."

A few years ago, as I mentioned previously, I was diagnosed with a small tumor on my neck—for a second time. Twenty years before, I had a tumor removed from the same place, underwent a rather painful, months-long recovery, but assumed that I would never have to worry about it again. After several tests, however, it was decided that this recurrence of the tumor, which physicians thought was probably benign, would require not only surgery but radiation, as a safeguard against a recurrence.

After the initial discovery of that second tumor, I had prayed hard that I wouldn't have to have the same surgery again. My mind flashed back to the difficulty of the first surgery: the long incision that traveled from under my left ear to my Adam's apple, the swelling, the pain, and the weeks of recovery. I wept in front of my spiritual director as I said, "I'm so disappointed." The word itself made me cry. But it wasn't a general disappointment. It was more specific: it was a disappointment *in God*.

That word kept coming up in my prayer: *disappointed*. Although I know that we can't bargain with God and that our relationship with God is not transactional ("If I do this for you, then you will do that for me in return"), it was hard not to feel let down. In the end, I made it through the surgery—the tumor was benign—and did the six weeks of radiation.

After the relief of the results, I remembered the disappointment. And I wondered whether Martha might have felt the same emotion: an intense, almost *burning* disappointment in the God she trusted. In this chapter's key passage, she seems to express faith and disappointment at once when she says, "Lord, if you had been here my brother would not have died!"

Martha's disappointment would have been even more intense than mine, and her feeling of being let down almost total: her brother was dead, and the person who could have helped was her great friend Jesus.

Throughout that medical ordeal, I never stopped being in relationship with God. Even when disappointed in God, I still believed in God. Even with those feelings burning in my heart, I sought to find God, listen to God, and follow God. I'm not implying saintliness on my part, just saying that, to me, cutting off a relationship with God even in the midst of pain was unthinkable, as it would be for many believers. I still believed.

So did Martha, who in her sadness was still in relationship with Jesus even as she protested his absence. And what a beautiful thing she utters: "Even now I know that God will give you whatever you ask of him." Even now she believes.

In her humility and desperation, Martha seems to say that she is finished praying. She asked for as much as she could, and her brother died. Now she turns to Jesus, the one in whom she is disappointed, and asks him to pray. "Even now I know that God will give you whatever you ask." In other words, "Jesus, pray for me!"

Martha and Mary's Honesty

When he arrives at Bethany, Jesus seems to be alone. Where are his friends? After all, he has invited them to join him, saying, "our friend Lazarus" has fallen asleep, not simply "my friend Lazarus."

In his book *Lazarus, Come Forth! How Jesus Confronts the Culture of Death and Invites Us into the New Life of Peace*, John Dear points out that Jesus's friends seem to stay put, while Jesus risks his life. Even Thomas, who said, "Let us also go that we may die with him," is nowhere to be found once Jesus arrives in Bethany. Dear links this absence with the actions of many Christians, who say that they worship Jesus, or follow Jesus, but shrink back when things become difficult and they are asked to face death, or the culture of death. "We don't lift a finger in the effort to end war," he writes, "disarm our nation, dismantle our nuclear arsenal, or abolish poverty."

Many of us fear even more ordinary things: we don't bother visiting friends in the hospital, giving help to a homeless person, calling someone who is lonely, challenging the status quo on the job, or, more positively, asking for forgiveness or loving someone who may not love us in return. It's too much work. Sometimes it's dangerous. "I'm no saint," people say. We leave the heroic work of holiness to others. "Thomas and the male disciples say the right things, but can't get their feet to move," Dear writes.[1]

Jesus is in Bethany alone, four days after his friend's death.

It is thought that some Jews at that time believed that the soul hovered around the body for a few days. And it was Jewish custom to bury the body on the day of the person's death.[2] Jesus's arrival in Bethany after four days would have meant, to the disciples (and

Mosaic of Jesus's arrival in Bethany, Church of St. Lazarus, Al Eizariya.
COURTESY OF CATHOLIC TRAVEL CENTRE

to the later hearers and readers), that, as Jesus said plainly in the previous passage, "Lazarus is dead."

Mary and Martha knew this better than anyone. Presumably, they had cared for their brother as he fell ill and died, had prepared his body for burial, and had helped to place it in the tomb, probably their family tomb, in Bethany. Their grief and exhaustion would prompt their words to Jesus, first Martha (the active one) and then Mary (the more contemplative one, who initially "stayed at home"): "Lord, if you had been here, my brother would not have died."

Many New Testament scholars have surmised that both sisters saying the same thing to Jesus, word for word, indicates John's editorial artistry at work. However, we can imagine the two women sitting at home as their brother is dying, and repeating the same words over and over, perhaps to one another, perhaps to their friends, until the words gained an incantatory power: "When Jesus gets here, he will heal Lazarus." And then in the days after his death, "If Jesus had been here, our brother would not have died."

And we do not know what Lazarus confided to them, as his strength slowly ebbed from him. For all the attention that the Gospel of John gives to Lazarus—his raising is the crowning "sign" in the Fourth Gospel—the man whom Jesus loved is given no words to speak. But it's not hard to imagine him lying ill, hoping desperately that his good friend would come to his aid. It's also not hard to imagine him asking his sisters over and over, "Is Jesus coming?" "Has he sent a message?" "Is he here yet?" Lazarus's own disappointment may have added to the sisters' frustration.

So perhaps Mary and Martha were united in their thoughts and in their words, and it is not surprising that they greeted him with the same words.

"Do You Not Care?"

Their words to Jesus work on several levels.

First, Martha and Mary are speaking honestly about their frustration to a friend who seems to have ignored their request for help. Sometimes good Christians object to this interpretation, saying that the sisters would never address Jesus so bluntly or, likewise, that their words would not be taken as being critical or in any way negative. "St. Martha and St. Mary would never speak to Our Lord like that!"

But remember Martha's earlier comments to Jesus, complaining about her sister's supposed laziness: "Lord, do you not care?" It is not beyond them—certainly not beyond Martha—to express frustration or anger. They may be saints, but they are also human.

Imagine that your elderly father is experiencing severe heart pains, and you have a friend who lives a few miles away who is a renowned heart specialist. He is the best cardiologist in the area. You phone him, text him, email him, and finally get through to him: "I think my dad is having a heart attack! Can you please come over?" But he never shows up. Three days later, at the funeral, he appears and consoles you.

With what emotion would you say these words?: "If you had been here, my father would not have died." Would you have said them sweetly, calmly, or reasonably? Especially under the stress of losing a loved one, you would probably say them with disappointment, frustration, resentment, anger, even rage. These are normal human emotions. Why would we assume Martha and Mary didn't feel them?

Brendan Byrne has noted that the Raising of Lazarus is as much about Jesus's great miracle as about the universality of Martha and Mary's experience: "Both women give expression to an aspect of grief virtually universal amongst those who mourn the recent death of a loved one: a numbing sense of God's absence." The story "is not just about the fate of individuals who die. It is also addressing the grief of those who mourn their loss."[3]

More often, however, Mary and Martha's words are presented as a statement of belief in Jesus. And they are that. Martha calls Jesus "Lord" (*kyrie*) and says that she believes what he says: her brother will rise again on the last day, expressing a widely held Jewish belief. And, as Stanley Marrow notes, Martha believes that the mere presence of Jesus would have held back "the rapacious hand of death."[4]

St. John Chrysostom praises both sisters for not collapsing in grief but focusing on Jesus: "See how great is the heavenly wisdom of the women, although their understanding be weak. For when they saw Christ, they did not break out into mourning and wailing and loud crying, as we do when we see any of those we know coming in upon our grief; but straightway they reverence their Teacher."[5]

At the same time, some New Testament scholars say that Martha's faith is meant to be seen as incomplete. She professes her faith in Jesus as a miracle worker, but in John's Gospel he is far more than that. John Meier sums this up: "'I know,' says Martha bravely—and, as so often in the Fourth Gospel, when people affirm what they know they actually betray their ignorance." Martha's faith, says Meier, is "not yet perfect."[6] As with the rest of the disciples, her faith is in a lifelong process of development.

These interpretations are not contradictory but complementary. We can be angry at others and still trust them. We can believe in God and still not understand God completely. Anger and trust, belief and unbelief can coexist. How often this is the case with us and God.

One of the most succinct summaries of this experience came during the Funeral Mass of the mother of my Jesuit friend Steve Katsouros. His mother, Suzette, died at age ninety-three and was laid to rest in Silver Spring, Maryland. For the Gospel reading that day, Steve chose the story of the Raising of Lazarus and, in the process, reflected on his mother's life and Martha's life.

Like Martha, Steve said, his mom was a social woman and also very close to her own sister. And, like Martha, she was also "complicated." His summary of Martha and her connection to believers today moved me:

> The Ancient Near Eastern author of our Gospel has presented us with a multifaceted human being with the capacity to hold a variety of emotions all at once. Martha is hopeful in Jesus. Martha is angry at Jesus. Martha loves Jesus. Martha has faith in Jesus.
>
> Like Martha, Suzette was complicated. Who isn't? Take a number! Like Martha, Suzette was also capable of holding strong, often conflicting emotions, simultaneously. Suzette was stubborn and charming. She was demanding and loving. She was critical and open-minded.

We are all like Martha, capable of holding "a variety of emotions all at once," whether in Bethany or Silver Spring.

Into the Deep

A few months after the surgery, and after I'd spent a few prayer periods expressing my gratitude to God, my spiritual director suggested another prayer for me: imagine yourself in a boat with Jesus and speak with him about your disappointment.

This form of prayer is common for Jesuits and is well-known to anyone who has been to a Jesuit retreat house. It goes by many names—"Ignatian contemplation," "imaginative prayer," or "composition of place"—and it forms the bulk of the prayer in St. Ignatius Loyola's manual for prayer, the *Spiritual Exercises.* Essentially, we imagine ourselves in a scene—usually a Gospel scene—or in conversation with Jesus. Using our imagination can be a great aid to prayer, and often what arises in the prayer—emotions, insights, memories, feelings, images, or words—becomes a means of God communicating with us.[7]

My spiritual director, Damian, knew that I had been praying with the boat image over the previous few weeks, since the initial diagnosis. It came to me one morning: an image of Jesus and me aboard a boat in the Sea of Galilee. Picturing it was easier because I had been to the Holy Land several times already, and even had taken boat rides on the Sea of Galilee.

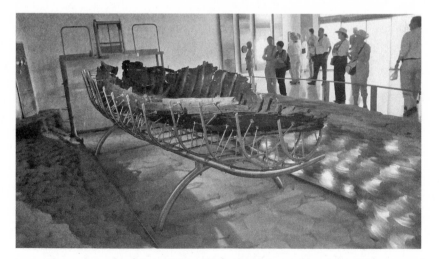

The "Jesus Boat," Yigal Allon Center, Kibbutz Ginosar, Ginosar, Israel.
COURTESY OF THE AUTHOR

There we were, in a wooden fishing boat of the kind that they used in Jesus's time, with a tall mast and wooden slats for seats. A few years earlier I had seen what is called the "Jesus Boat" in a museum near Capernaum, in Galilee. It was a fishing boat recovered, nearly intact, from the time of Jesus. Lower water levels in the Sea of Galilee had revealed the boat stuck in the mud, two thousand years after it had sunk.

In my imagination, Peter was steering. Jesus and I were seated close to each other. The water, in my prayer if not always on the Sea of Galilee, was cerulean blue.

Then Jesus said, "Put out into the deep," something he says to Peter in the Gospels.[8]

I knew what he meant. For many years I had struggled with mild hypochondria. I'd not reached a point of debilitating obsession but tended to focus too much on my own physical health and often catastrophized anything that happened. Every doctor's diagnosis led me to imagine the worst possible outcome and focus on myself even more. I knew my hypochondria was unhealthy, what St. Ignatius would call a "disordered attachment," but it was hard to let it go.

In my prayer, I felt Jesus asking me to let go of my obsession and "put out into the deep." This seemed to mean becoming more mature, more adult, and overall more "matter of fact" about my health. It was an invitation to more freedom. Freedom from the excessive focus on myself.

During radiation treatments a few summers ago, every weekday for six weeks I would hail a cab near my Jesuit community in Manhattan and say, "Sixty-Eighth and York, please." Once there, I would stop into a nearby church to pray. Afterward, walking to my appointment in a neighborhood jammed with hospitals, I passed cancer patients who had lost their hair, exhausted elderly men and women in wheelchairs pushed by home health-care aides, and those who had just emerged from surgery. But on the same sidewalks were busy doctors, smiling nurses, and eager interns, and many others in apparently perfect health. One day it dawned on me: we're all going to Sixty-Eighth and York, though we all have different times for our appointments. Clearly, I wasn't the only person facing illness and stress. Being around patients at the hospital reminded me of that.

Once, when I was complaining about some physical problems, Damian said to me, "You don't like the Incarnation very much, do you?" (The Incarnation is the doctrine that God became human in Jesus.)

"What are you talking about?" I said, somewhat offended. "I just wrote a whole book on Jesus. Of course I believe in the Incarnation."

"Yes," he said, "but you don't like your *own* incarnation very much!"

As a boy I had thought of Jesus primarily as divine (which he is), and so later, during my Jesuit formation, encountering books such as those of South African theologian Albert Nolan, which focused on the "Historical Jesus"—his humanity—transformed my faith. And what seems an obvious idea, but is often downplayed in some Christian circles—that is, Jesus had a body—also helped to deepen my faith.

If you had asked me before I entered the Jesuits whether Jesus had a body, I would have said, "Of course!" But I had never really considered that body outside of the suffering he endured during the Crucifixion. And yet—again this is obvious, but I had ignored it—he had a human body from conception. After his birth, Jesus needed to be nursed, held, and burped and his diapers changed. During his thirty or so years on earth, he would have experienced everything that every human being does: getting colds and flus, having headaches and stomachaches, spraining ankles and wrists, and so on. He got tired, hungry, and thirsty. Sleeping by the side of the road, as he did with his disciples, meant that he may have woken up with a stiff neck more than once. After the Wedding Feast at Cana, he might even have had a hangover! And during a time with only rudimentary health care and poor sanitation and hygiene, Jesus may have suffered even more than we do today in our bodies. This was part of his full humanity, part of his incarnation.

Over the years, then, I came to understand the incarnation in a much deeper way. But what about my own? My own incarnation in a human body?

Damian's words to me were a challenge but also a comfort. I had a body too, and I needed to accept that bodily reality, as Jesus had. We all have bodies that break down, get sick, and have problems. They need to be cared for, maintained, and sometimes fixed. When we get older, often our bodies cannot be fixed, and we must live with some pain. And even if we're not near death, we are all on our way to death—perhaps today, or perhaps years from now.

In my prayer that day, I was aboard the boat with Jesus, "into the deep," on the calm blue water, and ready to speak with him about my disappointment. I had already spent several days speaking with him about my gratitude. Now it was time to revisit those earlier feelings.

In putting out into the deep, I felt that I had to leave some things on the shore, as it were: my excessive focus on my body and health concerns, my childish attitude toward illness, and my need for perfect health. We all need to leave things behind before we "put out into the deep."

Suddenly I felt Martha in the boat with me. She was a vivid presence, dressed as she was in the mosaic at the Church of St. Lazarus in Al Eizariya, heavily robed and veiled, but for some reason in lavender tones.

I felt a kinship with her. Here we both were, two people who had been disappointed in God, yet for whom Jesus had done an act of mercy: for Martha, by raising her brother, for me, by accompanying me in my struggles.

I was torn. Grateful as I was, I didn't want to say that believing in Jesus had made everything work out just as I had wanted. The temptation is to say that because both Martha and I believed in Jesus, we both got what we had asked for: she, her brother returned to life; me, a good diagnosis. It was an easy mistake to make, the fundamental mistake of the "Prosperity Gospel," which claims that if you believe in God, nothing bad will ever happen to you, which is manifestly false, and if you ask for something in prayer, you will always get it, which is also not the case.

I was in a muddle, with feelings of gratitude and relief and embarrassment and confusion thrown together. Maybe Martha felt some of the same things in Bethany. I didn't know what to say.

So, I simply sat there and imagined the waves bumping against the side of the boat. After some time, I heard Jesus say four words to both of us, which put our disappointment and sadness in perspective, and which have stayed with me, and which I hope I will remember the next time:

"Can you trust me?"

This doesn't mean that I will never get sick again or that nothing bad will ever happen to me. But it does mean that I'm being asked, invited, through all of life, to trust. As Martha tried to do.

It's natural to be disappointed by life and even disappointed by God. "Don't you care?" we sometimes want to say to God.

We might feel that God is not coming to our aid in a time of distress, as Martha and Mary may have feared during their brother's illness. We might feel that God is not paying attention, as Martha did when she was doing all the *diakonia* during Jesus's visit and asked, "Don't you care?" Or we might feel that God is simply indifferent, as the disciples did on a boat on the Sea of Galilee, during the "storm at sea," when Jesus was fast asleep. "Teacher, don't you care that we are perishing"? they asked—or probably shouted—over the wind and waves.[9]

To feel such emotions about a God whom we love, trust, and rely upon can elicit intense, sometimes overpowering, feelings of disappointment.

In these times, it's helpful to consider the experiences of Martha and Mary and the other disciples and to remember that these are natural emotions. If disappointment was something that these people experienced during the time of Jesus's public ministry, even in his very presence, it is not surprising that we, who do not have the benefit of Jesus standing physically before us, experience them today. They are natural emotions for even the devout believer.

The key is to acknowledge these feelings, express them honestly in prayer (or to a trusted friend or spiritual director), and continue to be in relationship with God, remembering a few things, which Martha and Mary would discover in Bethany and the disciples discover on the Sea of Galilee. While God might seem late, God is on the way; while God might seem inattentive, God sees everything you are experiencing; and while God might seem indifferent, God cares deeply about your life, even if it is sometimes difficult to appreciate these things in the moment. In these times, it helps to look back at similar moments in your life when you were disappointed and remember how God eventually showed up, by showing his care.

God cared so much about us that he became one of us, eating with us, laughing with us, and weeping with us. God cared so much about us that he spent some thirty years living a human life, taking himself all over Judea and Galilee, to preach and do wondrous things, showing us what life was all about, even to the point of death on a cross. That is how much God cares for us. And how much God cares about you.

Soon, Martha and Mary will discover just how much God cares for them and for their brother.

For Your Reflection

1. Have you ever felt deep disappointment in God? How did you handle it?

2. New Testament scholars still debate the meaning of Martha and Mary's words to Jesus when he arrives—"Lord, if you had been here, my brother would not have died." Do you see these words as a profession of faith or as an expression of disappointment?

3. What do you think enabled Martha and Mary to speak so honestly to Jesus? What might you learn from this about your own relationship with God?

4. Have you ever thought of Jesus suffering in his body *before* the Crucifixion? How else would having a body have influenced his public ministry and his teaching?

5. How accepting are you of your own "incarnation"?

You Are the Messiah, the Son of God

Who Is Jesus?

Jesus said to her, "Your brother will rise again."
Martha said to him, "I know that he will rise again
in the resurrection on the last day." Jesus said to
her, "I am the resurrection and the life. Those
who believe in me, even though they die, will live,
and everyone who lives and believes in me will
never die. Do you believe this?" She said to him,
"Yes, Lord, I believe that you are the Messiah,
the Son of God, the one coming into the world."

One of the most impressive medieval depictions of Jesus can be found in the tympanum, the space over the main entrance, of the majestic Cathedral of St.-Lazare in Autun, in the Burgundy region of France.

This vivid depiction of the Last Judgment is often called one of the masterpieces of Romanesque sculpture. The art historian Don Denny says that the tympanum is "in several respects without precedent in Western depictions of the Last Judgement."[1] A massive, elongated,

Tympanum of the Cathedral of St.-Lazare, Autun, France.
WIKICOMMONS

placid Christ is seated in a kind of aureole, which may represent an episcopal seal—a symbol of the authority of both Christ and his church. To the right of Christ, seated in majesty, are the apostles, angels, a depiction of the Heavenly Jerusalem, and Mary at the Annunciation. To his left is St. Michael, weighing souls in a balance, along with the damned souls being tortured by an assortment of terrifying demons. Beneath Christ are various souls, which the art historian Linda Seidel describes in her book *Legends in Limestone: Lazarus, Gislebertus, and the Cathedral of Autun* as "emotionally differentiated souls, grieved and relieved," emerging from their tombs.[2]

The tympanum, as well as the sculptures on the exterior and in the interior of the cathedral, draw pilgrims from around the world, some on their way to Santiago de Compostela, the great pilgrimage site in Spain.

The relics kept at the cathedral are supposed to be those of

Lazarus. The fascinating story of the relics, the building, and the supposed sculptor is told in Seidel's marvelous book, which untangles threads of fact and legend surrounding the building.

The cathedral was consecrated by Pope Innocent II in 1130. Yet at the time there was already a fully functioning cathedral in Autun, just a few steps away: the Cathedral of St.-Nazaire. The new cathedral seems to have been built to house the relics of Lazarus, transferred from the older cathedral. These relics included, according to a transcription made in the fifteenth century, a body, a head, and an arm. Another head, or at least part of it, was also supposed to reside in a cathedral in nearby Avallon. (Competing claims to the relics are not unusual in the church, even today.) The new cathedral functioned essentially as an "annex of the cathedral" to house those relics. A series of miracles was said to be linked to those who had prayed near the relics, including the cure of an archdeacon from Reims, who was, it is reported, cured of leprosy.[3]

Lazarus's purported relics followed a circuitous route. According to the *Golden Legend*, a wildly popular medieval compendium of the (often legendary) lives of the saints by Jacob de Voragine, Mary (who is conflated with Mary Magdalene), Martha, and Lazarus are portrayed as high-born people, descended from royalty, who own castles in and around Jerusalem. In the story, some "miscreants" cruelly cast the three on a ship without sails, rudder, or oars, with the intention of drowning them. Instead, they miraculously arrive in France by sea. The three landed in current-day Aix-en-Provence, and all three preached the Gospel to the people of the region.

In this tradition, Lazarus becomes the first bishop of Marseille, eludes the Roman persecution under Nero by hiding in a crypt, but is then beheaded under the Emperor Domitian. His body was supposedly taken to Autun in the tenth century. The saint's head, however, remained in Marseille, in the Abbey of St.-Victor; later it was taken to the cathedral there, where the relics are still venerated. As Sister Vassa Larin, an Orthodox liturgical scholar, said to me, "Marseille claims only his head, while Autun claims all of him."

The Catholic Encyclopedia, originally published between 1907 and 1912, has another explanation for these relics: It proposes, on the basis of a fifth-century epitaph in the crypt of the Abbey of St.-Victor, that these are the relics of another man, St. Lazarus, bishop of Aix, who was consecrated in Marseille in 407. This Lazarus had to abandon his position and then spent some time in the Holy Land before returning to Marseille.

By contrast, a thirteenth-century manuscript notes that the relics were "translated" to Marseille after Lazarus died not in France but in the Holy Land. Yet it was clear that by the early eleventh century, people believed that Lazarus's relics, however they had come there, were in Autun. (Around that time the people of Avallon, Vézelay, and even Marseille also believed that *they* had the relics.) In 1120, plans were made for the Cathedral of St.-Lazare. As Seidel puts it, "By constructing a monumental structure in Lazarus's honor, not simply commissioning a new reliquary or building a sepulchral chapel, the see of Autun enforced its assertion that it was the official abode of the first-century holy man's body."

For me the most fascinating aspect of the cathedral in Autun is its surprising link to the Holy Land. Inside the cathedral is a sort of church within a church, the tomb holding Lazarus's remains. This chapel-like structure, destroyed in the eighteenth century, may have been, according to one scholar, "fashioned in conscious imitation of the tomb in Bethany that marked the site of Lazarus's resurrection."[4]

Pilgrims to the Holy Land had brought back reports of what they had seen in Bethany, and these were used to construct the shrine to Lazarus—but not just the small inner mausoleum that held the relics; the entire cathedral was constructed to imitate the church that was dedicated to Lazarus in Bethany. Seidel points out that this was not unusual. The many pilgrims (not to mention participants in the Crusades) "would have had no difficulty connecting the buildings [in the Holy Land and in Europe] so long as some elements of the structures seemed, in some way, to be comparable."

Cathedral of
St.-Lazare,
Autun, France.
WIKICOMMONS

In this, the cathedral somewhat mirrors the tradition of the Stations of the Cross, whereby those who could not visit the Holy Land and walk the Via Dolorosa, the path that Jesus took on the way to his Crucifixion, could experience it in the sculpted or framed stations in their local church or cathedral. In Autun, the connection was to Lazarus.

Over the transept door in the original cathedral, now destroyed, was a depiction of the Raising of Lazarus, and on the tomb-within-a-tomb that stood in the church the words "Lazarus, come out" were inscribed. In a beautiful summation, Seidel writes, "Precisely because he was no longer buried in the Bethany cave, Lazarus could be here, in Burgundy," presumably ready to be raised again, on the Last Day.

On the Last Day

In response to Jesus's assurance that her brother will rise again, Martha professes confidence in Lazarus's rising on the "last day," a commonly held belief. As Francis Moloney explains, *she* tells *Jesus* what resurrection is: something for the "end times."[5]

Then Jesus responds. And what he says must seem extraordinary to Martha. His words appear in Latin in the mosaic in the Church of St. Lazarus in Al Eizariya in foot-high letters:

EGO SUM RESURRECTIO ET VITA

"I am the Resurrection and the Life." Notice that Jesus doesn't say, "If you believe in me, you will experience new life and the resurrection," which he says, in so many words, elsewhere in the Gospel. Nor does he say, "I can cause you to have new life and ultimate resurrection." Instead, he says something more dramatic: He is resurrection itself and life itself.

John Meier points out how this differs from what Martha believed: "I know that he will rise again in the resurrection on the last day." Martha is hoping for something in the future. But Jesus is the resurrection *now*. Jesus doesn't talk about the Last Day, as Martha

Main altar, Church of St. Lazarus, Al Eizariya.
COURTESY OF CATHOLIC TRAVEL CENTRE

does; he talks about today. Theologians call this a "realized eschatology"; what we hope for in the end times is made present to us now, through the presence of Jesus. You can live today as if death has no power over you, no authority over humanity, no sway in the reign of God. Meier sums up Jesus's words as, "Martha, the resurrection you are looking for is looking at you."[6]

John Dear notes that Jesus is not simply inviting us away from the death that humans face but from a whole *culture* of death. We are now free to renounce it, to walk away from it, to challenge it. Resurrection means "the freedom to break the unanimity of our repeated and rabid rush towards war and all the methodologies of death." Dear quotes the theologian Monika Hellwig, who suggested that Lazarus represents all of humanity, and so all of humanity is called to hear Jesus's voice calling us to challenge death and its worldview.[7]

Wes Howard-Brook, a peace activist and theologian at Seattle University, believes that it is the possibility of death that keeps even the most devout of Jesus's disciples from following him completely. The opponent to be overcome, therefore, is the same one that "empires and other oppressors" have always used: the threat of death.[8] And the response to that threat, our safety from that danger, our assurance of life, is Jesus.

In his book on the Fourth Gospel, Brendan Byrne says that "Jesus sweeps the perspective from the indefinite future ('the last day') to the present: 'I am . . .' The statement is also more general in the sense of having not just Lazarus in view but all believers—and also all those who, like Martha and Mary, will mourn the loss of loved ones."

Byrne's comments are worth quoting in full:

[Jesus] does not deny that believers will continue to die—that is, die in a physical sense. But their "believing" in him while presently living (v. 26) will ensure that physical death is not the end of the story. In *this* sense they "will live" and "will never die"—that is, die eternally. It is not just a matter of rising "on the last day." Faith in Jesus and living in that faith communicates to believers a share here and now in the eternal life of God. The whole aim of the mission Jesus has from the Father is to communicate life in this exalted sense to human beings.[9]

Jesus says all this and more: "I am the Resurrection and the Life."

"I Am"

This is one of the great "I am" statements in John's Gospel (Greek: *ego eimi*), which reveal Jesus's identity to his disciples. Jesus speaks about himself often in the Fourth Gospel and uses the commonplace words "I am" in other situations, but the traditional list of the seven *ego eimi* statements includes more formal revelations. And these are emphatic declarations. In Greek you don't need the word *ego*; the *eimi* is sufficient. It is something like using *I myself* as an intensifier. The seven are:

1. "**I am** the bread of life. Whoever comes to me will never be hungry, and whoever believes in me will never be thirsty" (6:35).
2. "**I am** the light of the world. Whoever follows me will never walk in darkness but will have the light of life" (8:12).
3. "**I am** the gate. Whoever enters by me will be saved, and will come in and go out and find pasture" (10:9).
4. "**I am** the good shepherd. The good shepherd lays down his life for the sheep" (10:11).
5. "**I am** the resurrection and the life. Those who believe in me, even though they die, will live" (11:25).
6. "**I am** the way, and the truth, and the life. No one comes to the Father except through me" (14:6).
7. "**I am** the true vine, and my Father is the vinegrower" (15:1).

Often added to the list is an eighth statement, which caused "the Jews" to threaten to stone Jesus. After Jesus seemed to place himself on the same plane as Abraham, "the Jews" say, "You are not yet fifty years old, and you have seen Abraham?" And Jesus responds, "before Abraham was, I am."[10]

Although often omitted from the standard list, this is one of the most theologically significant of the *ego eimi* statements. Several are metaphorical ("I am the good shepherd"), with Jesus only obliquely equating himself with the Father. By contrast, "before Abraham was" seems to give him the same status as the God of Abraham, Isaac, and Jacob, who said to Moses, "I AM WHO I AM."[11] It's not hard to see why some people—perhaps among the most devout Jews of that time—would oppose Jesus.

Later on, another of his utterances, "The Father and I are one,"[12] which also would have struck any devout Jew as blasphemous, causes "the Jews" to threaten him with stoning again. This leads to his escape "across the Jordan," where we find him at the beginning of the Lazarus story.

Navajo Compassionate Christ, by John B. Giuliani. Father Giuliani, a Catholic priest and artist from the US, hoped to depict Christian scripture and biblical figures as Native Americans to "honor them and to acknowledge their original spiritual presence on this land." USED WITH PERMISSION

Who Was Jesus for His Disciples and Friends?

Who did Jesus's disciples and friends think he was? There are many indications in the Gospels that they know exactly who he is: the Son of God. There are other indications, particularly earlier in his public ministry, that they don't know, or it took them some time to "come to believe," as Jesus later says.

The question must have been constantly on their minds, in their hearts, and on their lips. After all, they would want to know who they were following and for whom they were making (and would make) great sacrifices. Jesus himself asks them this very question, in a dialogue so important that it is recorded in all three Synoptic Gospels.[13]

Remember when Jesus and the disciples are walking to Caesarea Philippi, a town in Galilee, and he asks them something.[14] (I'll use Mark's version here since it's the earliest.) Often I imagine Jesus walking ahead of the disciples and hearing them discussing this as they trail him, perhaps *sotto voce*. "He's the Messiah!" "No, he can't be. He's a man. He's a prophet, but not that!" "What are you talking about? He's a carpenter!"

Perhaps wanting to end the speculation, Jesus turns around and says, "Who do people say that I am?"

It's a canny question. Rather than asking who *they* think he is (I imagine their red faces as he catches them discussing the question), he asks what *others* are thinking.

They answer with what was a fair summary of what people were saying at the time: "John the Baptist; and others, Elijah; and still others, one of the prophets." The tetrarch of Galilee, Herod Antipas, thought that Jesus might be John the Baptist come back to life. Many Jewish people thought that Elijah's return would herald the reign of God, which some in the region thought was imminent. And a comparison to a prophet like, for example, Jeremiah seemed reasonable because of the similarities between him (and other prophets) and Jesus. But notice that the disciples are careful not to say what *they* believe.

So, Jesus asks them directly. I imagine him smiling at their reluctance but also knowing the stakes involved. He is revealing himself to them, gently, using their own insights.

"But who do you say that I am?" he asks.

In response, Peter says, "You are the Messiah."

But Jesus is divine, far more than the traditional Jewish definition of the Messiah at the time. Far more than Peter—or Martha or Mary—could comprehend.

It should not surprise us that his disciples and friends struggled with comprehending Jesus's identity. They knew him as a man—a friend with whom they ate and drank, whose family they knew, who got tired and frustrated and angry. They knew he was human. That was, in a sense, the "easy part." But they also witnessed the extraordinary "signs" (in John's Gospel) and "works of power" (in the Synoptics) that he performed, and they heard him at times speak of himself as no (sane) man ever had: "Before Abraham was, I am."

The question that the disciples ask aboard the ship during the storm at sea is apposite: "What sort of man is this, that even the winds and the sea obey him?"[15] Throughout the Gospels the disciples toggle between understanding and misunderstanding the man they are following.

Jesus's Self-Consciousness

How did Jesus understand his own identity? There are several schools of thought about Jesus's "self-consciousness," that is, his conception of himself as the Son of God. Obviously, he was conscious of his mission. But what does that mean in terms of his understanding of his identity? Some theologians, such as St. Thomas Aquinas, believe that he understood this from the moment of his conception, that from the earliest moments of human consciousness, thanks to the action of the Holy Spirit, he knew that he was the Son of God, he understood his relationship to the Father, and he grasped what his mission would be.[16]

Other theologians, such as the Anglican bishop and New Testament scholar N. T. Wright, have a different way of looking at Jesus's self-consciousness:

> I do not think Jesus 'knew he was God' in the same sense that one knows one is tired or happy, male or female. He did not sit back and say to himself, 'Well I never! I'm the second person of the Trinity!' Rather as part of his human vocation, grasped in faith, sustained in prayer, tested in confrontation, agonized over in further prayer and doubt, and implemented in action, he believed he had to do and be, for Israel and the world, that which according to scripture only YHWH himself could do and be.[17]

This mirrors the approach taken by theologians like Karl Rahner, SJ, and more recently Elizabeth Johnson, CSJ. In her book *Consider Jesus*, she suggests that Jesus grew in his consciousness of who he was. In this view, Jesus came to reflect on his mission and his identity over time. He may have been helped by Mary and Joseph, who had years to think about their own revelations of who he was. The line from the Gospel of Luke, after the birth of her son, is important: "Mary treasured all these words and pondered them in her heart."[18] Joseph must have as well.

And why would they not have shared their religious experiences and their later reflections with Jesus? Why do we think that Mary and Joseph would be, as the Catholic writer F. J. Sheed wrote, "tight-lipped" with Jesus as he tried to understand his mission and identity?[19]

Much of the discussion concerning Jesus's consciousness about his identity falls along the lines of Jesus's two "natures," human and divine. If we believe that Jesus was fully human and fully divine (as I do), then two things follow. If he is fully human, then he has a fully human consciousness, and a fully human consciousness knows only what it learns. But if he is fully divine, he has a fully divine consciousness and therefore does not need to learn anything, for a fully divine consciousness knows all things.

Ben Witherington emailed me his version of how to understand this reality of Jesus's life: "I tell my students that while remaining the divine Son of God, in order to be fully human, he accepted in the Incarnation our normal human limitations of time, place, power, knowledge and mortality. He had access to more knowledge and power, etc., but did not draw on it. In short, in his divine condescending he limited himself. His human life was not a charade." Witherington said that when Jesus asks in Mark's Gospel, "Who touched my clothes?" when the woman with the hemorrhage grabs his cloak, "he really meant it."[20] And, "When Luke says he grew in wisdom and stature, he did. When he says not even the Son knows the timing of the Second Coming, he was not kidding."

In *Consider Jesus*, Elizabeth Johnson describes how the early church struggled to understand who Jesus was. In a chapter titled "Jesus' Self-Knowledge," she lays out the conundrum: If Jesus knew he was God, then he could hardly be said to have lived a human life. But if he was God, then how could he not know his identity, since God knows everything? Johnson says that however he understood himself, Jesus would not have used the theological language of the early church. And, as the Protestant theologian Krister Stendahl has written, the ancient world did not have the same idea of "self-consciousness" that we do today.[21]

We cannot know for sure what he thought about himself, writes Johnson. "Obviously, Jesus did not wake up in the morning saying, I am the Son of God with a truly human nature and a truly divine nature." In other words, Jesus, so goes the argument, did not see himself as the kind of image depicted at the cathedral in Autun. Nor is it likely that he arrived at an understanding of his identity and mission in one moment. Rather, Johnson argues, like all of us, Jesus gradually grew in his knowledge of who he was. "It takes his whole life for him to understand himself in concrete terms."[22]

This is the approach that seems the most sensible to me. (Although with any of these theories, the best theological answer may be "Who knows?")[23]

It is difficult to imagine that as a boy at home and then an adolescent working in Joseph's carpentry shop in Nazareth, Jesus arrived at the notion that he was the Messiah all at once. Although, who knows? Mary and Joseph may have shared with him the experiences that happened to them before his birth, and he may have understood his identity immediately and completely—he had a relationship with the Holy Spirit that can only be guessed at.

But it seems more likely that this understanding—something that no person had ever had to understand—dawned on him gradually. As an adolescent, Jesus would have learned the Hebrew Scriptures, studying the traditional history of his people and the oppression they suffered in Egypt—and continued to suffer at the hands of the Romans. Later, as Jesus took up his carpentry work and traveled around Galilee and the surrounding areas, he would have encountered firsthand the suffering of the Jewish people and felt his heart, as the Gospels say of him later in life, "moved with pity."

Perhaps the builder from Nazareth, while feeling a growing sense of compassion for those who suffered, also noticed within himself the desire to help in some yet undefined way.

Yet about this critical period in the life of Jesus of Nazareth, the time between the ages of twelve and thirty—when he began what is called his public ministry—we know nothing and can only speculate. Today we can know much about the daily life in Galilee at that time and more specifically in Nazareth, thanks to some recent archaeological discoveries. But as to Jesus's own life, none of the four Gospels mentions anything about his young adulthood, a time when even today people are focused on questions of identity. For this reason, this period of Jesus's life is called the "Hidden Life" or the "Hidden Years."

Christ Emmanuel, by Kelly Latimore. Here Jesus is portrayed as an adolescent, a depiction that Latimore based on youth he saw in Palestinian territory.
COURTESY OF THE ARTIST

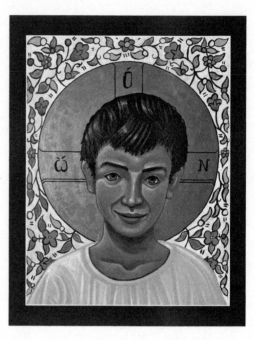

Even when he reached the age of thirty (according to Luke) and began his public ministry, Jesus of Nazareth may still have been unclear about his identity. Let's look briefly at clues about Jesus's self-consciousness as presented in the Gospels.

At the beginning of his public ministry, Jesus is baptized by his cousin John the Baptist. But why? Jesus is sinless and John is proclaiming a "baptism of repentance for the forgiveness of sins." One could argue that Jesus went to the Jordan River to be baptized by his cousin because he was attracted, like many Jews at the time, to John's fiery preaching. Jesus may have gone to hear what John had to say and to see if it would help him understand what he was meant to do. And for a time, many scholars now agree, Jesus was probably a disciple of John. (This is where he meets Philip and Andrew, in John's Gospel—in the company of John the Baptist.)[24]

Whatever drew Jesus to the banks of the Jordan River, something happened at his baptism that was so profound for him (the

Gospels describe it as the heavens opening and a voice speaking) that it convinced him of his divine mission. Afterward, Jesus journeyed into the desert to continue his process of discernment. In the Gospels, he is described as fasting for "forty days and forty nights," another way of saying "a long time."[25]

Clearly, Jesus was tested in some way during his time in the desert, though interpretations of what happened vary widely. Traditional artistic representations (including those in Martin Scorsese's *The Last Temptation of Christ*) have Satan appearing in some physical way. Others surmise that Jesus experienced these tests, or temptations, within himself.

Traditionally, Jesus is tempted to take up a life of power, security, and status, in contrast to the hard life of service that he eventually undertakes. While there are varying understandings of what Jesus's temptations in the desert involved, it is not an episode that one can dismiss as irrelevant to the Gospels. The Scripture scholar William Barclay suggests that this episode was most likely passed along to the disciples by Jesus himself, and so should be considered seriously.[26]

Biblical narratives of the testing in the desert are complicated and obscured for the modern person by centuries of paintings that depict small demons and animals tempting Jesus. (In *The Last Temptation of Christ*, Jesus is tempted by a snake, a lion, and a flame.) Yet this may be the easiest part of Jesus's life for the contemporary reader to understand. Jesus, thinking intently about his mission, was subject to some very human temptations: for power, for security, and for easy answers. In the end, though, he rejected these temptations and returned to Galilee to begin his ministry. For Johannes Baptist Metz, a German Catholic theologian, this is a critical point in the life of Jesus of Nazareth, as it reveals his fundamental acceptance of his own humanity. "Jesus subjected himself to our plight," writes Metz. "He immersed himself in our misery and followed our road to the end. He did not escape from the torment of our life. . . . He was not spared from the dark mystery of our poverty as human beings."[27]

Ben Witherington noted to me that these are not, however,

entirely human temptations. Each one, he points out, starts with, "If you are the (divine) Son of God . . ." No human being can truly turn stones into bread. "In short these are temptations for Jesus to push his God button, which he has, but if he does so, he will obliterate his true humanity."

Even after his sojourn in the Judean wilderness, Jesus may have experienced a lingering reticence about his vocation, about embracing his unique identity. Perhaps even *he* was asking himself, "Who does the Father say that I am?" After all, what is considered his first miracle seems a reluctant one.

We find this story, of the Wedding Feast at Cana, in the Gospel of John.[28] Jesus has gone to a small town called Cana, still in Galilee today, to attend a wedding, and the wine runs out. When Jesus's mother points this out to him, suggesting that he do something, Jesus asks her a question that is revelatory of this period in his life, when he may still be discerning who he is.

In Greek the question is, *"Ti emoi kai soi, gynai?"* Literally, "What to me and to you, woman?"

One translation might be, "What concern is that to you and to me, woman?" It's a forceful response.[29]

At Cana, he seems to be saying to his mother, "I'm not the person you think I am." Here Jesus may still be grappling with his mission, his vocation, his identity, and what the Trappist monk Thomas Merton called the "true self."

In response, his mother calmly gives him the freedom to do what he wants. "Do whatever he tells you," she says to the hosts' servants. Interestingly, John's Gospel portrays Jesus's mother as somehow understanding her son's mission earlier than Jesus does.

As John tells the story, Jesus grasps what is required of him. He tells the servants to fill large stone jars with water and serve the guests. But it is not water that comes out of the jars; it is wine. Jesus's career as a miracle worker has begun.

Was even Jesus surprised by his first miracle? If there was ever a time when he might have been surprised in his journey toward self-knowledge, it is in Cana.

At the same time, the miracle at Cana seems to strengthen Jesus's understanding of his mission, to inspire him to trust in his own discernment and in his ability to do miraculous things in the name of God.

As the Gospel stories continue, Jesus is shown as growing in confidence in his mission, which flows from his relationship with his Father, and in his identity. His miracles are a sign of this. In other passages, his self-confidence and his understanding of his own divine power virtually leap off the page, as in a story that is told in Matthew, Mark, and Luke.

"If you choose," says a man with leprosy, "you can make me clean."

"I do choose," says Jesus. "Be made clean!"

My own way of understanding his self-identity relies on these clues from the Gospel, as in the Wedding Feast at Cana, which aligns with what Elizabeth Johnson has suggested: Jesus's understanding of his mission and his identity grew over his lifetime. Even on the Cross, perhaps even he didn't understand what the Father had in store for him after his death. Only after he says, "Remove this cup from me" is he able to say, "Not my will but yours be done."

Earlier in the Gospels Jesus predicts that he will rise again. He says clearly in the Gospels of Mark and Matthew: "The Son of Man is to be betrayed into human hands, and they will kill him, and three days after being killed, he will rise again."[30] And in Luke he even says that he will rise "on the third day."[31] He may have in some way known and alerted the disciples.

Yet according to the Gospels, the disciples seem not only despairing after the Crucifixion but also stunned to see him again. And, according to Mark and Matthew, on the cross Jesus cries out, "My God, my God, why have you forsaken me?"[32]

So, did he know or not know that he would rise?

In all the Synoptics, Jesus predicts that he will rise "on the third day." But we can entertain the possibility that Jesus did not know precisely what would happen at Easter, which for many people makes Jesus's offering on the Cross more powerful, the final step in his understanding of his identity. Then, on Easter Sunday, as Elizabeth Johnson says in her beautiful words, "his ultimate identity burst upon him in all clarity."[33]

Is it any wonder that Jesus's disciples and friends, like Martha, may have struggled with understanding his identity? Imagine the disciples constantly trying to recalibrate their understanding with each word Jesus says and action he takes. The question aboard the boat resounds: "What sort of man is this, that even the winds and the sea obey him?"[34]

All this makes Martha's profession of faith in her friend Jesus, with whom she ate and drank and to whom she complained, even more moving and inspiring, especially in her grief over her brother's death.

Who Is Jesus for You?

Almost thirty years ago, when I was thinking about entering the Jesuits, I was invited to make a retreat at the Campion Center in Weston, Massachusetts, not far from Boston. I had never made a retreat before and didn't know what to expect.

When I arrived, my retreat director, a kind and soft-spoken priest named Ron, asked me, "Who is Jesus for you?"

I didn't understand the question. *For me?* What did it matter who he was for me? Jesus was Jesus, someone I followed, but he had little to do with me, other than as someone who told me how to live.

Or maybe he was the Judge, like the Jesus over the tympanum of the Cathedral of St.-Lazare, ready to have St. Michael weigh my soul in the balance, to see if my life measured up. If not, maybe I'd be given to one of those surly looking demons that probably terrified the people of Autun as they passed through the doors of their great cathedral.

As a suggested assignment for prayer, Ron asked me to pray about that question. Dutifully, I went outside and lay down on the broad green lawn next to the retreat house and thought about that question. I thought hard about it. My mind wandered a bit, and I had a tough time focusing.

The next day, I returned to Ron with a list. Jesus was Savior, Messiah, Son of God—almost as if I were giving answers to a quiz. This was how I saw my discernment, unfortunately: as a "test" I had to pass.

Ron asked me to return to the question for the next day's prayer. I had the vague feeling that I had somehow failed. But he

Veronica Copies the Face of Jesus, Stations of the Cross, by Engelbert Mveng, SJ (Hekima University College, Nairobi, Kenya).
COURTESY OF HEKIMA

also told me not to worry if my mind wandered and to see where that might lead.

I sat again under the sun, working on my tan, and thought about that question again. Who was Jesus for me? The same words kept coming up in my mind: *Savior, Messiah, Son of God.*

Then suddenly into my mind another word popped up: *friend.*

Friend? I had never thought of that before. I spent a few minutes thinking about how nice it would be to have Jesus as a friend, someone I could talk to, someone I could share my problems with, someone who would help me. It would be great, I thought, to have as a friend someone who could heal illnesses, still storms, and raise the dead; but it was more than his power—it was wanting to be with someone who was so loving and compassionate. Thinking of him in such a casual way seemed absurd, and borderline sinful, but I enjoyed thinking about it.

Then I returned to the question at hand and came up with a few more words: *Healer, Raiser of the Dead.* I was running out of titles.

The next day, I met with Ron and reported some of the new titles I had come up with. Then I said, "You know, the funniest thing popped into my mind: *friend.* I thought of how good it would be to have Jesus as a friend." Then I described what I had felt.

Ron leaned back in his rocking chair and said, "I think you're beginning to pray."

I've told that story many times, usually to illustrate how a person might begin to pray. But I'm telling it here to highlight how important it is to understand how *you* see Jesus. "Who is Jesus for you?" is essentially the same question that Jesus asked his disciples on the way to Caesarea Philippi: "Who do you say that I am?"

This question is an essential one for believers: Who do we believe Jesus is? Is he just another prophet, or is he more? Is he truly the Son of God, is he fully divine, or just someone who preaches inspiring sermons? "What do you believe?" is what Jesus is asking his disciples as they make their way to Caesarea Philippi. This is what Jesus is implicitly asking Martha at Bethany when he declares himself the "Resurrection and the Life." Do we believe this?

And how do we relate to him in daily life? Even if we believe him to be the Son of God, we may reach out to him in more familiar ways. Is he a friend, as he was for me on that day thirty years ago? Is he our brother? Our liberator? The answers to that question may change over a lifetime. And we may find ourselves moving from one image to another: for a time, when things are going well and we simply need companionship, Jesus might be our friend. A few months later, during a time of turmoil in our life, he is the Crucified One. Years later, as we face the end of life, he may be the Resurrection and the Life. Or these images may overlap, as perhaps they did for the disciples, who struggled to understand who Jesus was, even when he was with them.

Messiah and Son of God

It is impossible to know exactly how Martha thought about Jesus, the person whom she welcomed into her house but who also stilled storms. And after he raised Lazarus, her awe and admiration would have grown even more.

Jesus's disciples and friends likely struggled with the question of his identity, understanding him to be somehow divine but also knowing him as human. Martha's words—"I believe you are the Messiah, the Son of God"—were said to a friend with whom she had spent time, whom she had seen eat and drink. Perhaps she had a sense of his fully human and fully divine natures. Or these words may simply have been placed on her lips by the Gospel writer. The New Testament scholar Sandra Schneiders said to me, "I do not think this is a historical transcription of an actual conversation."

But it's not unreasonable to think that Mary and Martha would have passed along these stories in some form. So let's look at the two names Martha gives him in this passage: *Messiah* and *Son of*

God. And then let's look at the two names Jesus gives himself: *Resurrection* and *Life*.

What would Martha have meant by the terms "Messiah" and "Son of God"? Schneiders described to me those words as Martha's "lapidary Christological confession—parallel to Peter's confession in Matthew ["You are the Messiah, the Son of God"] but more significant in my opinion."[35]

Raymond Brown provides a succinct definition of "Messiah" in his commentary on the Gospel of John: "the expected king of the House of David."[36] John's Gospel uses the Greek form of this title (*Christos*) more frequently than any of the Synoptics and is the only Gospel that uses the transliterated form from the Greek rendering of the Hebrew *messias*. Jesus's messiahship is a central theme of his Gospel. In chapter 20 he says, "These things are written so that you may come to believe that Jesus is the Messiah, the Son of God."[37] Clearly this was an important title for John.

But what would it have meant to the people of the time? Often, scholars say that it was someone who would "restore the fortunes of Israel." But how?

As ever, Amy-Jill Levine's work can help us. AJ notes that often Christians have promoted the idea that the Jewish people were looking forward to a "warrior messiah," someone who would, perhaps through violent means, eject the Roman occupiers from Judea. Therefore, goes the thinking, "the Jews" rejected Jesus because he was not a militaristic messiah.

But "Jewish messianic speculation was as diverse as Jewish theology and practice," she told me. She offers a summary of what might have been meant by "the Messiah" (the word comes from the Hebrew *māšîaḥ*).

"Some Jews expected a messianic king, others a priest, others an archangel or some other heavenly figure such as Enoch, and others the coming of the world to come by divine fiat; still others were quite happy with the way things were."[38]

Expectations about how the Messiah would fulfill his role were diverse. Some hoped for the removal of the Roman occupiers from Judea and Galilee ("if not from the earth," as AJ says); some were more concerned with how fellow Jews who did not follow their way of living were to be "corrected" in some eschatological way; and others looked forward to the end of poverty, disease, and death. "There was," she says, "no single view of a messiah other than the sense that his coming would manifestly change the world."[39]

For Martha, grieving the loss of her brother, a change in the world may have meant not only the restoration of the fortunes of Israel but also her own personal world.

We must be open to the possibility that these were words placed in her lips by John, as Sandra Schneiders suggests. By the same token, as one of Jesus's friends, Martha would have thought long and hard about this title as applied to him. Everyone else seemed to be using it. Why wouldn't she have used these words as well?

What about "Son of God"? What would Martha (or John) have meant by this?

In John's Gospel, Jesus often refers to himself as the Son, especially in relation to his Father in heaven. The intimate relationship between the Father and Son is one of the primary themes of Jesus's Farewell Discourse to his disciples, covering four chapters in John's Gospel and coming only a few chapters after the story of Lazarus: "Father, the hour has come; glorify your Son so that the Son may glorify you,"[40] he prays toward the end of this long passage. Jesus is praying before his disciples to the Father.

Some of the construction and the language of the Farewell Discourse that deal with the Father and Son may come from John's hand. But we can't ignore the fact that this is a key element in Jesus's self-understanding. At the Baptism in all three Synoptics the voice that comes from the heavens says some variation of "This is my beloved Son."[41] In John's Gospel, Jesus is described by John the Baptist as the "Son of God." And at the beginning of the story of

Lazarus, Jesus tells his disciples that the purpose of this illness is the glorification of the "Son of God."

Jesus's relationship with the Father was profound—and intimate. In Mark, the earliest Gospel, written around AD 65, Jesus uses the Aramaic word for "father," *abba*, in Gethsemane, when he asks that he not have to suffer: "Abba, Father, for you all things are possible; remove this cup from me; yet, not what I want, but what you want."[42] Still earlier, in Paul's letter to the Galatians, written around AD 50, Paul writes, "And because you are children, God has sent the Spirit of his Son into our hearts, crying, 'Abba! Father!'"[43]

Scholars disagree on the most accurate translation of *abba*, but we know that it was a term children used for their father, and so it's safe to say that this was a term of intimacy.[44]

Clearly, the language of sonship was part of Jesus's vocabulary, and perhaps expressed to Martha and Mary. But what would Martha (or John channeling Mary) have meant by "Son of God"? Besides having heard Jesus speak this way, she might also have been aware of its use in the Old Testament, typically in reference to angels but also in relation to Israel, for example, in the Book of Exodus: "Thus says the LORD: Israel is my firstborn son."[45] At the same time, it could be said that everyone is a child of God. We can see this clearly in Luke's genealogy, which goes backwards from Jesus to "Adam, the son of God."[46] Because Adam is the son of God, all his descendants are as well.

Martha may also know that by calling Jesus the "Son of God" she is making a statement both theological and political. In the realm of the Roman emperors, divine sonship was conferred by the Roman Senate, if not an inherited trait. Julius Caesar was proclaimed divine, and that divinity was passed on to Augustus, his adopted son, who was then the "Son of God." *Divi filius* was a favorite title. In 2016, a nineteen-hundred-year-old gold Roman coin was found in eastern Galilee with the head of Augustus on the front and the legend *Divus Augustus*. Martha might have known some of these traditions.

Mainly, however, Son of God, in addition to expressing Jesus's relation to the Father, was used, as Amy-Jill Levine explained to me recently, by the Gospel writers as a kind of "synonym for Messiah." This, she said, includes not only the Davidic connection, since in 2 Samuel God promises David's royal descendant a son, but also as a kind of retort to Rome.[47] In effect, the Gospels ask: Do you want to worship Jesus or Caesar?

But what Martha meant by "Son of God" is probably what Jesus meant.

Resurrection and Life

Now let us turn to the terms that Jesus uses for himself and one of his most important "I am" statements: "I am the Resurrection and the Life."

These terms may be easier to explain but harder to understand. Messiah and Son of God relate more to Jesus's identity—his roles or titles. In using the terms "Resurrection" and "Life," he takes onto himself not a role but a *concept*. It is akin to the difference between saying "I am a friend" and "I am friendship itself." The terms must also be seen as a unit. Jesus does not say, "I am the resurrection. And I am the life." But "I am the resurrection and the life." The two are coupled. Both parts of that statement invite us to believe.

At the time, belief in the resurrection of the body was commonplace among many Jewish people. In fact, when the Gospel writers introduce the Sadducees, a religious group associated with the upper echelons of the priesthood, they describe them as those who don't believe in the resurrection. "Some Sadducees, who say there is no resurrection, came to him and asked him a question," reads the Gospel of Mark.[48]

As Amy-Jill Levine notes, both the Gospels and Josephus, the Jewish historian writing at the time, mention this aspect of the belief of the Sadducees, and so they suggest that their view was in the minority. Thus, she concludes, "The majority belief was that the dead would rise, although some thought that all people would rise to face a final judgment, and some believed that only the righteous would rise while the wicked would just stay dead."⁴⁹

Yet Jesus is offering Martha more than she can imagine. She believes that her brother would rise on the last day. Brendan Byrne says, "What Jesus announces here is of universal significance— a gift for the human race for which the raising of Lazarus will only be a sign and a symbol." What Jesus offers Lazarus—resurrection and new life—he offers to all of us. And what Jesus offers Martha— a remedy for her grief—he also offers to all of us. "This simple miracle story," writes Byrne, "is at this point becoming a revelatory discourse with significance for us all."⁵⁰

Jesus and Martha and the whole group who are mourning, Byrne says, are confronting the mystery of death and suffering. But it is focused on one person and one family. On the surface, what Jesus is about to do is raise that one person to life and comfort one family. But Martha is being invited, as is the reader, to grasp a deeper truth. Lazarus will die again—he is not raised at this point to an eternal life, something that his friends must have wondered about. (Recall Peter's question to Jesus about the Beloved Disciple.) It will be a "marvel but not a lasting remedy," says Byrne.⁵¹

I love what Byrne says next: "Jesus uses this present predicament to draw Martha, and all who share both her faith and her grief, to a vision where death is seen to be conquered, not by a return to present mortal life, but by the gift of 'eternal life,' which perdures even in the face of death. Lazarus's death—and shortly his raising—are a sign of this wider truth."⁵²

This truth—that Jesus offers us resurrection and new life not only in the future but here and now, through faith—is what I want to communicate most through this book. And this happens through belief, through the concept stressed in John. The entire emphasis of the Gospel is that it is written so that you may not only come to believe in Jesus as the Messiah and Son of God, as Martha attests, but that in believing him you may have "life in his name."

. . .

How can this wider truth penetrate the lives of believers?

First, it helps us know that Christ promises eternal life to those who believe in him. Even some devout believers say that this is hard for them to accept: eternal life in company with God. And it often is hard to understand.

The reality of Jesus Christ helps us understand this in several ways. First, Jesus *promises* us this—not only here, explicitly in the story of Lazarus, but throughout the Gospels—in John to be sure, where he declares himself the "living bread" that offers eternal life;[53] and in perhaps the most famous of the Johannine quotations, 3:16, which promises "that everyone who believes in him may not perish but may have eternal life"; and in his promise that believers will abide in his "Father's house," where there are many "dwelling places."[54] These are Jesus's verbal assurances of eternal life.

Second, Jesus *shows us* this in his miracles, like the Raising of the Widow of Nain's Son and the Raising of the Daughter of Jairus, and, most dramatically, the Raising of Lazarus. We have already explored how the raising of the dead was a central part of his ministry and is even mentioned to John's disciples ("the dead are raised") as an indication that Jesus is the "one who is to come."

Third, Jesus *reveals* this in his own resurrection. As what St. Paul calls the "first fruits," the forerunner of humanity, Jesus manifests what God has in store for believers.

But there is another way of understanding the life that awaits believers after death. And that is to remember the intimate relationships that we have with God. God created us, loved us into being, and sustains us throughout our lives, blessing us and nourishing us every day we take breath. One of the hallmarks of that love is the relationship into which God invites us. One reason that God incarnates himself in Jesus is so that we can enter even more deeply into that precious relationship.

Why would God allow death to end that relationship? It makes no sense.

Let the intimate relationships that Jesus had with Martha, Mary, and Lazarus serve as examples. One way to understand the Raising of Lazarus is as a sign that Jesus would not let death sever their love. It is similar in the Resurrection of Jesus. God will not let death have the last word. The relationship between the Father and Son is not ended by death.

And with us as well: God will not allow something like death to end our relationship. As Paul wrote, "For I am convinced that neither death, nor life, nor angels, nor rulers, nor things present, nor things to come, nor powers, nor height, nor depth, nor anything else in all creation, will be able to separate us from the love of God in Christ Jesus our Lord."[55]

Yet even *that* is too limited a notion of how Jesus is "Resurrection and Life" because it is limited to what happens at the end of our lives, or the "end times." Thus far, we have been talking about an eschatological hope—a hope for future times, ours and the world's. But resurrection and life are what Jesus offers us now.

This is what theologians call a "realized eschatology," meaning that the promises of new life as part of the reign of God are present now. You can see this in the patterns of death and resurrection that happen to us almost daily. It is also a participation in the Paschal Mystery, the process of dying and rising, of death and new life. (The word "paschal" comes from the Greek word *paschō*, which means to suffer or experience.) The forerunner is Jesus, and the event par excellence is Easter.

Much of this is related to "dying to self," letting any parts or aspects of your life that keep you from moving close to God "die" to experience new life. At the beginning of this book, we talked about "leaving behind" in Lazarus's tomb, at least imaginatively, whatever keeps us from more closely experiencing new life.

This may sound abstract, so let me give you an example.

Freedom from the Need to Be Liked

One of the biggest challenges in my life has been facing the need to be loved, liked, and approved of. Of course, I'm loved by my Jesuit brothers, my friends, and my family. I don't lack for love. Perhaps it's better to say that for many years I felt a need for *everyone* to like or approve of me. Others feel the same. We want others to like us. It's a human desire, probably born of our primitive need for community, protection, and safety.

Problems come, however, when the need to be loved, liked, or approved of prevents us from being who we are, from doing the right thing, or from simply getting on with life. And for some time, I felt bound by that desire, always asking myself, "What will people think if I do this? Will I become less popular? Will anyone disagree with me?" Even worse, I would ask myself, "What can I do to get people to like me more?" It could be paralyzing as I tried to gauge the best "path" to more and more approval. It prevented me from living life freely, from making healthy decisions, even from being myself.

One year on retreat, I was praying over the Gospel passage called the "Rejection at Nazareth," where Jesus preaches in his hometown and proclaims himself the Messiah (in so many words), whereupon the townsfolk turn on him, drive him out of the town, and try to kill him.[56]

While meditating on that passage, something dawned on me. Nazareth was a small town, perhaps of two hundred to four hundred people, where Jesus had lived for some thirty years. He must have known most if not all the inhabitants. Some were probably members of his extended family. Consequently, Jesus must have known or had some idea of how people would react to his proclaiming himself the long-awaited Messiah. So, I asked Jesus in my prayer, "How were you able to stand in front of that crowd and say that?" All I could think of was what it would mean to be rejected.

And in my prayer, I heard him say, "Must everyone like you?"[57]

With a laugh, I told my retreat director that the answer was "Yes!" Then, more seriously, I told her how limiting that need had been for me. Because it was preventing me from new life, I started to think more deeply about what it would mean for that need to "die." Over the next few years, I worked to identify places where I could let go of that need.

A few years later, I wrote a book on LGBTQ (lesbian, gay, bisexual, transgender, and queer) Catholics, which garnered a great deal of opposition from some quarters of the church, including personal attacks, canceled talks, and frequent protests. The book had the approval of my Jesuit superiors and was endorsed by several cardinals and bishops and said nothing against church teaching. Nonetheless, I was labeled a "heretic," an "apostate," a "false priest," and a "wolf in sheep's clothing." I also received what I call Catholic death threats: "I hope you die and go to hell," read a typical note. At the same time, the book received a great deal of support from other parts of the church, and I was invited by cardinals and bishops to give lectures in their dioceses and the next year was invited by the Vatican to address the World Meeting of Families, in Dublin, Ireland, where they asked me to speak on LGBTQ Catholics and their families. Eventually I was invited to a private audience with Pope Francis, where we spoke for thirty minutes about LGBTQ Catholic ministry. At the end of the audience, Pope Francis said, "Continue your ministry in peace." So I had a great deal of support.

But early on, as I was beginning to be attacked and vilified both online and in person, I realized that I no longer needed everyone to love, like, or approve of me. How had this happened? For one thing, I had been thinking about that question I heard in prayer: Was it necessary that everyone like me? For another, I knew I had the support of my Jesuit superiors and now the pope. Finally, I knew that some of the opposition I was receiving was motivated by simple homophobia and a real hatred of LGBTQ people. It was easier to not take such attacks personally.

Still, the freedom from the need to be liked, and the recognition that the opposition didn't disturb me, was a grace. It was like being healed from an illness. And being tied to the opinions of others was a form of enslavement. When I realized this, I felt tremendously free.

Why am I bringing this up in a book on Lazarus? Because the pattern was one of death and rebirth. The part of me that craved constant approval had to die so that I could experience new life.

All this was grounded in my desire to follow Jesus but also in my confidence that he is the Resurrection and Life. And that resurrection, at least in part, may be experienced now—by all who believe in him.

What does it mean for you? Maybe you'll never be called hateful names on social media. Indeed, I hope not. And I certainly hope that you never receive any death threats. It is something I would not wish on any person.

But most of us, to take the example I just offered, want other people to like, love, or approve of us. That's probably part of our human nature—wanting to be part of the crowd. We experience that as children on the playground, wanting to be "in" and not "out," wanting to be picked for the team, wanting others to see us as part of the group. An ancient part of the human brain probably craves social approval and acceptance as a way of keeping us closer to the community. For our prehistoric ancestors, being tightly bound to community would have meant increased safety, and so natural selection probably favored human beings who craved approval.

Taken to the extreme, however, a desire for the approval of others can, as I discovered, be crippling. Like Lazarus, I felt bound up in my grave cloths, unable to move freely. Once I set those cloths aside, however, I experienced a great deal of freedom—and life.

Maybe what keeps you bound is not an overreliance on the approval of others. Perhaps you are largely free of that desire. Perhaps what keeps you bound is something else: a need always to be right, a burning desire for more wealth, an overemphasis on your physical appearance. We all wear grave cloths that prevent us from moving around freely, keeping us in our own "tombs."

The key is to recognize these unfreedoms and set them aside—even if the process takes years—so you can experience new life. And in this recognition and setting aside, we let these unfreedoms "die." Only then can we experience the freedom that God offers us. These small "resurrections" are not as earth-shattering as the one that Jesus experienced on Easter Sunday, nor is this "new life" as dramatic as what Lazarus experienced a few days before in Bethany. But these everyday experiences of dying and rising offer us new life right now and help us glimpse the abundant life that God has prepared for us in the fullness of time.

The more you can see this pattern in your own life, the more you will be able to trust in God's ability to bring about new life, and the more you will be able to say with Martha, "Yes, Lord, I believe."

For Your Reflection

1. Does the image of Christ as depicted on the tympanum of the Cathedral of St.-Lazare console, terrify, or fascinate you? Is this close to your image of Jesus?
2. Martha says, "Yes, Lord, I believe that you are the Messiah, the Son of God, the one coming into the world." How would you describe Jesus? With what words or titles?
3. Which of Jesus's "I am" statements in John's Gospel are the most meaningful to you?
4. Do you think Jesus knew who he was, how he would suffer and die, and that he would rise again "on the third day"? What do you think about his "self-consciousness" as the Son of God? Do you think he knew who he was from the time he was born, or did he have to learn it throughout his life?
5. Have you ever felt the desire to be freed from the need to be loved, liked, or approved of? Where are you on that journey? If not, what keeps you "bound"?
6. Where do you see signs of the pattern of dying and rising in your own life?

When She Heard It

Waiting, Patience, and Growth

*When she had said this, she went back and
called her sister Mary, and told her privately,
"The Teacher is here and is calling for you." And
when she heard it, she got up quickly and went to
him. Now Jesus had not yet come to the village,
but was still at the place where Martha had met
him. The Jews who were with her in the house,
consoling her, saw Mary get up quickly and go
out. They followed her because they thought
that she was going to the tomb to weep there.*

In his commentary on John's Gospel, the theologian Wes Howard-Brook proposes that Mary remains in the house not only to mourn but out of fear as well.[1] Jesus had recently been threatened with stoning (the reason for his being on the other side of the Jordan when the story begins). So Howard-Brook suggests that Martha's telling her sister about Jesus's arrival "privately" was not simply because it was a personal matter but so the opponents of Jesus would not hear.

Notice too that Martha meets Jesus outside Bethany, another sign that their meeting is surreptitious. Is this evidence, as Howard-Brook proposes, of an "underground" movement?

As Howard-Brook sees it, Martha leaves the house alone so as not to "arouse the Judeans' suspicion." When she returns, she reports to her sister that the "Teacher" wants to see her. The Greek word used to describe their communication, *lathra*, can mean "privately," which suggests private family matters, or "secretly," which fits with Howard-Brook's idea of the two sisters' concern about being watched and "death threats" in Judea.

Amy-Jill Levine strongly rejects this interpretation. "Jesus has already made a public appearance at the tomb," she explained to me, and so Jesus's presence was already well-known in Bethany. Plus, the people have no problem following Mary when she goes to the tomb, which again argues against any kind of "hidden" movement. "There is nothing 'underground' in John," said AJ. "Jesus is much more public here than in the Marcan Messianic secret." There is no reason, she said, to see any hostility among the Jews who came to offer their support.

Mary, for whatever reasons, waited. She may have been angry at Jesus for not coming sooner. Or she must have been just as eager as her sister was to see Jesus, the one at whose feet she had sat so lovingly in Luke's Gospel.

As we consider this part of the story, we must remember that some of it may reflect John's construction of the narrative, where the "active one" rushes out and the "contemplative one" waits in the house. And we have to remember John's general antipathy toward "the Jews." Still, Martha's departure before Mary, whether historically accurate or John's creation, sets the two sisters apart, in terms of not only action versus contemplation but also doing versus waiting.

Who knows how long Mary waited for her sister's return—an hour? Once her waiting is over, however, she springs up and rushes to meet Jesus.

John presents her in a positive light, now hurrying to be with him. John also uses a significant word to indicate what she does. The usual translation is she "got up quickly." But the original Greek is *ēgerthē*, she "rose up," used in John elsewhere to describe Jesus's rising from the dead. We may be meant to see a kind of transformation in Mary.

Mary's waiting in the house came after three days of waiting for Jesus to come. This part of the passage, then—Mary remaining at home—reminds us of the value of waiting, an often-overlooked spiritual virtue. Most of our lives are spent waiting. In fact, that is an essential part of the Christian life.

Christian Waiting

In the previous chapter we talked about the Paschal Mystery—the dying and rising of Jesus and our continual participation in what theologians call in anodyne language the "Easter event." To use that image, we might say that much of our lives are spent not in Good Friday or Easter Sunday but in Holy Saturday. That is, most of our days are not filled with the unbearable pain of a Good Friday. Nor are they suffused with the unbelievable joy of an Easter. Some days are indeed times of great pain and some great joy, but most are in between: they're spent in Holy Saturday, when the disciples simply waited.

From the perspective of Mary and Martha, most of our lives are not spent in the horror of seeing one's brother die, or the joy of seeing him risen from the dead, but in between.

The excitement of a visit by Jesus was not something that happened every day to Martha and Mary, but only when he visited nearby Jerusalem, and then only when he had time to relax at their house. Though the sisters were probably wealthy, they likely spent their lives doing simple tasks, common to the people of their time: waiting for bread to rise, waiting for the weather to change, waiting for an illness to pass. In their religious lives there was waiting as well: first waiting and wondering when the longed-for Messiah would come, and then, after coming to know Jesus, waiting for the "Teacher" to return.

The Two Marys Watch the Tomb,
by James Tissot (Brooklyn Museum).

Waiting is a dominant theme throughout the Old Testament, as Israel first waits for release from bondage and slavery in Egypt, then waits to enter the Promised Land, and finally waits for the coming of the Messiah. The psalms are replete with odes to waiting:

Wait for the LORD;

be strong, and let your heart take courage;

wait for the LORD![2]

Much of our own lives are times of waiting. Waiting to get into a good college. Waiting to meet the right person to marry. Waiting to get pregnant. Waiting to get a job. Waiting for a diagnosis from the doctor. Waiting for things at work to improve. Waiting for the results of our physical therapy to help us feel better. Waiting for a relationship to improve. Waiting for life to get better.

But there are different kinds of waiting.

There is the wait of despair. Here we know—or at least think we know—that things could never get any better, that God could never do anything with our situation. Nothing will, or could, ever change, we think. So, we just wait and endure life. It is a kind of negative, even dead, waiting, closer to dread than to hope.

This may be the kind of waiting that forced the fearful disciples to hide behind locked doors on Holy Saturday, cowering in terror after Jesus's crucifixion.[3]

They could be forgiven for their fear. After Jesus was executed, they probably were terrified, with some justification, of being rounded up and executed by the Roman authorities. This kind of wait—which edges toward despair—is a common human experience.

In an alternate turn of events, we can imagine Martha and Mary not waiting expectantly for Jesus but giving up after the death of their brother. Rather than meeting Jesus when he arrives, the sisters could simply have withdrawn, bitterly, into resentment against the supposed healer who failed to show up. We may be so familiar with this Gospel story that we forget that these characters in the story were human beings who had the freedom to respond in any way they wanted. Those who encounter God have the freedom to respond any way they choose. Mary could have said "No" to the Angel Gabriel in Nazareth. Peter could have said "No thanks" to Jesus at the Sea of Galilee. And Mary and Martha could have refused to see Jesus in Bethany. "He's too late," they could have said. "Nothing can be done now."

But Mary and Martha knew that this kind of attitude, which says

"Nothing can ever change," is not the mark of a disciple. This is not the waiting we are called to.

Then there is the wait of passivity, as if everything were up to "fate." In this waiting, there is no despair but not much anticipation of anything good either. It is the wait of "Whatever." It denies God's involvement with humanity. Or even God's interest in humanity. It is an empty waiting. This is not the waiting that disciples are called to.

Christians are called to the waiting that is called hope. It is an active waiting that knows even in the worst situations, even in the darkest times, God is powerfully at work, even if we cannot see that clearly. The disciples' fear after Good Friday was understandable. But we, who know how the story turned out, who know that Jesus will rise from the dead, who know that God is with us, who know that nothing is impossible for God, are called to wait in faithful hope. And to look carefully for signs of life that are always right around the corner—to look, to seek, to expect, just as a few of the disciples, especially the women, were doing on Holy Saturday.

Mary waited in this way in her home at Bethany. Because she knew that change is always possible, renewal is always awaiting, and growth is always happening. This is why, when her sister returned with word from the "Teacher," she "got up quickly" and rushed out to see Jesus. She was waiting in hope.

Weeds and Wheat

We may wait for a long time, however. Change, renewal, and new life take time.

This is one reason why so many of Jesus's parables are about slow growth. Many of the parables feature themes of sowing, planting, growing, and harvesting. The New Testament scholar C. H. Dodd defined a parable as "a metaphor or simile drawn from nature or common life, arresting the hearer by its vividness or strangeness, and leaving the mind in sufficient doubt about its precise application to tease it into active thought."[4]

Common life in Jesus's time meant a largely agrarian existence. Certainly Jesus spoke with people who made their living from other trades, as well as to more formally educated people. He spoke not only to farmers but to fishermen, millers, potters, tax collectors, bakers, and textile workers as well as scribes and Pharisees. Jesus also used images from his own trade. Think about the parables of the man who builds a house on sand, the builder who constructs a tower and fails to calculate its cost.[5] But many if not most of his parables, which were designed to help people of the day understand the concept of the reign of God, are about farming.

More to the point, many of the parables are about *growth*—often slow growth. Here, in full, is the Parable of the Growing Seed, from the Gospel of Mark:

> The kingdom of God is as if someone would scatter seed on the ground, and would sleep and rise night and day, and the seed would sprout and grow, he does not know how. The earth produces of itself, first the stalk, then the head, then the full grain in the head. But when the grain is ripe, at once he goes in with his sickle, because the harvest has come.[6]

Notice that the sower sleeps "night and day" while the seed grows, "he does not know how." Patient waiting is involved, as well as the recognition that it is not the sower who is causing the seed to sprout and grow, but God. In other parables about growth—the Sower and the Seed, the Woman with the Yeast—we also see themes of hopeful waiting and expectation. Waiting is part of the Christian life. So is patience.

It's natural to be impatient. We wonder why things aren't changing more quickly in the world, in the church, or in our families. Social movements, to take one example, take time. Consider how long it took, several generations, for women to win the right to vote in the United States. The women who finally saw victory in that struggle had not even been born when the fight began. We know how long it took, even longer, for African Americans to gain their civil rights, a struggle that continues.

But it's still hard to wait for these things to happen, things that seem so just, so right, so obvious. We wonder: Why isn't God making this happen faster?

We also find it hard to wait for change in ourselves. And most of us want to change. Most of us have a sense of the kind of person we would like to become. But something holds us back. Maybe we tend to take a negative view of life. Or we cannot forgive someone against whom we hold a grudge. Or we admit we're addicted to something: drinking, drugs, gambling, overeating, pornography. Or maybe we simply keep repeating unhealthy and selfish patterns of behaviors with others: we're angry, jealous, or vindictive. Beneath all this, however, is a desire to change, to grow, to renew. And we have an image of the person we'd like to be.

We want to become the person we think that God would like us to become. But it is a call that often takes a long time to reach fruition. Like the seeds in Jesus's parables, it takes time for that call to "sprout and grow."[7]

In another parable about growth, the Parable of the Weeds and the Wheat, which appears in Matthew's Gospel, Jesus tries to help his hearers grasp the concept of the "reign of God." The Greek *basileia tou theou* is less about a kingdom, which can have geographic overtones, and more about a reign. Matthew calls it the "kingdom/reign of heaven," *basileia tōn ouranōn*.[8]

Jesus says that the reign of God is like a man who sows good seed in his field. While everyone is sleeping an enemy comes and sows weeds among the good seeds. After the crops grow, his servants notice the crime and ask the man whether they should pull up the weeds.

The Greek word used for "weed" is *zizanion*, a plant that would have looked almost exactly like wheat until it ripened—called today "darnel" or "tares." Thus, the owner replies, "No; for in gathering the weeds you would uproot the wheat along with them. Let both of them grow together until harvest; then at harvest time I will tell the reapers, 'Collect the weeds first and bind them in bundles to be burned, but gather the wheat into my barn.'"[9]

After the disciples ask Jesus for an explanation, he gives them one: the good seeds are those who follow Jesus's word; the bad, the "children of the evil one"; and the harvest, the final judgment.[10]

Parables work on many levels. This one is about growth, patience, and judgment in the reign of God. But I am reminded of a hero of mine, whose story illustrates this parable.

"A Changed Man"

John Lewis was an icon of the civil rights movement and a US politician who lived from 1940 to 2020. While still in his twenties, he helped organize the famous March on Washington in 1963 and spoke to a crowd of hundreds of thousands of people shortly before Martin Luther King Jr.'s "I Have a Dream" speech on the steps of the Lincoln Memorial. Two years later, Lewis led a march from Selma to Montgomery, which took him and many other activists over the Edmund Pettus Bridge, where armed Alabama police beat the unarmed marchers, including Lewis, who suffered serious injuries.

Later in life, John Lewis ran for the US Congress and served seventeen terms, from 1986 to his death in 2020, and was often called the "Conscience of the Congress."

His extraordinary life is impossible to summarize in a few paragraphs. But I would like to focus on one aspect, which relates to this parable and our theme of waiting—specifically on the patient trust in God's final judgment and patient tolerance of the present.[11]

Every year Lewis traveled to Selma to mark the events of the day now known as Bloody Sunday. (In his obituaries, almost every newspaper and website featured the photo of Lewis, wearing a simple raincoat, suffering under the blows of a club-wielding police

Congressman John Lewis. In
time he would meet with and
forgive men who had opposed
him and beaten him.
US HOUSE OF REPRESENTATIVES:
WIKICOMMONS

officer.[12]) At the ceremony in 1998, he was greeted by Joseph T. Smitherman, Selma's mayor, who was also the city's segregationist mayor in 1965. Smitherman—now repentant—gave Lewis the key to the city.

"Back then, I called him an outside rabble rouser," said Mr. Smitherman. "Today I call him one of the most courageous people I ever met." The *New York Times* noted that Mr. Smitherman had been engaged in a decades-long effort to show people that he and Selma had changed.[13]

Lewis, an ordained minister and deeply religious Christian, knew a lot about patience and growth. In 1998, the same year that Smitherman awarded him the key to the city of Selma, Lewis wrote an op-ed called "Forgiving George Wallace," about the famously segregationist governor of Alabama and presidential candidate who thundered at his inauguration in 1963, "Segregation now, segregation tomorrow, segregation forever!"

John Lewis met George Wallace in 1979. He wrote about that meeting: "I could tell that he was a changed man; he was engaged in a campaign to seek forgiveness from the same African-Americans he had oppressed. He acknowledged his bigotry and assumed responsibility for the harm he had caused. He wanted to be forgiven."[14]

Thirty years later, in 2009, Lewis also had the opportunity to forgive another person, this time a man who had beaten him at a bus terminal in Rock Hill, South Carolina. Elwin Wilson, then a supporter of the Ku Klux Klan, who had an "awakening" after Barack Obama was elected president, said that a friend had asked him, "If you died right now, do you know where you would go?" To hell, said Mr. Wilson. Seeking forgiveness, he eventually met with John Lewis, who in a later interview said, "He started crying, his son started crying, and I started crying." The two men later made several appearances together to talk about reconciliation.[15]

There are stories about the Weeds and the Wheat—about God's slow ways. Most of us would be tempted to condemn Mayor Smitherman, Governor Wallace, Elwin Wilson, and their fellow segregationists to hell, as weeds. But God had other ideas for them, ideas that would take a long time to germinate. This vision presented by Jesus in the parable is not only a vision of the reign of God but also directions for how to help cultivate the reign of God on earth.

Does this mean that we shy away from condemning evil acts, like racism? No! That was the last thing that John Lewis would do. "I can never forget what George Wallace said and did as Governor, as a national leader and as a political opportunist," he wrote in that same op-ed. But, he continued, "our ability to forgive serves a higher moral purpose in our society. Through genuine repentance and forgiveness, the soul of our nation is redeemed. George Wallace deserves to be remembered for his effort to redeem his soul and in so doing to mend the fabric of American society."

As I noted in chapter 7, the Greeks had two different concepts of time: *chronos* and *kairos*. "What time is it?" is a *chronos* question. "Strike while the iron is hot" is a *kairos* expression—about the right or opportune time. When Jesus talked about time, it was about *kairos*, not *chronos*. God's time is more important than our own. In fact, the very first words out of his mouth, in the earliest Gospel, Mark, are *Peplērōtai ho kairos*, "The time is fulfilled."

The time of harvest, as in the Parable of the Weeds and the Wheat, is *kairos* time. This is the word used by the master, who speaks of the "time of the harvest," not the *chronos tou therismou* but the *kairos tou therismou*. John Lewis knew that all sorts of things can happen in *kairos* time that seem impossible in *chronos* time.

God's time is God's time. And good and evil are often so intertwined that, as Jesus says in the Parable of the Weeds and the Wheat, it is impossible to separate them and eradicate that evil.

It is the same within us. We must be patient for God to uproot the evil in us and invite us into healthier, more flourishing lives. But it happens in God's time.

Why does it take so long for these things to happen? Why doesn't God act more quickly?

At heart these questions are variations on one of the primary questions in the Christian life: "Why do we suffer?" Even if you are not a great civil rights activist or a character in a Gospel narrative, you will probably ask these questions of God at some point in your life.

These are the questions we ask, that John Lewis probably asked himself at Selma, and that Mary asked herself as she waited in the house in Bethany.

Key to being able to wait, whether for John Lewis, Mary, or us, is being in relationship with God. It is not simply waiting for some-*thing* to happen, but for some*one* to come. Otherwise the waiting makes little sense.

This is one reason why the Christian faith is not simply faith in a set of rules—as important as rules are for any group. Christians believe in certain creeds, dogmas, and doctrines, of course. But in the end, our faith is about belief in a *person*, Jesus Christ. We wait because we trust in him, trust in his judgment, and trust in his coming, often in ways that seem confusing, mysterious, or even devastating—and often on a timetable not of our choosing.

Mary, she waited in hope, ready for the Lord. Waiting for the *kairos*. And when that time came, she was ready to rush out and greet it. Or, more accurately, greet him.

For Your Reflection

1. Why do you think Mary waits, staying behind in the house? Is she fearful? Humble enough to let her sister go ahead? Waiting for Jesus's invitation?
2. Consider the different kinds of waiting. How would you describe "Christian waiting"?
3. How does the idea of slow growth work in your life?
4. How do you experience the two types of time—*chronos* and *kairos*—in your life?
5. What is your response to John Lewis forgiving Governor George Wallace? Do you need to forgive anyone? Where do time, waiting, and growth fit into this process?

She Knelt at His Feet

Is Everyone Wrong About Mary?

*When Mary came where Jesus was and saw him,
she knelt at his feet and said to him, "Lord, if you
had been here, my brother would not have died."*

At this point in our story, after hearing that the Teacher has
called her, Mary rushes from the house to greet Jesus, who is
still outside of Bethany. Kneeling at his feet, as she does in Luke's
story of Jesus's visit to her house, Mary repeats the precise words
that her sister used: "Lord, if you had been here, my brother would
not have died."

On the surface, her greeting, while heartfelt, seems like little
more than a repetition of her sister's words. Does this mean that
we are to see Mary in a somewhat lesser light? After all, her sister
greeted Jesus first and pronounced him as the "Messiah, the Son of
God, the one who is coming into the world." Some scholars point to
Martha's proclamation as the theological climax of the story. Mary
seems to be running a distant second to her sister, a kind of copycat.

Other New Testament scholars disagree. Indeed, one of the
most surprising divisions in scholarship about this story is who
John is setting forth as the ideal disciple. For some scholars that

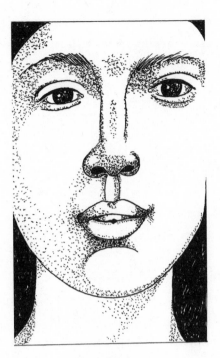

Mary of Bethany,
by William Hart McNichols.
COURTESY OF THE ARTIST

person is not the traditional candidate, Martha, with her bold profession of faith, but Mary.

In a provocative article titled "Can Everyone Be Wrong?" Francis Moloney makes a persuasive case for why John intends for us to see Mary in the more positive light.[1]

At the outset, John identifies Mary as the one who anointed Jesus's feet with ointment and wiped them with her hair (an event that had not taken place in the narrative but would have been known by John's readers, a point that suggests that John expected his readers to have some knowledge of Luke's Gospel). The naming of Mary first (the sisters are introduced as "Mary and her sister Martha") and the reminder of the anointing instructs the reader on the importance of Mary for the story being introduced. "The reader must keep an attentive eye on Mary," says Moloney.[2]

Moloney believes, contrary to what scholars like Sandra Schneiders suggest, that Martha's confession in Jesus as "Messiah and Son of God" is meant to be seen as incomplete. Let's look again at that interchange between Jesus and Martha, but this time from another angle:

> **Jesus:** "I am the Resurrection and the Life. Those who believe in me, even though they die, will live, and everyone who lives and believes in me will never die. Do you believe this?"
> **Martha:** "Yes, Lord, I believe that you are the Messiah, the Son of God, the one coming into the world."

Jesus asks whether Martha believes he is "the Resurrection and the Life." But Martha answers with terms that can be seen as "acceptable messianic categories": Messiah and Son of God. On the one hand, those are impressive titles. However, earlier uses of these expressions, says Moloney, were seen as signs of the "limited faith" of those who uttered them.[3]

In other words, Jesus is asking Martha to believe something larger than almost anyone can imagine. But Martha answers with standard categories.

Some of this argument turns on grammatical analysis. In her Greek response, "I believe," Martha answers in the perfect tense. That is, she has *already* believed in this. Her faith preceded Jesus's identification as the Resurrection and Life. "She affirms her long-held view that Jesus fulfills her messianic expectation," Moloney says. She knows this, but often in John's Gospel it is those "who know" who are shown as lacking in faith. "Repeatedly in the Fourth Gospel," Moloney points out, "the 'we know' of prior certainties about the identity of Jesus are mistaken."

Martha's "lack of faith," according to Moloney, is also reflected by the word she uses for Jesus when she calls her sister: "Teacher." Finally, she seems not to have understood Jesus when she protests at the tomb, "there is a stench because he has been dead four days."

But instead of needlessly denigrating Martha for what may (or may not) have been her lack of faith (or John's presentation of it), let's look at what Moloney says about Mary and her faith.

Mary responds immediately when she is told Jesus is "calling" for her and kneels at his feet in their encounter that day in Bethany. Her physical posture indicates her complete trust in him and her sense of worship. While Martha goes to see him on her own, and presumably speaks to him face to face, Mary waits for his invitation and then prostrates herself. "Her attitude," Moloney says elsewhere, "is highlighted by receptivity and respect for the person of Jesus."[4]

Yet Mary joins "the Jews" in their weeping. Soon we will see that John may be indicating that this means not simply mourning but a lack of belief in Jesus's power. And so Mary may have blotted her copy book.

Trying to Get It Right

Let's return to what Mary does after her brother is raised from the dead (in John 11): she anoints Jesus's body (in John 12). The Passion of Jesus was set in motion by the Raising of Lazarus—in John's Gospel this leads directly to his crucifixion—and Mary's anointing of Jesus's feet is a preparation for his death.

Moloney has a beautiful way of understanding this as an act of faith: Mary is the first to accept that the illness and death of Lazarus will lead to the glorification of the Son of God. Jesus's supportive explanation of Mary's anointing (where he defends her against naysayers) indicates that, at last, one of the characters in the story "got it right."

Moloney ends his analysis by saying that we should not "divide characters" in the story, much less divide readers. We don't want to fall into the same trap that so many have fallen into concerning

Martha and Mary—arguing "Who is the better sister?" or "Who is the better disciple?" What is better—action or contemplation? Who really believes in Jesus—the one who on her own initiatives goes to see him and perhaps imperfectly confesses her faith or the one who falls at his feet in prostration and then anoints his feet at a dinner?

The desire to grasp the intent of John's Gospel is understandable. And it's natural to ask such questions. But such divisions ignore several important points.

First, we may be reading a construction of the two sisters by John. We've already established that Martha and Mary were real people, yet the writer of John's Gospel might have embellished some aspect of this story—even if it came from the Beloved Disciple, who was perhaps their brother. Themes of misunderstanding, which run through John's Gospel, may have been overlaid on a story in which both sisters understood Jesus in the same way.

Second, if the story happened precisely this way, then the varying responses of both grieving sisters to Jesus are understandable. So what if Martha used the wrong phrasing or imperfectly confessed her faith? So what if Mary stayed behind? They had buried their brother and would be excused for anything that we might see as a lapse. Besides, do we expect them to have at this point a full and complete "Christology," or understanding of the person and work of Jesus Christ?

Finally, something to remember when considering the disciples' response to Jesus: How could any of them truly have understood what was going on? Even if they had heard of Jesus's Raising of the Widow of Nain's Son and Jairus's Daughter, how could they have understood, or predicted, or even dared to hope for what he was about to do? God's ways are always too wonderful and—to use an overused word—too mysterious for us to anticipate. Martha and Mary lived in hope, but they also lived in the real world, where dead people didn't walk out of their tombs.

Once again, we are all Martha and we are all Mary, struggling to believe, struggling to hope, and struggling to understand Jesus. None of us is perfect—and neither was Martha or Mary. Most of us are trying to get it right, sometimes failing to do the right thing and sometimes doing what we believe is right, even though we may question our course of action afterward, wondering, *Was that really the right course of action?* This is part of the human condition, even for the devout believer: living with an imperfect faith and imperfect knowledge in an imperfect world.

Who got it right: Mary or Martha? As I see it, both sisters were doing their best, trying to believe in God's ways during a difficult time. And so in that sense, they both got it right.

We are all Lazarus, too, who also must have wondered in his last moments why his friend hadn't come and why the man who had healed so many others hadn't healed him as well. Imagine his own disappointment and his sorrow for his sisters. No matter which sister is "right" in expressions of faith and grief, we have all felt the same emotions during times of stress and struggle—fear, doubt, faith, hope, trust, confusion—and yet still listen for Jesus's voice.

For Your Reflection

1. Do you think that Martha's confession of Jesus—"Yes, Lord, I believe that you are the Messiah, the Son of God, the one coming into the world"—is somehow incomplete?

2. The responses of Martha and Mary to Jesus's appearance in Bethany are contrasted in this chapter. Which sister do you feel "got it right"? Or is that question too judgmental for you? Are we meant to see them struggling to understand in their own ways?

3. When have you felt your own faith to be "incomplete"? What helped you in those moments?

See How He Loved Him

Why Does Jesus Weep?

*When Jesus saw her weeping, and the Jews who
came with her also weeping, he was greatly
disturbed in spirit and deeply moved. He said,
"Where have you laid him?" They said to him,
"Lord, come and see." Jesus began to weep. So the
Jews said, "See how he loved him!" But some of
them said, "Could not he who opened the eyes of
the blind man have kept this man from dying?"*

In his classic manual for prayer, *The Spiritual Exercises*, as well
as in his spiritual journals, St. Ignatius Loyola refers to the "gift
of tears," an experience that came when he was so overcome with
feelings of God's presence that he wept. In fact, he wept so often
during prayer that a physician told him that unless he stopped, he
would harm his eyes. So he did. Ignatius was nothing if not practical.

For most of us, though, weeping is not often associated with
being moved by God's presence, but rather with sadness or frustration. Even as an adult, I have been surprised to find how emotions
can often spill out as tears.

Not long ago, during a Mass in our Jesuit community, I prayed for my mother, who had just been diagnosed with cancer. The diagnosis had come a few days before and when I started to voice my prayer, I was fine. But hearing myself say the prayer brought a lump to my throat and then tears to my eyes, which I could not control. I left the chapel to compose myself for a few minutes, and afterward my brother Jesuits were kind and solicitous. This was one of many times when I felt my utter humanity. The next week, when I was told that my mother's cancer was untreatable, I wept for her and for me: I would miss her so much.

Weeping is probably one of the most human things we do, and it connects us to people around the world. Everyone weeps. So did Jesus on that day in Bethany. And he wasn't the only one.

Jesus Began to Weep

Martha and Mary probably felt a welter of emotions on that day, common to all who mourn, which elicited many tears. Sadness over their brother's death of course, but also sadness over what he had to endure during his last few days. When my father died over twenty years ago, I wept not only because I would not see him on earth again, but also out of sadness over the suffering he endured as cancer ravaged his lungs. On top of their grief for their brother, Martha and Mary may have felt another emotion, about their friend Jesus, which Paul McCarren points out, "They may feel Jesus has let them down."[1] And so they wept.

St. John Chrysostom notes in his homily on Lazarus that even those close to God suffer: "Many men, when they see any of those who are pleasing to God suffering anything terrible, as, for instance, having fallen into sickness, or poverty, and any other the like, are offended, not knowing that to those especially dear to God it belongs to endure these things."[2]

So even those close to God, as Martha and Mary were, suffer and weep. (And "the Jews" who were with the sisters weep, showing real sympathy for their grief.)

Raising of Lazarus, mosaic, Basilica of Sant'Apollinare Nuovo, Ravenna, Italy.
WIKICOMMONS

Someone else weeps in this passage as well, reported in one of the shortest sentences in the Bible. It has imprinted itself on the popular imagination and is notable for its brevity and power. In many translations it reads, "Jesus wept."

These two words are sometimes used as an expression of frustration or an exclamation over a tragic event. In the 1962 film *Lawrence of Arabia*, an American journalist named Bentley stumbles onto a group of massacred Turkish soldiers in Syria and at the sight of the bloodbath mutters, "Jesus wept. Jesus *wept*."

The words are also sometimes set forth as an example of Jesus's humanity. Christians believe that Jesus is fully human and fully divine, but they often focus more on what are often seen as signs of his divinity: the healing miracles, the nature miracles, and his resurrection. Signs of his humanity may seem harder to find, especially in John's Gospel, where Jesus can appear more divine than human. Though the God of Israel surely weeps, and first-century Midrash, ancient commentary on the Jewish Scriptures, portrays God weeping, the tears of Jesus are for many a window into his utter humanity.

We cannot divide moments of his life between those that are human and those that are divine since he is always both. Jesus is human when performing a miracle and divine when sawing a piece of wood. But it's natural for people to see the more supernatural aspects of his life (the miracles and the Resurrection) as signs of his divinity, and the more natural aspects (his tears, his anger) as signs of his humanity. Thus, the words "Jesus wept" are offered as a clear sign of his humanity. What could be more human than crying?

Jesus's weeping demonstrates that he is assuredly a *physical* human being—that is, he does something that is part of human physiology: he sheds tears. An old heresy, Docetism, suggested that Jesus was simply God "appearing" to be human.[3] Even though Docetism is not as much of a threat to contemporary Christianity, Jesus's tears are important for the believer's understanding of who he is: weeping is a completely human action. But it's also something he does as the Son of God. You could say that God wept at Lazarus's tomb out of love for his friend.

This reading is often used at funerals for that very reason. We chose it for my father's Funeral Mass, to help those gathered focus on the promise of new life and also to show a Jesus who suffers with us in our grief. Christians don't believe in a God who is apathetic or who doesn't feel, but rather one who understands the human condition in the most intimate way. Many Christians point to this verse to show that whatever else we know about Jesus, we know that he could be sad, just as we are sometimes sad.

But many Christians may have it wrong: Jesus may *not* have been weeping out of sadness over the death of his dear friend or even because he felt sorry for Martha and Mary, as human as those emotions would be.

Moreover, perhaps the most beloved part of this story—"Jesus wept"—is the aspect about the Raising of Lazarus about which there is the most scholarly discussion and disagreement. No part of the story comes close in terms of controversy among New Testament scholars. Open any Bible commentary and you'll be surprised at lengthy sections treating these few words. And the reasons behind that statement have to do with the Greek words that are used.

Come and See

First, let's remember what is happening at this point in our story: Mary has just raced from her house to meet Jesus on the outskirts of Bethany. Her Jewish friends have accompanied her. Jesus sees Mary and "the Jews" weeping and asks to see the tomb.

Jesus, familiar with Bethany after having visited Mary and Martha's house, but perhaps unfamiliar with the location of the tombs, asks, "Where have you laid him?"

They answer with the words that early hearers and readers would have recognized from the beginning of John's Gospel: "Come and see" (*Erchou kai ide*).[4] In that earlier passage, in the first chapter of the Gospel, Jesus is in the company of John the Baptist. To his own disciples John points out Jesus as the "Lamb of God who takes away the sin of the world."[5] Then he describes an event that has already occurred: the Baptism of Jesus.

We can only imagine the reaction of John's disciples at such a dramatic announcement. John also subordinates himself to Jesus, saying, "After me comes a man who ranks ahead of me because he was before me." John had attracted a huge following by the Jordan River, and now he was pointing to not his successor but his master. The next day, John is with two of his disciples and again makes that startling claim, "here is the Lamb of God." Naturally the two approach Jesus. They ask, "Rabbi, where are you staying?"

Jesus responds with history's most famous invitation: "Come and see."

Had Jesus used these words (and there's every reason to think that he did), then hearing them on the lips of Mary and Martha after Lazarus's death would have been deeply moving. And we can see the richness of its use in the Gospel. At the beginning of his public ministry, Jesus uses these words to invite the disciples to new life. Here, the sisters use the same words to invite Jesus to a place of death, which paradoxically, will lead to new life for Lazarus. In turn, this new life will lead to Jesus's death, which will lead to new life for all.

But what are we to make of being asked to "come" and "see"?

As Wes Howard-Brook notes, there is a great deal of "coming and going" in the story of the Raising of Lazarus, physical movements that symbolize the people's journey to faith. Here are the main movements that he identifies:

1. The sisters send a message from Bethany to across the Jordan, asking Jesus to come.
2. Jesus comes to Bethany; Thomas offers to go with him.
3. "The Jews" come from Jerusalem to console the sisters.
4. Martha goes from the house in Bethany to meet Jesus.
5. Martha comes back to the house to alert Mary.
6. Mary goes from the house to meet Jesus, with "the Jews" coming along.
7. Jesus goes to the tomb.
8. Lazarus "comes out."[6]

Each movement represents part of a journey of faith, and a journey of life and death. In each movement God says to us, "Come and see."

Now let's return to those tears.

What Was Jesus Really Feeling?

Upon hearing his own words repeated by Mary and Martha, Jesus weeps. Or he begins to weep: *edakrysen ho Iēsous* can mean either. The verb *dakryō* means to shed tears, with *dakry* being a teardrop. It is the only place in the New Testament where the verb *dakryon* appears.[7]

The first thing we notice is that Jesus's weeping is described differently from the weeping of Mary and "the Jews." The word John uses for them is *klaiontas*, which is to weep aloud, even to wail. It connotes loud lamentation of the kind that one might expect at a funeral.

By contrast, Jesus simply sheds tears. As Brendan Byrne notes, John is careful to distinguish Jesus's response from the more intense

Take Away the Stone, by John August Swanson. Swanson was an American artist who painted many Christian-themed works, including several depictions of Lazarus.
USED WITH PERMISSION

grief of Mary and "the Jews."[8] It's the first sign that the common understanding of this part of our story may be amiss.

Of greater importance are two other phrases, much debated by New Testament scholars, that describe Jesus's emotional state. And what scholars say may surprise readers used to thinking of Jesus as being sad over Lazarus's death or over the grief of Martha and Mary.

After he sees the weeping of Mary and "the Jews," Jesus is described by the English-language translators of the NRSV as "greatly disturbed in spirit and deeply moved." We might conclude that Jesus is sad over the death of Lazarus and is participating in the grieving going on around him. This is the human response that has made such an impression on believers throughout the centuries. The response from "the Jews" seems to underline this interpretation: "See how he loved him!"

Colm Tóibín's novel *The Testament of Mary* captures some of this approach when Mary explains what happens when Jesus saw her weeping: "As she wept, so did he, because he had known Lazarus all of his life and had loved him as all of us did."

This approach, however, does not accurately convey what the original Greek means.

Let's look in detail at those words, "greatly disturbed in spirit and deeply moved," in the original Greek: *enebrimēsato tō pneumati kai etaraxen heauton*. The key words to focus on are *enebrimēsato* and *etaraxen*. The first word, *enebrimēsato*, is used twice in this story: once here, when Jesus sees Mary and "the Jews" weeping, and a few sentences later, when he stands before Lazarus's tomb.

But "greatly disturbed in spirit" is maddeningly vague. Moreover, almost every scholar says that *enebrimēsato* doesn't mean "sad." Rather, it points to something more complicated: to make a sound displaying *anger*. In classical Greek it means to snort like a horse.[9] Raymond Brown writes, "The basic meaning of *embrimisthai* seems to imply an articulate expression of anger."[10] The translation is often surprising to people accustomed to thinking of Jesus's emotions at the tomb in other ways. Finally, the phrase *tō pneumati* means "in [the] spirit."

So Jesus is, perhaps more accurately, "angry in his spirit."

This translation becomes clearer when we look at the other places in the Gospel where *enebrimēsato* and other forms of the same verb are used—and where they are usually translated very differently from the way they are in the story of Lazarus. In Mark 1:43, Jesus has just cured a man with leprosy and sternly (*embrimēsamenos*) warns him not to tell anyone (he also "sternly" orders people to stay silent after healing blind men in Matt. 9:30). Then in Mark 14:4–5, ironically a connection to Mary and Martha, is the description of the crowd's reaction to the woman who has anointed Jesus's head. The crowd first expresses "anger" and then they "scolded her": *enebrimōnto.*

In neither case does the word convey sadness. Rather, it connotes anger or frustration.

Moloney translates *enebrimēsato* in John 11 as "severely disappointed."[11] Byrne notes, "the expression has a clear reference to anger." More specifically, anger "in his spirit."[12]

But why would Jesus be *angry* at the Tomb of Lazarus?

Some scholars surmise that Jesus, at least as portrayed by John, may be angry at the lack of faith shown by Mary and "the Jews." In this interpretation, the wailing (*klaiein*) of Mary and her friends shows that they do not understand who Jesus is or what he can do.

Raymond Brown suggests that the passage might indicate anger at death and suffering itself. When the word is used in Mark's Gospel, after the healing of a man with leprosy, we might conclude that Jesus is angry at the manifestations of "Satan's kingdom of evil."

Jesus's anger, according to Brown, may have been over the sadness of his friends that is brought on by death, or simply by death itself. His comment suggests the rage we sometimes feel when we see a loved one or friend who is suffering. We are not just sad but angry. When my father was dying of lung cancer, I was sad but also furious at the reality of death.

Yet Jesus's tears, an utterly human reaction, still seem to point to an underlying sadness. It's hard to get away from the simple fact that he is weeping.

What is going on? Is Jesus angry? Sad? Frustrated? All three? I've heard many beautiful interpretations of his weeping over the years. My friend Anita Lustrea told me that she imagined Jesus crying because he has to bring Lazarus back from the dead, from heaven, where he knows Lazarus is happier. In his book on Lazarus, John Dear suggests that Jesus is weeping not only for the unbelief of those around him, but because people have rejected his promise of life. We are comfortable with the "culture of death," with war, violence, and killing, and would prefer not to change.[13]

John Meier sums up the many possible ways to interpret Jesus's tears: the weeping of Mary and "the Jews" moves him in a human way to share his own emotions; the unbelief of the crowd moves him to frustration; his confrontation with the power of death moves him to anger; or finally "the miracle-worker must stir up his spirit within to prepare himself to perform a mighty miracle."[14]

A key to understanding all this may be the second phrase, *etaraxen heauton,* which means to be "troubled" or to "shudder," again "in himself." The phrases *tō pneumati,* "in his spirit," and *heauton,* "in himself," parallel one another. These words are also much debated by scholars.

Jesus utters this phrase in the next chapter in the Gospel, in the face of his impending death. The verse is usually translated as "Now my soul is troubled [*tetaraktai*]."[15] The verb next occurs during the Last Supper when one of the disciples is about to betray him: "After saying this Jesus was troubled in spirit [*etarachthē*]."[16]

His emotion in both cases seems connected with his own death, which he would have anticipated at Lazarus's tomb. So perhaps in Bethany he was experiencing a combination of strong feelings—about Lazarus, his sisters, and the crowd—mixed with trepidation over what he knows this miracle will lead to: his own death.

But it's important not to downplay Jesus's anger, suggested by the Greek. "There is no need to resort to a softening of the context, suggesting that Jesus is moved by his sympathy for the sufferers," says Moloney.[17]

At this point, it's good to step back and not get overly engrossed in the Greek. The story may have been from one of the Aramaic oral traditions about Jesus. Indeed, Brown, quoting other sources, suggests that both phrases are "variant translations of the original Aramaic expression which meant 'to be strongly moved.'"[18]

Perhaps it's best to say that, as Mary invited him to "come and see," Jesus felt a mixture of powerful emotions: grief over his friend's death and the sadness of his friend's family; apprehension or fear knowing that this miracle would lead to his own suffering and death; anger at the seeming lack of faith of his friends; and frustration at the human condition that had led to all this. Jesus is under incredible stress, which Byrne captures well:

> Jesus, then, weeps at their grief, but their very grief intensifies the pressure on him to restore Lazarus to them. At the same time as he feels this pressure, he also knows that performing such a miracle will invariably set in motion forces leading to death for himself. He is torn, then, between love for his friend and sympathy for the bereaved, on the one hand, and the shrinking from death that is part of human nature, on the other. His anger arises out of the impossible situation he is in and out of the conflict with the power of darkness now before him.[19]

Here we read—whether in Aramaic, Greek, or English—the divine one experiencing human emotions. How could he not have felt deep emotion as he stood before his friend's tomb, heard the wailing of his sisters and friends, prepared to perform a great miracle, worried about his own death, and confronted the power of suffering? Who wouldn't be reduced to tears? At Lazarus's tomb, God weeps.

Byrne also speaks of Jesus's "strong and tangled feelings" at the tomb:

> For myself, I've come to see it as a Johannine echo of what the Synoptic gospels present as Jesus' pre-passion agony in the garden. . . . Aware that the raising of Lazarus will come at the cost of his own life, he shrinks from the prospect of death. Yet love for his friend will impel him to go ahead with the raising. Hence his strong and tangled feelings at the dilemma in which he is caught. As in the Synoptic account of Jesus' agony in the garden, what emerges here with particular force is the cost to Jesus of his saving action in our regard.[20]

Does it diminish our sense of his humanity to know that Jesus is not just sad but angry and apprehensive and fearful and frustrated? Here his humanity intersects with our own in times of stress, when we are overwhelmed with a mixture of feelings that we may have a hard time identifying, much less managing.

Inside the Tomb

One of the most vivid experiences of this phenomenon for me was in the Tomb of Lazarus. It came during my first pilgrimage to the Holy Land with America Media.

This was my first time back in Al Eizariya since my initial trip with George, and I was filled with emotion—mainly a certain nervousness. I was worn out from worrying about the pilgrimage— even though all was going well. Yes, I know that Jesus asked whether we can "add a single hour" to our lives by worrying, but I

Entering the Tomb of Lazarus.
COURTESY OF CATHOLIC TRAVEL CENTRE

was worried anyway.[21] And it was worry about someone else's experience, not mine. Now, standing at the Tomb of Lazarus, with a group of forty pilgrims, I remembered how steep the stairs were and how slippery. I had a vision of people tumbling down the stairs. Someone made a dark joke about one of us needing to be raised from the dead in case we died in the tomb.

I stood at the top of the stairs and helped people enter the narrow chamber, five or six at a time, and then helped them as they emerged. Earlier in the day, I had asked them to pray about what they wanted to "leave behind in the tomb," which I had done several years earlier. As they emerged from the tomb, some were in tears. Others seemed happy to have made it out unscathed.

Finally, most of the pilgrims had made their visit, and I figured I would go down with the last group. Descending the stairs, I was focused on the few pilgrims in front of me, who held the metal railing with death grips while they carefully walked down. As during much of the pilgrimage I was focused not on the place, or my own reaction to it, but on the pilgrims.

One carefully descends the stone steps to a small landing, where a few people can stand in the hollowed-out stone cavity. There is a small hole in the floor, into which you must crawl. This leads to a kind of chamber, roughly ten feet high, with ledges on the walls, on which, presumably, the corpses were placed. The entire space is lit by dim fluorescent lights.

Inside, I was surrounded by several other pilgrims whom I had come to know over the previous few days. Some stood with their foreheads pressed against the damp, grainy stone wall, lost in their thoughts and prayers.

Suddenly I was overwhelmed with emotions: I couldn't believe I was here again, at the site of Jesus's supreme miracle; and I felt aware of my own sinfulness in this holy place (not that I had done anything awful—just a sense of my own failures to live up to my call as a Christian); and I was still worried about the safety of the pilgrims; and I was thinking of all the people who had asked me to pray for them back home; and I was also worn out from the stress of our first trip.

Kneeling heightened both my sense of the holiness of the place and my feelings of fatigue, and I started to sob. Several of the pilgrims surrounded me and put their hands on my back. And if you had asked me why I was weeping, I doubt that I could have told you.

So when I read the lines "Jesus wept" and I study the various interpretations of why he wept, I can well understand how he could have been dealing with a mix and surfeit of emotions. As he stood by the tomb, the intensity of his emotions would have outstripped mine a thousand-fold. I wasn't about to raise a friend from the dead. Nor would anything I did lead to my crucifixion. At that moment I think I understood Jesus's complicated and hard-to-define feelings. "Jesus wept" for many reasons.

Human and Divine

For those who lament the fact that Jesus may not have been sad but perhaps angry in this passage, it's important to note that none of these discussions about translations, and about what Jesus was feeling, take away from the significance of the moment. Jesus, riven with feelings both human and divine, weeps, perhaps out of an overflow of feeling.

So perhaps the words "See how he loved him!" are not part of John's normal negative portrayal of "the Jews" but the genuine response of people who saw Jesus's emotions close up. Raymond Brown suggests that this more positive portrayal of "the Jews" may represent "different strata of Johannine tradition," a part of the oral tradition behind John's Gospel where "the Jews" are regarded in a less negative light.[22]

The final words of "the Jews" in this passage, however, may seem less laudable: "Could not he who opened the eyes of the blind man have kept this man from dying?" John seems now to return to his negative portrayal of "the Jews." Yes, Jesus did love Lazarus, and they correctly perceive this. But some scholars see this as John portraying "the Jews" as taunting Jesus. It is reminiscent of Martha and Mary's complaint about Jesus's late arrival: "If you had been here . . ." But it may not be a taunting at all, but a genuine sympathy for the sisters and their grief over Lazarus's death. Here we can see "the Jews" as truly friends of the sisters, expressing their own confusion and grief.

Did Jesus let his friend die? This is a difficult proposition to stomach, especially knowing the affection that Jesus had for Lazarus, Martha, and Mary. But whatever the reasons for his delay, it will lead to something greater than anyone in the crowd could imagine. And this will all happen, as the crowd rightly says, because of love.

• • •

Why is this important for the believer? Why should we care about Jesus's tears? Besides the fact that knowing more about the possible causes of his emotions helps us understand him better—which is always a good thing—this part of our story reminds us, as few Gospel passages can, of his utter humanity.

As I've mentioned before, some Christians remain uncomfortable with the true humanity of Jesus, a man who could feel intense emotions, like anger, sadness, or frustration. But if we are uncomfortable with this part of his identity, it can mean that Jesus, or God, may feel distant from us. Thus, Jesus's tears can narrow the distance between us.

Jesus is about to do something that we cannot do: raise someone from the dead. But shortly before that he does something that we all do: weep. At this moment in our story our lives perhaps most intersect with his. Jesus is both beyond us and one of us.

For Your Reflection

1. After surveying the evidence, why do you think Jesus wept at the Tomb of Lazarus?
2. Does it change your understanding of Jesus if he was not sad but angry in Bethany?
3. What moments in this narrative so far reveal Jesus's humanity for you? What moments most reveal his divinity? Do you think of divinity as impassive or unemotional? Why or why not?
4. When a loved one has died, were you ever not only sad, but angry? How did that emotional response influence your relationship with God?
5. Have you ever wept not simply out of sadness but for a mixture of reasons? Can such weeping bring you closer to Jesus?

Take Away the Stone

Turning Away from the Negative

*Then Jesus, again greatly disturbed, came to
the tomb. It was a cave, and a stone was lying
against it. Jesus said, "Take away the stone."
Martha, the sister of the dead man, said to him,
"Lord, already there is a stench because he has
been dead for four days." Jesus said to her, "Did
I not tell you that if you believed, you would see
the glory of God?" So they took away the stone.*

A few years after my tearful time in Lazarus's tomb, on a subsequent pilgrimage to the Holy Land, I was eagerly anticipating a return to Al Eizariya. Over the years, it had become for me a place of deep devotion, not only because of my experiences there but because of what it meant to the pilgrims.

As we walked up the hill in Al Eizariya, on a bright and sunny day, I spoke with several people who were afraid of the staircase (I had perhaps warned them too often about its slippery steps) but also the experience itself. They were concerned that they weren't ready to enter the tomb, that they would be overwhelmed, or that nothing would happen. Maybe, I thought ruefully, I had built it up

Entrance to the Tomb of Lazarus, Al Eizariya.
COURTESY OF CATHOLIC TRAVEL CENTRE

too much, which is a cardinal sin of pilgrim leaders. It never pays to say, "You're going to find this extraordinary," or "This will be the high point of our trip," because what moves one person may leave another cold. I reminded them: "Have no expectations. Whatever happens, happens."

It's advice that I could have used myself.

Our group of a hundred pilgrims chatted away at the top of the hill. I decided to wait until the end of the line, after most of the group had visited the tomb, so that I could have some quiet time to pray, maybe even by myself. A few struggles were on my mind, and I wanted to "leave them behind" in the tomb. I stood at the top of the stairs and helped pilgrims climb down and then out of the dark space.

After almost all of the group had visited, I started down the staircase, holding on to the railing for support. Several of the other pilgrims passed me on the left, going up the narrow stairwell. As I looked behind me, a group of tourists from another pilgrimage were gathering at the top of the stairs. "Hurry up!" they shouted. "Don't die in there! Ha, ha, ha, ha!"

I was beginning to think that this would not be the prayerful experience I was hoping for. And I started to grow angry, focusing on their loud voices and what I saw as their rudeness. Maybe they were trying to be funny, or were having a good time, but it struck me as probably the last place I would make jokes.

Inside the quiet and cool space were only a few pilgrims from our group. I knelt down on the dirt floor to pray. There was so much I wanted to leave there, and I had looked forward to this moment for many months. I took a deep breath and closed my eyes. Then I heard loud, braying voices from the top of the stairs.

"Hey, Lazarus! Come out!" Peals of laughter rang down the stone stairwell. "Lazarus, come out! Ha, ha, ha, ha, ha!" My fellow pilgrims sighed, crossed themselves, and made their way out of the tomb. My anger grew. I was alone in one of my favorite places in the world to pray, but I was unable to concentrate, the voices now not only loud but insistent. And I was angry that the other group had forced my fellow pilgrims out.

"Maybe he's still dead down there! Ha, ha, ha, ha, ha!" The tourists kept talking loudly, waiting for their own time in the tomb. "Hurry up, Lazarus! Are you dead? Come out!"

I started up the stairs, furious.

"Look, here comes Lazarus! He's alive, after all! Ha, ha, ha, ha, ha, ha!"

Honestly, I wanted to punch them. The tour leader, a beefy blond-haired man, perhaps thirty, grabbed on to the side of the entrance with a big hand, and leaned in, barking out orders to his group. I climbed farther. "Hurry up!" he hissed. I had been in the tomb for no more than a few minutes.

Next to me ten people from their group crammed inside on the left side of the staircase, pushing me aside and chattering away.

"Lazarus, what took you so long? Get out of the way!" On their way down they laughed and snapped photos and selfies.

Why am I telling you this? Not to evoke sympathy. Failing to have a meaningful experience at a holy site on pilgrimage is not a tragedy. And I've had other deeper experiences in the tomb before and since. Spiritual experiences are not ours to plan or schedule.

Rather, it's to say that it's easy to focus on the negative at any time, even in places where you would least expect it. Sometimes life makes it almost impossible to see the positive.

Here is where we find Martha at this part of our story. Standing before her brother's tomb, beside the person she has identified as the Messiah, she focuses not on what he might be able to do, but on something else: the stench. She focuses on the negative.

Martha couldn't help herself. She's human. Just like us.

A Cave and a Stone

Archaeologists attest to the kinds of caves and stones described at this point in our story: first-century tombs with a stone that can be "taken away." The Greek in John's Gospel calls the tomb (*mnēmeion*) a *spēlaion kai lithos epekeito ep'autō*. Literally, a "cave and a stone lying against it." The stone would have been there to keep the smell in and the animals out.

Some of us may imagine the Tomb of Lazarus as akin to that of Jesus, covered by a circular stone to be "rolled away" from the opening on Easter. But the Greek here is "taken away" (*arate*), which means that the stone might have been a cork-shaped plug that was pulled out.

Tombs at the time would have been accessible through a horizontal or vertical shaft.[1] Inside would have been two spaces: an outer vestibule, with a stone seat, and an inner chamber, with niches, which held the body—or bodies if it was a family tomb—carved into the rocky walls. Once the bodies had decayed, the bones were placed in ossuaries, small stone boxes, thus creating space for more bodies. Overall, there is a great deal of archaeological evidence for the precise kind of tomb described in John's Gospel: first-century cavities cut into rock and sealed with a stone.[2]

Historical details like this remind us that much of what people may dismiss in the New Testament as unreliable often turns out to be historically accurate. Such details ground us in the reality of the time, place, and story. This is often a surprise to people who dismiss the Gospels as fictional, either in whole or in part.

My favorite example from the Gospel of John is the story of the Pool of Bethesda, where Jesus heals a man who has been paralyzed for thirty-eight years.[3] For many years, the pool, which could not be located, was thought to be allegorical. It was described in John's Gospel as having "five porticoes," with the porticoes perhaps representing the five books of Moses. William Barclay noted that John's reference to the thirty-eight years was also considered to be allegorical, representing the time the Jewish people had wandered in the desert.[4] Such connections lent credence to the idea that the entire story was simply an allegory.[5] But in the late nineteenth century, excavations in Jerusalem revealed not simply a pool in the location

Inside the Tomb of Lazarus (shelf for bodies visible).
COURTESY OF YAMID CASTIBLANCO, SJ

described by John, but the foundations for colonnaded walkways or "porticoes"—exactly as John's Gospel had described it.

Lazarus's tomb may also tell us something about the economic status of Martha, Mary, and Lazarus. As Amy-Jill Levine told me recently, in Jesus's time only the wealthy could afford rock-cut tombs. "Poorer families," she explained, "buried bodies in what are called 'trench graves,' which are exactly what they sound like: trenches, often lined up along an axis, dug into the ground." So we can presume that Mary, Martha, and Lazarus were wealthy.

Jodi Magness, whose fascinating and marvelously titled book *Stone and Dung, Oil and Spit*, looks at Jewish daily life in the time of Jesus, agrees with AJ. In an extensive chapter on tombs and burial customs she quotes another scholarly paper noting that fifty days of work by "experienced professionals" were required to hew a rock-cut tomb, placing such tombs out of reach for those who were not wealthy. Also, the association of rock-cut tombs with the upper classes is indicated by a few other factors. First, these tombs are concentrated around areas of "elite presence," primarily Jerusalem and Jericho, with a few exceptions. Second, the tombs date from times when there was an "autonomous or semiautonomous Jewish elite in the city." All this points to Lazarus's family as one of wealth.[6]

Also, as AJ pointed out, John's Gospel has Mary anointing Jesus with a "hefty amount" of expensive perfume and the household hosting Jesus and his entourage for a feast. "Even if we didn't have the story of the Raising of Lazarus to tell us that these folks were wealthy," AJ says, "you'd know it from the anointing scene."

"There Is a Stench"

As ever in John, Jesus is in control. Notice that he is not taken to the tomb; he *comes* to the tomb. He does not shrink from death, much less deny it. It is a reality that he confronts by going to the tomb.

Standing before the rock-cut tomb in Bethany, Jesus is described by John for the second time with the vivid phrase we encountered in the previous chapter. Jesus is *palin embrimōmenos*, greatly disturbed or angered. The surfeit of emotions is still with him.

Or perhaps, the physicality of the place hit him. At the beginning of the story, in the company of his disciples, he is told of Lazarus's illness, while he is "across the Jordan," far from the event. Next, as he stands outside of Bethany, Martha and Mary describe the death of "he whom you love." But now, as he stands before the tomb itself, the quiddity, the essence or *thisness*, of the place may have gripped him.

No amount of time can prepare us for something so vivid. It is one thing to know that we will be confronted with such a scene; it is quite another to confront it. Before my father died, I had seen many dead bodies and been to many wakes and funerals. I had prayed before open caskets and looked at powdered faces, lips drawn tightly over clenched jaws, and even touched the cold hands that were tightly gripping rosary beads. Nothing, however, prepared me for the shock of seeing my own father's body in the casket: mute, cold, lifeless, immobile, uncomprehending. Dead.

In Bethany, Jesus is standing before the place of the dead. "We face the awful prospect of opening a tomb," says Brendan Byrne.[7] Finally, he is moving even closer to the performance of a "sign" that he expects will lead to his own suffering and death. So he is again *embrimōmenos*.

But we notice different reactions: those of Martha and those of Jesus. Martha is focused on the earthly: "Already there is a stench," she says. (Or as the King James Version has it, "Lord, by this time he stinketh."[8])

It's unfair to fault her. Several days after they had laid their brother's body in the tomb, there would indeed have been a stench, and Martha, the "practical one," would know this. Death was a constant companion in antiquity; people would have been well acquainted with the physical reality of decomposition, especially in the climate of Judea. In many paintings and icons, people in the crowd cover their faces with their hands or with cloths to protect against the smell.

In Richard Beard's novel *Lazarus Is Dead*, the sick man suffers from a variety of diseases, including scabies and diarrhea. "He stinks of suspended flesh and innards leaking," Beard writes, and people recoil from the stench. In the novel, Lazarus must be *known* to be sick, so that Jesus's miracle will not be misunderstood: "His sickness should be horrific, definitive, undeniable. It should be both recognizable and worse than anything anyone has seen." The stench is part of this.[9]

In a page from the gorgeously illuminated manuscript *Les Très Riches Heures du Duc de Berry*, a book of prayers created for a wealthy French patron in the fifteenth century, Lazarus climbs out of a marble tomb as three men slide the lid off. The exquisite scene takes place under a royal blue swirling sky that Van Gogh could

Les Très Riches Heures du Duc de Berry, folio 171r: *The Raising of Lazarus.* In this fifteenth-century depiction, Lazarus crawls out of his marble tomb, as one man covers his face against the "stench." (Musée Condé, Chantilly, France).
WIKICOMMONS

have painted, in the shadow of either a ruined cathedral or perhaps a building insinuating that we are in a cathedral. Jesus has a full head of chestnut hair and matching beard, all surrounded by a golden halo. He raises an arm as if commanding Lazarus to come out, staring at him, chin tucked. The delicately drawn men and women in the scene are clad in soft, elegant gowns, many of them trimmed and decorated in gold, as if they had just come from an evening of dancing. But as Beard points out, "of the fourteen by-standers, four are covering their noses, three with their hands and one with the bunched front of his tunic."

Yet there is a mystery about the stench, which Beard's novel prop-erly identifies: we are told later in the Gospels that Mary possesses a huge amount of expensive nard, with which she will anoint Jesus's feet at a meal. Was this nard left over from the anointing of their brother after his death? That is the most likely explanation of why they had so much in the house at the time. If so, why wouldn't the practical and hardworking Martha have anointed Lazarus properly?

No, in Beard's novel her protests about the smell come not from his death, but from his life:

> Lazarus is wrapped in sweet-smelling herbs and perfume and linen, Martha having doggedly observed every ritual of cleansing, every bitter gesture of interrupted love.
>
> Martha does not take shortcuts. It is not in her character. Therefore, the corpse of Lazarus will not smell, not if it was prepared by Martha, not after only four days. The memory of the smell, like the memory of his decaying body, comes from the period before the death of Lazarus.[10]

Raymond Brown doubts this. Even with careful preparation, the decay of the body would have begun: "The oils and spices employed in Jewish burial practices prevented unpleasant odor for a while, but there was no real embalming, such as practiced in Egypt, which prevented decomposition."[11]

For whatever reason, Martha is focused on the smell. John's Gospel is often interested in appealing to the reader's senses: hearing, seeing, talking, tasting, and, here, smelling. Her blunt response to Jesus suggests not only her practicality but something else that John wants us to see: she has not grasped the full significance of the words "I am the Resurrection and the Life."

She seems stuck. John Dear links this passage to our inability to change our minds about the culture of death: "Seemingly secure at our stasis point, we do not want authentic change." Or stuck in a cycle of greed, as we continually pursue money. Or security. Or fame. All these things, society tells us, make sense. As a result, we fear disruption, change. Taking away the stone would only make our lives worse, we fear. Social pressures encourage us to believe that: "This is the way things are," or worse, "This is way things should be."[12] Better to keep the stone tightly over the tomb.

But to follow God, we must withdraw from those impulses that would keep the tomb closed, that would focus on the stench of change.

In Colm Tóibín's novel *The Testament of Mary*, Jesus's mother also professes a reluctance to "disturb" Lazarus, now in the ground. Most of the crowd, says the fictional Mary, believed that such a raising shouldn't even be tried.

"No one," she says, summing up the feelings of the crowd, "should tamper with the fullness that is death."

Catastrophizing

It may be unfair to fault Martha, but John's Gospel doesn't let her off the hook either. Even as Jesus, the man she has professed as the Messiah, the person capable of healing the sick and raising the dead, is standing before her, about to perform his greatest miracle, she is focused on the stench. In the face of the positive, Martha focuses on the negative.

For many years, I struggled with that same inclination: focusing on the negative. Occasionally, it all but overshadowed the positive. One of my spiritual directors used an image of a paint can to help me with this. Imagine, he said, a single drop of red paint dropped into a can of white paint, somehow turning all the white paint red. If you picture the drop of red paint as the one negative thing in life, and the white paint as all the positive, it would be as if one single drop turned everything from positive to negative. In other words, the paint was white, not red. But I kept focusing on the single red drop.

I would focus not on my many friends but on the one person who seemed not to like me. Not on the many blessings of living in Jesuit community but on one minor inconvenience. Not on my overall good physical health but on the one minor health concern. Not on the many times that God had blessed me but on the few challenges in my life. Not on the many people who said they enjoyed my books but the one anonymous critic on social media.

Likewise, I would engage in what some psychologists call "awfulizing" or "catastrophizing." A bumpy airplane ride meant that we were crashing. A mildly critical remark from a friend meant that he hated me. A spot on my skin meant that I was dying from skin cancer. All of this was unreal. The pilot didn't say we were crashing; the friend didn't say he hated me; and the doctor didn't say I was dying. The focus on the negative is a lie. There's a reason they call Satan the "Prince of Lies." If Satan can get you to focus on only the negatives, you're living a lie.

Such attitudes can have serious effects on our emotional, mental, spiritual, and even physical health. For me, they distracted me from the good that was going on and tempted me to see life as a series of problems, to feel sad, and to complain more. But on balance, my life was good, not bad.

This is not to say that problems don't exist. Or that on that day in Bethany Martha wasn't devastated by the loss of her beloved brother and probably had a hard time thinking clearly. Nonetheless, she was standing next to the person whom she knew would always help her, and she was focused on that one drop of red paint: the stench. She most likely had heard rumors of Jesus's miracles, even if they go unrecorded in John's Gospel, including the Raising of the Widow of Nain's Son and of Jairus's Daughter.

In Beard's novel the knowledge of Jesus's two life-giving miracles intensifies the sisters' desire for his presence: "Jesus brought two people back to life," Mary says. "He can't just leave us like this."[13]

The two sisters must have heard the stories of Jesus's power. It strains credulity to think that, so shortly before his death, when Jerusalem was abuzz with tales of what he had done, two of his closest friends would not have known of his wonder-working. But Martha is focused on the smell. She is, as Francis Moloney says, telling Jesus how things are in *her* world.[14]

It is similar to her focusing on her sister not pulling her weight in Luke's Gospel, where she complains about Mary not helping and says to Jesus, "Lord, do you not care?"[15] At least as Luke presents things, her sister Mary is focused on the "better part" at that time: being with Jesus. Martha is taken up with the negative.

Maybe it's more accurate to say that in both cases Martha is taken up not so much with the negative as with the purely practical. In the story of the visit, she is focused on her work, her *diakonia*, whatever needed to be done to welcome Jesus, rather than on the presence of Jesus. In this story of her brother's raising, she is focused on the stench rather than on Jesus. In both cases we could say that she's right. Someone does need to work, and there will be a stench.

But there is more to life than the practical, as Jesus points out to Martha when she is complaining about her sister, and as he is about to show her, before her brother's tomb.

It's easy to focus on the negative and cling to the practical, even in the most spiritual of places and the most spiritual of times. It's a reminder of our humanity. And how much we need God.

What Is "Rotten" Inside of You?

Another way of approaching this passage is from an even earthier point of view: rotting flesh. That's an unpleasant image to conjure up, but it is part of the story: Lazarus had a human body, had been ill for some time, and after three days in the tomb, no matter what anointing had been done, his body would have started to decompose and to stink.

But let's think about this more metaphorically.

Do you remember my friend Michael Peppard? He is the Fordham University theology professor who told me about the scholarly conversation about Lazarus being the Beloved Disciple. As I was writing this book, I attended Mass with Michael and his wife, Rebecca. At lunch afterward, they asked about my writing, which led to yet another discussion about Lazarus.

Rebecca said that she loved this story because there are some things in our lives that we think are "rotten" or "decaying."

Something about what Rebecca said made me hear that part of the story in a new way. Throughout this book we have talked about God calling us into new life, as Jesus called Lazarus. There are parts of us that we want to "let die" or "leave behind" in the tomb.

But Rebecca's comment reminded me there are also parts of us that we see as "rotten." Not exactly dead, but so awful that we can barely look at them: unpleasant, unsavory, disgusting, embarrassing, even shameful. Sometimes we believe these parts of us are so rotten that God wouldn't want to look at them either.

Some of us struggle with an addiction: to drugs, pornography, gambling, sex, drinking, overeating. Or perhaps we are engaging in an unhealthy pattern of behavior that isn't an addiction but still makes us feel disgusted with ourselves. Perhaps we can't help saying mean things about people, or we're always passing on the hard work to others in the office, or we can't be bothered to visit friends who are in the hospital, or we always cheat on tests, or we post nasty

The Raising of Lazarus, by Eduard von Gebhardt
(Museum Kunstpalast, Düsseldorf).
WIKICOMMONS

comments on social media. Even though the behavior makes us feel rotten, we can't stop doing it.

Or maybe we feel we've done something in the past that is so horrible that we fear it can't be forgiven. We can barely stand to think about it. Perhaps we were cruel to someone in our family or betrayed them. Perhaps we cheated on our spouse or partner. Perhaps we did something awful that we've never told anyone about.

Part of us feels rotten, putrid, foul inside. There is a "stench." Like a person turning away from rotting flesh, we can barely stand to look at it, much less think about it. We want to keep the stone tightly shut over that part of us.

It is to this part of us that God calls. It is this part of our lives that God wants us to confront and to examine. More important, God wants to confront it with us.

But what exactly does that mean? In many cases, it means first admitting to ourselves that it is part of us and that it feels rotten. Then it may mean admitting it to a trusted friend, then to a therapist, and then to a spiritual director.

Then it may mean looking at how that part of us became so rotten. Something causes meat to rot—it's taken out of the refrigerator, it's exposed to air, it encounters bacteria or mold, which causes it to decay. A trusted friend, counselor, or therapist can often help us see how that rottenness came about, help us to confront it, deal with it, and then avoid it in the future. A priest may hear our confession and offer us forgiveness for whatever we might have done. Or we simply decide not to do it any longer. In all this we hear God's voice.

God is not afraid of the stench, just as Jesus was not afraid of the stench of Lazarus.

"I Like You the Way You Are"

Sometimes the parts of us that we think are rotten are perfectly healthy, and it's our way of looking at our rottenness that needs to be examined.

In my ministry with LGBTQ people, I sometimes meet people who believe they were created in a faulty way, that there is something deeply wrong with them, that they are "rotten." Sometimes it takes years for them to realize that this part of themselves is healthy, whole, and perfectly normal. Often all it takes is for someone to accept them with love. Love calls them out of the tomb. Knowing that they are loved and lovable enables them to "come out," in common parlance. And they see that they are not rotten at all but beloved children of God and valuable members of the community.

Likewise, some of us may be ashamed of some sort of disability, physical or otherwise. Rick Curry, a Jesuit brother who was born without a right arm, often told a story about growing up in the 1950s as a boy with a disability. In those years, the right arm of St. Francis

Xavier, a relic from the famous Jesuit missionary, was coming to Philadelphia to be venerated. (Catholics often find comfort in the physical connection to the saint that a relic provides.[16]) Not surprisingly, Rick's Catholic school classmates were eager for him to visit the relic so he could be "cured." After all, Rick was missing an arm, and here was St. Francis Xavier's arm coming to Philadelphia. His class started to pray for a miracle.

Rick made the trip to the cathedral in Center City and pressed himself against the glass case that held that body part of the saint. Perhaps proximity to this famous right arm, and the prayers of this great saint, might miraculously restore Rick's own right arm.

When he returned home, he was the same as ever. His younger sister, Denise, said, "I'm so glad that nothing happened, because I like you the way you are."

It was a pivotal moment for Rick, which he spoke of often. Love had called him out of the tomb. What seemed rotten to others was perfectly healthy to his sister, and to him. And, of course, to God.

God's Reassurance

Jesus's reassuring response to Martha's mention of the stench, however, is puzzling: "Did I not tell you that if you believed, you would see the glory of God?" This comment functions less as a direct response to Martha's question and more as a general reassurance to this troubled sister and to the crowd mourning with her.

This reassurance is reminiscent of the Angel Gabriel's response to the Virgin Mary at the Annunciation. In Luke's Gospel, Mary, "much perplexed" by the news that she will give birth, asks, "How can this be?" Mary is also focused on the practical: she's a virgin. In response, the angel reassures Mary by reminding her that her cousin Elizabeth, previously thought to be unable to give birth, is pregnant. "For nothing will be impossible with God," the angel reminds her.[17] God reassures Mary, as Jesus reassures Martha by Lazarus's tomb.

In moments of confusion, doubt, or fear, such reassurance jolts us out of our focus on the practical, the negative, the seemingly impossible. This is what Jesus does in both cases for Martha: in the house and at the tomb.

In our own lives, there are several antidotes to a misdirected focus on the obviously negative, the purely personal, the seemingly impossible. To be clear: I'm not saying that we should never feel sad or discouraged. Sadness, frustration, and discouragement are natural reactions to times of loss, pain, or a disappointing turn of events. What I'm talking about here is a frequent, persistent, or habitual tendency to focus on the negative to the exclusion of all else. What can help counteract those tendencies?

First, *gratitude*. Nothing counters negativity as much as gratitude. As St. Ignatius Loyola said, ingratitude is the worst, the most abominable of sins and the origin of sins. Ingratitude blinds us to the blessings that God is giving us, even in the middle of tough times. Ongoing ingratitude can make us tetchy, negative, complaining, and even despairing. In those moments of negativity, doing an honest inventory on the blessings in our lives can help restore some balance.

Second, *memory*. This is something of what the Angel Gabriel does for Mary. "And now, your relative Elizabeth in her old age has also conceived a son," says the angel, "and this is the sixth month for her who was said to be barren."[18] As I see it, the angel isn't revealing something new to her—Mary most likely would have heard of her cousin's amazing pregnancy even though Elizabeth was in "seclusion"—but is reminding her of something she already knew.

When we look back to see how God has been with us in the past, our memory reminds us that "nothing will be impossible with God." This can help us move past fear. Looking backward can help us move forward.

Third, *grit*. A friend, colleague, psychologist, or spiritual adviser can jolt us out of our negativity. "Stop complaining!" or "Stop focusing on the negative!" An honest friend's remark can be a pail of cold water in the face. However, we need to be careful not to simply tell people to "snap out of it" because there are legitimate reasons people are sad, angry, or frightened. But an overall attitude of negativity sometimes needs to be challenged.

Fourth, *perspective*. Reminding ourselves of the ways that others suffer helps put our own suffering in perspective. We can make an honest acknowledgment that when compared with many others, we sometimes don't have it so bad. A few weeks ago, I was speaking to my physician about some minor concern, and I asked how he was doing. Without breaking confidence, he told me he was dealing with several patients who were suffering from life-threatening illnesses. This put things in perspective for me.

Finally, *faith*. Remember, God is with us. The practical, negative, and frightening aspects of life are only parts of the picture. As St. Paul said, "We see only in a mirror. . . . I know only in part."[19] When we see only a small bit—work that needs to be done at home, the stench at the tomb—God sees the whole picture.

In every life, there will be a stench. But, as on that day in Bethany, God stands next to us, encouraging us to see the rest of the story.

Take Away the Stone

Jesus has already told those who have gathered with the sisters, "Take away the stone." Though he presumably could have done so, he does not ask the Father to shatter the stone or make it disappear. It's a reminder that Jesus often relies on others for help and that, in our own lives, others help us to be freed.

We're so familiar with this Gospel story that we can forget that the people at the time didn't know what would happen. It's easy to imagine people in the crowd struggling with the heavy stone but confused about what Jesus would do next.

They might have wondered: Why would Jesus ask that the stone be taken away? Does he want to see Lazarus one last time? Does he want to enter the tomb?

Jesus asks those around him to conquer death *with him*: "Take away the stone."

Moments of freedom come thanks to God's grace. Conversion or change happens because of God's activity. But there are also people who *participate* in these conversions, who help us to freedom. Who, in your life, has helped you take away the stone?

One person who helped me take away the stone was the assistant novice director in my novitiate, David Donovan, SJ. As a trained spiritual director it fell to him to teach me about prayer and the spiritual life. And I had a great deal to learn about both.

When I entered the novitiate at age twenty-seven, I was a bundle of fears, worries, and anxieties. At the time I was almost completely preoccupied with my parents' separation, as I have mentioned. Besides that, I was worried about how I would live the vows of poverty, chastity, and obedience, having joined the Jesuits in some haste. Mostly I was concerned about what others thought of me. Did the other novices like me? Was I acceptable? Did they approve of me? Would I fit in?

David helped me see how God was part of all those questions and how bringing God into the conversation could help me find a path to conversion. Here I'm speaking of conversion not in the sense of moving from unbelief to belief in God but in the sense of the *metanoia* that Jesus and John the Baptist spoke of in the Gospels: a change of mind and heart. *Metanoia* (from the Greek *metai*, meaning "after" or "beyond," and *nous*, meaning "mind") is a change of mind, a reorientation, an embrace of a new way of life.

As I talked to David about my parents' separation, I started to cry. But as a new novice, I felt that it was somehow inappropriate to do so.

"Why?" he asked gently.

"Because it doesn't have to do with the novitiate."

"But it does," he said. "Because it has to do with your relationship with God. You can't keep that part of yourself in a little box in a closet, tucked away from God. You have to bring it out into the light." David helped me take away the stone in my spiritual life, which had kept so many things closed off from God's light.

What was behind the stone? Essentially, the realization that I was not responsible for my parents' happiness—I couldn't fix their marriage. "You're not God," said David, bluntly. I could be supportive, but I wasn't able to work miracles. In time, they reconciled, but that had to do more with them than with any of my efforts. What was behind the stone was freedom from the idea that I should have Godlike powers.

St. Augustine, in a homily on the Raising of Lazarus, compares this part of the story to turning away from sin, the death of the soul being worse than the death of the body. He compares the stink of Lazarus's decaying body to the stench of sin: "But he who has become habituated to sin, is buried, and has it properly said of him, *he stinks*; for his character, like some horrible smell, begins to be of the worst repute."[20]

But there are other ways to think about the stone.

In her charming book *Lazarus Awakened*, the Christian evangelical writer Joanna Weaver tells us the meaning of the Greek word for "tomb," which comes from the verb *mnaomai*, to remember. A tomb is a remembrance or memory. Weaver talks about how painful memories can block us from being free. More specifically, she speaks of three "stones" that block our spiritual progress: the stone of unworthiness ("I don't deserve God's love or anything good to happen to me"), the stone of unforgiveness ("I refuse to let that hurt go"), and the stone of unbelief ("I refuse to believe that God can help me").[21]

All of us, then, have stones that block us from hearing God's voice. Stones keep us shut in our tombs. They can seem as immobile as the great stone that must have blocked Lazarus's tomb. But once they are rolled away, usually with the help of others, we wonder why we ever let them stand in our way. Sometimes the "rolling away" happens in an instant—as when David helped me see that I couldn't fix my parents' problems, that I couldn't do everything, that I wasn't

God. Sometimes the rolling away happens gradually, as someone comes to see that they are not faulty at all, but a beloved child of God. But whether at an instant or over years, an important part of the spiritual life is seeing those stones, confronting them, and rolling them away.

Like Martha, we often quail at rolling away our stones because we fear what we will discover. And while we may fear the "stench" inside, what God wants to offer us is a fresh, new, and vibrant way of life.

From Martha's point of view, the stone may have been not what blocked the entrance to her brother's tomb, but her inability to see who Jesus was. The stone prevented her from relaxing with him in her house. The stone made her focus on the stench rather than what Jesus could do.

For Lazarus, the stone blocked him from living, until Jesus asked others to take it away.

For Your Reflection

1. Why do you think Martha focuses on the stench? Is she being negative or just practical? Does the mention of the stench help us to take death seriously?

2. Do you ever feel that you focus too much on the negative in life? What do the events of Bethany tell you about that?

3. During moments when you feel focused on the negative, what helps to reassure you? What helps to move you away from negativity or despair?

4. What are the "stones" in your life? What keeps you from experiencing new life or hearing God's call?

5. Are there parts of you that you consider to be "rotten"? What are they? Are there ways that you can name them, bring them into the light (first on your own and then with trusted friends and counselors)?

Father, I Thank You

Jesus's Prayer and Ours

And Jesus looked upwards and said, "Father,
I thank you for having heard me. I knew
that you always hear me, but I have said this
for the sake of the crowd standing here, so
that they may believe that you sent me."

O n a hillside overlooking the Sea of Galilee, a few hundred feet from the shoreline and not far from the fishing town of Capernaum, which was Jesus's home base during his ministry in Galilee, is a large opening known as the Eremos Cave.

It's an easy site for tourists to miss, and the first time I visited the Holy Land my friend George and I missed it entirely. For one thing, it's impossible to see from the top of the Mount of Beatitudes, where we were staying in a guest house run by a group of friendly Franciscan sisters. For another, the tour buses speeding from the Church of the Multiplication of the Loaves and Fishes or the Church of the Primacy of Peter, both near Tabgha, on their way past the Mount of Beatitudes and heading to Capernaum, often miss it. Most eyes are facing away from the hillside, intent on taking in the usually sparkling waters of the Sea of Galilee. If you're walking, it's easier to spot. But in a big tour bus, you must crane your neck to

The Eremos Cave, beside the Sea of Galilee.
COURTESY OF THE AUTHOR

see it, halfway up a hill. And even if you see it, you might not think
it in any way special. There is no church, no plaque, no sign. It's just
an unremarkable hole in a hill.

What is supposed to have gone on there, however, is not unremarkable.

The cave, nestled into the rocky hillside, is roughly fifteen feet
long by ten feet wide. Adults can stand inside, but if they are tall,
they have to duck to enter. Just inside the mouth of the cave, a small
and not especially picturesque tree has grown, giving onlookers the
impression of a weed sprouting from a hole in the ground. Inside
the cave someone has placed a simple wooden bench, affording a
postcard-worthy (or social media–worthy) view. Despite the empty
water bottles and trash littering the dirt floor, the Eremos Cave is a
perfect place for prayer, and you can often see pilgrims meditating
there.

Another person who, by tradition, prayed in here was Jesus.

Jesus's Prayer

That Jesus prayed shouldn't surprise anyone who reads the Gospels,
which often tell of his withdrawing from the press of the crowds,

who were desperate for healing (and at times wanted to proclaim him king), to pray in a "deserted place."[1] In fact, this is the meaning of *eremos*: "desolate" or "deserted," from which we get the word "hermit."

The Eremos Cave is supposed to be one place where Jesus withdrew. We can't know for sure whether he did, but given its proximity to Capernaum, its secluded location, its sheltered setting, and its unobstructed view of the Sea of Galilee, it would be surprising if he didn't. It is also supposed to be the spot "on land" where, during the storm at sea, Jesus could see the disciples in the boat "straining at the oars."[2]

In the Synoptics Jesus prays frequently. He prays so often in the Gospel of Luke that it is sometimes called the "Gospel of Prayer." Besides Jesus's personal prayer, he speaks to his disciples about prayer, and in response to their request "Teach us to pray," he teaches them the Our Father.[3]

But as Daniel J. Harrington, SJ, notes, "In comparison with the three synoptic gospels, John's Gospel tells us very little about Jesus's practice of prayer."[4] Only when we reach Jesus's Farewell Discourse does prayer take center stage in the Fourth Gospel. Toward the end of that discourse, he offers his "priestly prayer" (so called because it is on behalf of the disciples and those who will follow them).

A few chapters earlier, Jesus prays in a similar way, pleading to the Father on behalf of the crowd—at the Tomb of Lazarus, and at this point in our story.

The way Jesus prays in Bethany mirrors his actions elsewhere in the Gospels. First, he looks "upward," which was probably a common Jewish practice. In Luke's Parable of the Pharisee and the Tax Collector, the tax collector does not feel worthy to make that same gesture. Jesus also looks to the heavens when he is about to multiply the loaves and the fishes in the Synoptics. And during his "priestly prayer" he looks up. But nowhere else in the Gospels does Jesus pray to the Father before performing a miracle.

So why does he pray before Lazarus's tomb? Perhaps the

knowledge that he was about to perform his greatest miracle intensified his desire for connection with the Father. Likewise, his awareness of where this sign would lead—to his death—may have heightened his desire to feel the Father's protection.

But this was also a way of communicating something to those who were with him. His prayer in Bethany was not only for him but *for them*. Jesus is praying on his own but is also offering thanksgiving so that those in the crowd might hear. His public prayer is an invitation for the crowd to participate in his act of thanksgiving, and an opportunity for him to announce publicly what his mission is: belief that the Father has sent him.

As Brendan Byrne notes, Jesus prays not for the ability to perform a miracle but for something else—the faith of those who are there: "That they will see beyond the miracle something of the fuller meaning bound up with the mysterious communion of the Father and the Son."[5] In John's Gospel the miracles are always signs that point to something greater.

The Ordinary Ways of Humanity

Jesus's prayer in Bethany begins with the most basic of prayers, gratitude: "Father, I thank you." This is not the only place where Jesus thanks the Father in prayer. In Matthew 11, which speaks about the mixed reaction Jesus's message receives and the hostility that sometimes greets him, Jesus, sounding a bit like the Johannine Jesus, says:

> I thank you, Father, Lord of heaven and earth, because you have hidden these things from the wise and the intelligent and have revealed them to infants; yes, Father, for such was your gracious will. All things have been handed over to me by my Father; and no one knows the Son except the Father, and no one knows the Father except the Son and anyone to whom the Son chooses to reveal him.[6]

As Harrington points out, the prayer here and at Bethany takes the form of a common Jewish prayer, one of thanksgiving: "In the Old Testament and in other Jewish prayers, a thanksgiving was a public witness and affirmation that God had been at work in rescuing the speaker from great danger or in revealing some important truth."[7]

We see this not only in the many psalms that praise God but also in the practices of other Jewish contemporaries of Jesus, for example, the community behind the Dead Sea Scrolls. The *Hodayot*, or Thanksgiving prayers, often use the first-person singular ("I") and then list the reasons for gratitude: "I thank you, Lord . . . for you have . . ."

Thus it would have been natural for Jesus to begin his prayer in Bethany with gratitude.

The Raising of Lazarus,
by Karl Isakson
(Göteborgs Konstmuseum,
Gothenburg, Sweden).
WIKICOMMONS

What a wonderful prayer this is—the Son thanking the Father. It calls to mind the thirteenth-century German mystic Meister Eckhart's famous comment: "If the only prayer you ever said was 'Thank you,' that would be enough."

Gratitude is one of the gateways to the spiritual life. It reminds us of our ultimate reliance on God. We can do nothing without God's help. Being grateful grounds us in this reality. Gratitude also serves as an antidote (not that Jesus would have needed this) to the common tendency to focus on the negative. By praising God, we move away from the despair that comes from ignoring God's presence to the hope that comes from recognizing God's grace.

When we are *ungrateful*, however, we tend toward jealousy, anger, and vengefulness, as we falsely perceive that others have it better than we do.

Here's an easy way to see this. If you are not aware of the blessings in your own life, you tend to look upon other people's lives as if they were perfect, which they assuredly are not. Everyone's life is a mixed bag of joys and struggles. But when we compare, something strange often happens. We tend to see only the *good* in other peoples' lives. Why? Because people often hide or downplay the not-so-good, such as medical problems, relationship worries, financial woes. This may be out of a sense of embarrassment, or discomfort, or simply the self-effacement that says, "No one wants to hear me complain." Also, some people may want to project an attitude of confidence and success. This is especially true on social media. Whatever the reason, our imperfections are often hidden. Thus, the "blessings" and successes are all we see of others' lives, leading to a dangerously skewed view of those lives.

But that's only the first step. Because if, as a result of ingratitude, we couple that skewed view with an inability to see the good in *our* lives, then our misery is compounded. Now we are comparing a falsely negative version of our lives with the falsely positive version of other peoples' lives. We will *always* lose out in this rigged game. The other peoples' lives will always seem better. "Compare and despair," as many Jesuits say.

This comparison leads inevitably to jealousy, as we look with longing on other peoples' lives, anger that we are not as fortunate, and even vengefulness as we feel the desire to reject or punish them for "having it so good." Those other people, unaware of what they have done (and in full knowledge of their own struggles), may wonder why we seem so jealous and angry!

Thus, ingratitude leads to our own misery but also to sin—the sins of jealousy and resentment. We see this clearly in the lives of some people—usually angry ones, who leave negativity in their wakes. Nothing is good enough for them. Everyone else has it easier. No one suffers as they do.

Ingratitude also means that we don't see what God has given us, which can lessen our faith. We say, "Why should I believe in a God who doesn't help me?" or "If God really exists, God would be helping me." This process feeds on itself. Ingratitude means less faith; less faith means less of a desire to look for signs of God's presence. Which leads to less faith.

"Father, I thank you" may be as important a prayer as the Our Father.

The second part of Jesus's prayer before Lazarus's tomb expresses a confident trust in God. Jesus knows that the Father hears him. Even as one of his closest friends lies dead in a tomb, even as he has been challenged by Martha and Mary, even as the crowd says he should have arrived earlier, he remains confident in the Father.

Where does this fierce confidence come from? Well, it is hard, if not impossible, for us to access or even begin to fathom the intimate relationship that Jesus had with the Father. After all, in the Gospel of John he says, "The Father and I are one."[8] But his confidence is grounded in that *relationship*. Jesus trusts the Father. As he approaches the end of his public ministry, Jesus has seen what the Father can do through him: heal the sick, still storms, feed vast crowds, and raise the dead.

We will never have the same intimacy that Jesus had with the Father in prayer, and so that level of confidence may remain inaccessible to us, but we can share in Jesus's experience of being able to look back and see what the Father has been able to do.

One of the best ways to gain confidence in God is by seeing the hand of God active in the past. In times of stress, when we remember other times that God has cared for us, we can often move on more confidently. Looking back can help us move ahead amid uncertainty. And we can then say with Jesus, "I know that you always hear me."

The third part of Jesus's prayer is more subtle. This part is meant for the crowd—a reminder that prayer is never solitary. It is done with other believers, even if we aren't around them or can't see them. Even if we are praying in the silence of our rooms, we are united with people praying elsewhere in the world—and with those who have gone before us and who pray for us now. This is one meaning of the idea of the "Communion of Saints." Here in Bethany, Jesus acknowledges the crowd by praying aloud. It is an act of solidarity with them.

His prayer is also an act of solidarity with humanity. Jesus prays as other people pray. Stanley Marrow, SJ, notes that he prays in this "traditional" way: "The Word did not become man to exempt himself from the ordinary ways of humanity."[9]

Jesus, the Model Pray-er

At the end of his lovely essay "The Prayer of Need," the German Jesuit Karl Rahner, SJ, one of the most influential theologians of the twentieth century, points to Jesus as the perfect model of prayer.

Father Rahner looks at three of the prayers that Jesus utters on three different occasions that beautifully sum up the stance of the one who prays.[10] One of these occasions is at Bethany.

The prayer of Jesus includes, says Rahner, "the word of realistic petition, the word of heavenly confidence and the word of unconditional submission." In the Garden of Gethsemane, over the hill from Martha and Mary's house, faced with a fate he does not want, he prays, "remove this cup from me."[11] In Bethany, before Jesus raises his friend from the dead, he prays in front of the crowd, "I knew that you always hear me." And in the garden again, after he seems to sense that the Crucifixion is coming, he prays, "Yet, not my will but yours be done."[12] Rahner writes: "Jesus wrestles with the will of God until he bleeds but is totally devoted to him. He shouts his need to heaven and is always certain of being heard. He knows that he will be heard always and in everything and wants to do nothing but the incomprehensible will of God."

This model has proved incredibly helpful in my own spiritual life. Understanding the three elements of Jesus's prayer—which I think of as *honesty, trust,* and *acceptance*—has helped me to frame my own prayer and my spiritual life.

And many of us tend to skip one or another of these steps.

Often people resist being honest with God in their prayer about what they need. "I should be grateful for what I have," they say, or "Others have it worse than I do." And while both of those are true (gratitude is important in the spiritual life, and others probably do have it worse than we do), it does not mean that we should not be honest with God.

Honesty, as we've seen in the case of Martha and Mary, is part of being in a relationship with God. If in our prayer we say only those things that we think are "appropriate" to say in prayer—for example, if we are unable to lament or ask for what we need—we may find our relationship with God growing cold and distant. Occasionally we leave out that step in the spiritual life. We trust that God hears us and we accept whatever is God's response, but in such cases, we are not honest.

Likewise, we might be honest in prayer—pouring out our hearts to God—and accept whatever comes, but we might skip the second step: trust. That is, we simply pray and pray and pray, not really believing that God is listening, not really trusting that God has our best interests at heart. Part of this is trusting that God is actively listening to us. To use the model of prayer as a personal relationship again, it is akin to trusting that when we are telling a friend a long and involved story about a problem we are facing, that the friend is listening carefully, paying attention, always with an eye to help.

Another way of looking at trust is believing that even if we don't feel God's presence all the time, God is still there. In the friendship model, it's akin to knowing that even though we may not have heard from a friend for a while—no visits, no phone calls, no emails, no texts, no DMs—that our friend still loves us and cares for us. The temptation is to assume that God is no longer listening, simply because we don't feel God's presence. There may be honesty and acceptance, but no trust.

Finally, the most common step skipped is acceptance. Most of us are honest in prayer and trust that God hears us, but we have a hard time accepting the answer. We've already talked about un-answered prayers, but here it's good to focus on Jesus's words, as highlighted by Karl Rahner: "Yet, not my will but yours be done" is one of the hardest things for a believer to say. Recently during a homily in our Jesuit community, I quoted this line but got it backward: "Like Jesus, we must say, 'Not your will but my will be done.'" Everyone laughed, and one Jesuit afterward teased me and asked, "Freudian slip?"

But if we're honest, it's hard not to wish that my will is God's will in all things. Can we, as a friend often says, "surrender to the future that God has in store for us," confident in God's love for us?

Rahner's profound image of Jesus at prayer—embodying hon-esty, trust, and acceptance—offers a realistic model for all who ask

God for help: in other words, for all believers. These days when I pray, this tripartite image helps not only to focus but to calm me. I feel that I can better emulate Jesus in prayer by remembering these three essential aspects of his prayer. Sometimes I even repeat these words to myself when I'm praying. Honesty encourages me to speak my mind; trust reminds me to believe that God is listening; and acceptance, perhaps the most challenging part, asks me to follow the path of Jesus, who accepted suffering because this was part of the mysterious future, still unseen, into which the Father was inviting him.

Can we pray for what we need? Yes. Will we always receive what we think we need? No. Does that mean we don't ever pray again or fail to trust in God? No.

Because, as Jesus said in Bethany, "I know you hear me."

For Your Reflection

1. Jesus may have prayed in the Eremos Cave on the shoreline of the Sea of Galilee. But even if he didn't pray in that exact spot, he prayed elsewhere. What does the fact that Jesus prayed often say about your own need to pray?

2. Why do you think Jesus pauses to pray before Lazarus's tomb? Jesus says it is for the crowd. Might there have been other reasons for his heartfelt prayer?

3. St. Ignatius Loyola called ingratitude the "origin of all sins." Do you agree? Why or why not?

4. Karl Rahner's presentation of Jesus as the model "pray-er" includes three qualities of the spiritual life: honesty, trust, and acceptance. Which one of these steps do you think you may need to deepen?

5. What enabled you to accept God's will in a difficult situation, where you might have preferred your own will "to be done"?

Lazarus, Come Out!

Dying to Self and Finding New Life

*When he had said this, he cried with a loud
voice, "Lazarus, come out!" The dead man
came out, his hands and feet bound with strips
of cloth, and his face wrapped in a cloth.*

I t's a big thing," said Sister Vassa Larin, who holds a doctorate in liturgical studies with an emphasis in the Byzantine Rite. She was answering my question about the importance of something I had never heard of: Lazarus Saturday, a special feast in the Orthodox Church. In a series of emails and subsequent conversations, she carefully explained the traditions. The daughter of a Russian Orthodox priest and host of "Coffee with Sister Vassa," an online catechetical program, she has lived in various Orthodox dioceses and monasteries and a convent in Jerusalem for two years; in addition to her studies, she was well positioned to tell me about Lazarus Saturday.

On the Sixth Saturday of Lent, also the Saturday before Palm Sunday, Orthodox churches (including the Eastern Orthodox, Oriental Orthodox, and Byzantine Catholic Churches) commemorate the Raising of Lazarus from the dead with a variety of fascinating customs, both cultural and liturgical. Interestingly, the hymnography (the liturgical prayers and hymns) used in the week leading up to Lazarus Saturday focus on both the Lazarus of Jesus's parable (the poor man who had gone to the underworld) *and* Lazarus of Bethany being raised from the dead, the latter being seen as a kind of fulfillment of the parable.

To distinguish Lazarus of Bethany from the man in the parable, most Orthodox use the term "Four-Day-Dead Lazarus" or the "Righteous Lazarus of Four Days Dead." (In Vienna one of the most beautiful Orthodox churches is known in the Russian community as the Chapel of the Four-Day Dead Lazarus at the Central Cemetery, or *Zentralfriedhof,* where Lazarus is commemorated at every service.)

"By raising Lazarus from the dead before Your Passion, / You confirmed the universal resurrection, O Christ God!" goes the Troparion, or main hymn, for the feast. "Like the children with palms of victory, / We cry out to You, O Vanquisher of Death, / Hosanna in the highest. Blessed is He that comes in the name of the

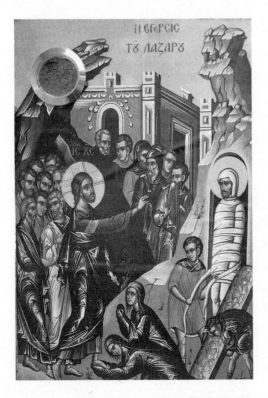

Traditional icon of the Raising of Lazarus, purchased from the shop across from the tomb in Al Eizariya. As Martha and Mary prostrate themselves before Jesus, a man covers his face with a cloth against the stench.
COURTESY OF THE AUTHOR

Lord!" Even though it is still a week before Easter and the Passion and Death of Jesus lie ahead, the prevailing mood is one of joy.

For Orthodox Christians, said Sister Vassa, the forty days of Lent end on Lazarus Saturday. In Palestinian monasticism it was customary for the monks to spend forty days in solitary prayer in the desert and to return to their monastery communities for the feast. Certain hymns sung only on Sundays are sung on Lazarus Saturday, and baptisms were also done on the day, though that is no longer the practice.

The liturgical color for the day, which is one of celebration, is sometimes green, but it differs from parish to parish. White, the color of resurrection, is often used, but sometimes red, said Sister Vassa. She explained that churches on Lazarus Saturday may not be "super crowded" in terms of the number of parishioners, because a few hours later the celebrations for Palm Sunday Eve take place. But, she said, most Orthodox Christians would know of this important feast.

Lenten fasting rules for the Russian Orthodox Church are somewhat relaxed for Lazarus Saturday, when caviar is allowed, along with wine and oil. On other Saturdays of Lent, wine and oil are allowed, but not caviar. Sister Vassa noted that "you can have caviar in addition to wine and oil, but no fish." She hazarded a guess, from some online research, that this might have something to do with the imagery of the egg as a symbol of life (as in Easter eggs) but admitted that she'd never heard that explanation from any reliable source and thought it sounded "fishy."

In terms of foodstuffs, the most charming tradition associated with Lazarus Saturday is the baking of pastries called *lazarakia*, or "Little Lazaruses," which originated in either Greece or Cyprus. The connection to Cyprus makes sense since, as we will see, there is an Eastern tradition that Lazarus, after his life in the Holy Land, later became the first bishop of Kition, now Larnaca, in Cyprus, where today you can find the Cathedral of St. Lazarus.

Greek Orthodox Christians make their *lazarakia* out of flour, sugar, yeast, cinnamon, olive oil, and cloves, but no dairy or eggs, so as to conform with the Lenten fasts. Mahleb, an aromatic spice made from the seeds of a particular cherry, is often added. Most marvelous of all, they are shaped like little Lazaruses: a tiny man bound up tightly in grave cloths, usually with whole cloves for his unblinking eyes.

Lazarus Saturday, with its brightly colored vestments, its relaxation of fasting, and its little sweet-smelling pastries, is a joyful time. Writing about Lazarus Saturday in his book *The Christian Way*, the Orthodox scholar and archpriest Alexander Schmemann notes, "The joy that permeates and enlightens the service of Lazarus Saturday stresses one major theme: the forthcoming victory of Christ over Hades."[1]

It is a time that focuses believers on the central part of our story, the Raising of Lazarus from the dead, which we have now reached.

"Come Forth!"

It is the dramatic high point of our story, the climax of the greatest of Jesus's signs in John's Gospel, and the scene that nearly everyone thinks of when they hear the name "Lazarus."

After the long and involved saga of the news of Lazarus's illness reaching Jesus, his delay in attending to his sick friend, his journey to Bethany, his encounter with the sisters, and his final journey to his friend's resting place, Jesus finally stands at the entrance to the tomb to perform his greatest miracle.

Here it is helpful to know a little about the Jewish traditions around the grave itself. As Jodi Magness points out in her book on daily Jewish life, referring to the Qumran sect, "Anyone entering the closed space of a rock-cut tomb [as Lazarus was buried in] or burial cave would have contracted corpse impurity."[2]

Amy-Jill Levine cautions us, though, against seeing Jesus as standing against purity laws, which she labels as a "typical

Jesus Raises Lazarus to Life, JESUS MAFA.
COURTESY OF THE VANDERBILT DIVINITY LIBRARY

misunderstanding." To the contrary, she told me, "You might want to see Jesus, in raising Lazarus, as restoring him to a state of purity," as he does with the man with leprosy and the woman with the hemorrhage. Moreover, Jesus does not enter the tomb here, nor does he touch a dead person. Rather, the person who emerges is alive.

After his public prayer to the Father, Jesus "cries out" or "shouts." The word *kraugasen* is used only eight times in the Gospels, six of which are in John's Gospel. (The word is used four times to describe the shouts of the crowd that wants to crucify Jesus.) And Jesus doesn't merely shout; he shouts in a *megale phōnē*, a loud voice, the same phrase used when he gives a "loud cry" on the Cross.[3] Earlier in John's Gospel, Jesus had promised, "the hour is coming, and is now here, when the dead will hear the voice of the Son of God, and those who hear will live."[4]

"Lazarus, come forth!" he shouts in a loud voice.

This is the second time in the story that Jesus's voice, his *phōnē*, elicits a positive response. The first is when Martha tells Mary that the Teacher is "calling for you" (*phōnei se*) and she rushes to see him, believing. Now Jesus calls Lazarus, and he too responds.

And, as in the other miracle stories, Jesus's mere word is enough to make this happen. In a homily about Lazarus, St. Athanasius says that this is the same voice that gave life to Adam, the same voice that brought the world into being.[5] There is a sense of creation or revelation.

Jesus's words give meaning to his actions, his actions to his words. And he needs no magic formula, incantation, or physical objects (a wand, incense, offerings) to accomplish this.

Lazarus has been raised from the dead.

He emerges from the tomb with his hands and feet bound with "strips of cloth." It is an unusual Greek word used in the Book of Proverbs to indicate bedcoverings. The *soudarion* covering Lazarus's face is the same type of cloth that Jesus leaves behind in the tomb on Easter Sunday. And remember the suggestion that Lazarus may be the mysterious Beloved Disciple: one reason that the Beloved Disciple is quick to believe in Christ's resurrection is that he sees the *soudarion* in the empty tomb on Easter Sunday. Just a few days before, Lazarus himself was wearing one. So it is easier for him, compared with Peter, the disciple who accompanies him to the tomb, to believe.

Brendan Byrne delineates an important difference in the two raisings, with the *soudarion* as a link. Lazarus's raising is more passive. The dead man is summoned by Jesus, and he responds; and then, still wearing his bandages, he needs to be "loosed" from those bonds. By contrast, when the disciples reach Jesus's tomb, they find the *soudarion* neatly rolled up and the linens carefully set aside, presumably by Jesus. As we've seen in the rest of John's Gospel, Jesus is in control. "It is hard to escape the conclusion that the evangelist wants us to see the contrast," writes Byrne.[6]

Byrne notes as well that the arrangement of the grave cloths

Mosaic of the Raising of Lazarus, Church of St. Lazarus, Al Eizariya.
COURTESY OF CATHOLIC TRAVEL CENTRE

also precludes the possibility that grave robbers have stolen the body. "Robbers do not leave things tidy," he writes. No, we are meant to see that, in contrast to the passivity of Lazarus, there has been a "calm, active reclaiming of life."[7]

Raymond Brown notes another theological reason for the emphasis on the burial garments in the Raising of Lazarus. Jesus's burial cloths remain in his tomb since he will never again need them. Lazarus still wears his since, one day, he will need them again.[8]

As an aside, some commentators puzzle over how Lazarus could have "come out" if his hands and his feet and head were bound in linen. It conjures up the unintentionally risible image of the dead man emerging from the tomb, unable to see or walk, hopping around in front of the crowd. Here we need not be so literal. The *soudarion* might have slipped down, and perhaps his feet were not bound so tightly. Or John could have been summing up a general tradition of Lazarus coming out still bearing the cloths that had been placed on him only a few days before.

Brown writes, sensibly, that the question of just how Lazarus emerged from his tomb with his head and feet bound is "really rather silly in an account that presupposes the supernatural."[9]

The important thing is this: Lazarus has been raised from the dead.

As a Child in the Freshness of the Womb

This is not only the dramatic high point of the narrative but the moment from the story most often represented in art and popular culture. In Giotto's vivid depiction in the Scrovegni Chapel in Padua, Lazarus comes out tightly bound, seemingly immobile, his gaunt and pale face a rictus of disbelief. Lazarus still stands at the entrance of the tomb surrounded by the crowd, some of whom cover their face with cloths. Those in Giotto's time would have known what a corpse smelled like. Icons of the event often show the crowd shrinking back in terror or awe, with Mary and Martha kneeling at the foot of a placid Jesus. He is, as in John's Gospel, in control.

Eugene O'Neill's allegorical play *Lazarus Laughed*, complete with Greek choruses and figures wearing symbolic masks (including Boyhood, Girlhood, the Simple, the Ignorant), has Lazarus emerge from the tomb laughing. Standing before the crowd, he utters a single word: "Yes."

In Nikos Kazantzakis's *The Last Temptation of Christ*, the famous scene is told by someone who had been present that day, an old man named Melchizedek. The crowd hangs on his every word. He describes the sisters prostrating themselves before Jesus, lamenting their brother's death and screaming, "If you had been with him, Rabbi, he wouldn't have died."

When Jesus stands before the tomb, says the old man, his eyes roll back into his head and he lets out a "bellow" such that "you'd have thought there was a bull inside of him" (a terrific way of describing *enebrimesato*). Then he utters a "wild cry, a strange cry,

The Raising of Lazarus, by Giotto di Bondone
(Scrovegni Chapel, Padua, Italy).
WIKICOMMONS

something from another world," and the crowd hears the earth in the tomb "stir and crack." Then two yellow arms and a green head, a "skeleton-like" body wrapped in a shroud, come out from the darkness.

Colm Tóibín, in *The Testament of Mary*, describes the rest of the scene beautifully, in the voice of Mary, Jesus's mother:

> Slowly, the figure dirtied with clay and covered in graveclothes wound around him began with great uncertainty to move in the place they had made for him. It was as though the earth beneath him was pushing him and then letting him be still in his great forgetfulness and nudging him again like some strange new creature jerking and wriggling towards life. He was bound with the sheets and his face was covered with a napkin and now he turned as a child in the freshness of the womb who turns knowing that his time there is up and he must wrestle his way into the world.[10]

Come Out!

Originally, I planned on calling this book *Lazarus, Come Out!* This is the simplest way for this famous clause in Greek, *Lazare, deuro exō*, to be translated. *Exō* means "out" or "away." When Jesus expels demons, *exō* is used and the English translation is "cast out."

As I have already mentioned, a few years ago, my book *Building a Bridge*, about LGBTQ Catholics, garnered a good deal of controversy, even though it didn't challenge any church teaching. So as much as I treasure the words "Lazarus, come out!," I was worried that the reference to "coming out" would be seen as a veiled comment on that earlier book, thereby serving as an occasion for snarky comments or distracting from this book, which is not focused on LGBTQ people but on everyone.

The message, however, is especially important for LGBTQ people. "Coming out" means to accept, embrace, and love who you

Take Away the Stone, by John August Swanson.
USED WITH PERMISSION

are, especially your sexuality and the way that God made you, and to reveal or share that part of yourself with others. Coming out is a critical step for LGBTQ people, who are sometimes told, either overtly or covertly, that they should not accept or love themselves. Or that they are a mistake, less valuable than straight people or less worthy of love and affection. Or, worst of all, that God doesn't love them. In many places this has changed for the better, with LGBTQ people finding more welcome and acceptance. But in some locales and countries, coming out is still made difficult by the hateful and harmful messages communicated to LGBTQ people, especially youth.

Often these messages come from religious people who believe that they're doing LGBTQ people a favor by speaking this "truth" to them: they are a mistake. This may be coupled with rejection from families, which can be devastating to a person who may already be facing bullying, harassment, and even violence outside of their families. In many places in the world, LGBTQ people are faced with the severest of persecutions, sometimes encoded in civil law. Mark Gevisser's powerful book *The Pink Line: Journeys Across the World's Queer Frontiers*, which looks at the plight of LGBTQ people around the world, offers at times shocking testimony from this community. Sometimes, in fear of being beaten to death or executed (same-sex relations warrant the death penalty in seven countries), they must escape their own countries. Gevisser details situations where these LGBTQ refugees are then harassed and beaten in the very refugee camps to which they flee.[11]

All of this can lead many LGBTQ people, especially youth, to reject an essential part of themselves, fall into despair, and even consider suicide.

When this happens in a religious context (that is, being rejected for supposedly religious reasons by families, friends, or church), it can turn LGBTQ people away from the church and from God. Tragically, this happens at the very time when such young people most need the support of God and their faith communities. Not long ago I read an article about a bullied twelve-year-old boy who had died by suicide. His distraught parents said, "He was told because he didn't necessarily have a religion and that he said he was gay that he was going to go to Hell. They told him that quite often."[12] Churches need to be aware of the real-life effects of stigmatizing language about LGBTQ people.

"Coming out," then, whenever it happens, is a key step in both their emotional maturation and spiritual growth. It is a sign of a healthy love of self, which is often a challenge for LGBTQ people. When I hear "Lazarus, come out!," I often think of LGBTQ people.

But love of self represents a challenge for many people, not just those in the LGBTQ community.

Not Enoughness

Loving oneself is a struggle for an astonishing number of people. Over the past thirty years as a Jesuit and especially in my ministry as a spiritual director, I've met dozens of people who face crippling doubts about their own value and worth. This happens even to people who would be considered by many as "successful." It is a contemporary disease that plagues almost everyone—feelings of what one professionally successful man in his thirties described as "not enoughness."

Often it manifests as feelings that one is inadequate, unintelligent, or a failure in life. It also manifests in embarrassment or shame about an aspect of one's body, personality, family of origin, educational background, or financial status. This may include highly negative perceptions about physical appearance, fear of being unable to succeed in one's chosen field, feeling unpopular, or simply having vague feelings of unworthiness. Sometimes these feelings can be traced to childhood, when people describe parents for whom nothing ever seemed to be enough (or at least this is the way that some people internalized their parents' expectations). Although it may sound like I'm copying this from a book on psychology, I'm describing multiple experiences with people who have seen me for spiritual direction and counseling over the years. And the number of people who must confront not enoughness seems to grow each year.

This feeling can influence the way people imagine, understand, and relate to God, thus having a profound impact on their spiritual lives. People's conceptions of God naturally are influenced by how they saw their parents: judgmental or accepting, gentle or harsh, demanding or accepting. These experiences, positive or negative, are often imported into their spiritual lives. Having judgmental parents, for instance, can mean that people may judge themselves severely—and believe that God does as well.

Often, they will say to me the same thing, word for word: "I know I shouldn't feel this way, but I feel like I'm just not enough." This moves beyond guilt over something they did and into an unhealthy sense of shame. Guilt says "I did a bad thing"; shame says "I am a bad person."

Such feelings can be crippling. How can we feel at peace if we are "not enough"? Nothing that we do, and nothing that anyone can say to us, can fill that need. No amount of success, no amount of money, and no group of friends can paper over that tear in a person's psyche.

Key to combating not enoughness is a healthy sense of the gifts and talents God has given us and the blessing we are for others. Often, I ask people simply to take time—hours, days, weeks—to focus on the blessings in their lives. What talents have you been given? What friends have you had? Where have you experienced love and support? What are your successes? What brings you joy? How have you helped others to flourish?

This is not a papering over of the "not enoughness." Rather, when we are stuck in feelings of inadequacy and unworthiness, it helps to see, in concrete terms, where we have been blessed, what gifts we have been given, and who we have been able to become with God's grace. Gradually, people can come to see how God loves them, which means they come to see *that* God loves them. They are invited to relate not to the God who has lived in their minds (harsh, angry, judgmental) but the God they experience in real life (loving and accepting, who has blessed them).

Often this recognition means a kind of smashing of "idols," that is, false images of God. When you ask people if they follow the Second Commandment, "You shall not make for yourself an idol,"[13] they look surprised, then appalled. They say, "Of course I don't worship idols! Or make little statues that I bow down before!" But sometimes people have created in their minds a false image of God—a God for whom nothing is ever enough, a God who disapproves of who they are, a God who condemns them. This is every bit as much an idol as a little clay statue. And these false images must be destroyed if they are to have an encounter with the Living God.

This approach is not a panacea for the disease of not enoughness, which may need to be treated with a psychotherapist to uncover its deeper roots. And it does not eliminate our need to look at our own sinfulness and failings—none of us are perfect. But this is the approach I have found most useful in helping people face this situation: centering people on blessings. It also invites them to detach from what society often considers valuable: financial status, educational credentials, perceived good looks (all of which, especially the last category, are subjective).

This approach helps people move away from unhealthy measures of value and, more important, reveals to them their essential goodness and the love that God has for them. This helps them, over time, to accept that they are enough.

Greg Boyle, a Jesuit priest who works with former gang members in Los Angeles at Homeboy Industries, once said: "We all think we are not enough. We all think we are an eternal disappointment." He says that one of life's key goals is to see things as God does. Because otherwise we end up creating God in our own image. "We measure, but God doesn't know what we're talking about. We evaluate outcomes, and we chart results, and chronicle progress and polish up success stories," Boyle says. "God doesn't."[14]

Wonderfully Made

In this battle against not enoughness, Psalm 139, one of my favorites, is especially helpful: "Wonderful are your works; / that I know very well."[15] The writer of the psalm praises God's marvelous works, which he sees all around him. In contemplating creation, we see the "wonderful" activity of God and God's care for humanity.

The psalmist marvels at his own creation as well, gratefully acknowledging himself as part of God's plan for the universe: "I am fearfully and wonderfully made," he writes.[16]

Few lines are as helpful for people who suffer from not enoughness. In this psalm we see an essential human impulse: giving thanks for God's creating us. In another psalm, we are invited to ponder God's care for us:

[W]hat are human beings that you are mindful of them,

mortals that you care for them?

Yet you have made them a little lower than God,

and crowned them with glory and honor.[17]

These lines can help people see that not only are they blessed by God, but that it's okay to feel that way.

Quoting Leviticus 19:18, Jesus also calls us to love ourselves when he says, "You shall love your neighbor as yourself."[18] For how can we love our neighbor as ourselves without an appropriate love for what God has created in us? As St. Thomas Aquinas writes, "Among these other things which man loves out of charity because they pertain to God, he loves also himself out of charity."[19] Some might think this view diminishes humility. Rather, it perfects it, by reminding us that God is the source of who we are. And we rely on a God who continues to "labor" in us, as St. Ignatius Loyola put it.[20]

God is continually working in us, laboring in us, as we live. Gratitude for having been created increases not only humility but a sense of own our goodness. A healthy love of self is part of a healthy emotional life and a healthy spiritual life.

"Come out!" is an invitation to all people who feel that they are not enough. That they are inadequate. Or even that they are a "mistake." These feelings and beliefs are something to leave behind in the tomb because they are a kind of death. Feelings of not enoughness can be death to the spiritual life, because you live under a cloud of self-hatred. So why not leave that death in the tomb?

We can imagine Lazarus's tomb in this way. We can leave behind those parts of ourselves that make us doubt God's love. We can leave behind our not enoughness. We can leave behind the idols we have created in place of the Living God. We can walk into the sunlight of God's love for us. And we can hear Jesus say directly to us, "Come out!"

The Raising of Lazarus,
by John August Swanson.
USED WITH PERMISSION

Dying to Self

For others, the words "come out" may focus on what spiritual writers call "dying to self."

Often I suggest to pilgrims that they might leave something behind in Lazarus's tomb. I now invite you to consider the question: What part of yourself—an old grudge, a failed relationship, a disappointment in life—do you want to "let die"?

To understand the concept of "dying to self," let's consider these lines from Jesus, contained in all three of the Synoptic Gospels: "If any want to become my followers, let them deny themselves and take up their cross and follow me."[21] What did he mean by that?

First, there is a literal way of understanding this, namely, that some of Jesus's disciples would be crucified, as happened, for example, to Peter. In Jesus's day (and sometimes in our own but certainly not as much) "taking up the cross" meant to be willing to give up your life for what you believe and proclaim.

Keep in mind that people in Jesus's day would have known about and seen crucifixions. "Taking up your cross" was not mere imagery. "Crucifixion was well known to Jews of Jesus's time," writes Daniel Harrington.[22] But in classic spiritual circles, these lines have been interpreted to mean something more universal: dying to self, one of the most important parts of the Christian life.

Let me distinguish "dying to self" from the phrase "take up your cross daily," which has a slightly different connotation, though the two ideas are related.

Today, to take up one's cross may mean to shoulder either the common burdens of daily life or the burdens of special responsibilities or sufferings. A man caring for an aging parent struggling with memory loss might think of his cross as the constant energy needed to be kind, generous, and hopeful in the face of someone who no longer remembers him or even rejects him. A woman who is an attorney committed to the rights of poor people might think of her cross as the opposition she faces when fighting an unjust economic system. A teacher in an inner-city school might think of his or her cross as working in a system with limited resources. People who live with physical disabilities or a long-term illness might consider these things as their own crosses. A lack of friends or support system can become a cross for someone who is lonely. Everyone has their own crosses, big and small.

Some of these things can be changed: injustice can be combated, physical ailments can be treated, and emotional situations can be addressed. But what cannot be changed may be your cross. And we are asked, as the prayer says, to accept these things, or as Jesus says, to "take up" that cross.

That is part of Jesus's command. The other part, about "denying ourselves," is slightly different. And there are a few ways to understand this.

First, denying oneself is a kind of *humility*. As the *New Jerome Biblical Commentary* says, with admirable brevity, "Self-denial means submission of one's will to God's."[23] We deny ourselves but accede to God. When we confront something that we wish were not the case and that we cannot change, we may have to "deny ourselves" by accepting God's will, hard as it may be, and trusting that God is present. The "denial" is the denial of what we would want for ourselves. As Jesus says in Gethsemane, "Not my will but yours be done."[24]

Second, it is a kind of *asceticism*. We "deny" ourselves things that are not good for us, that will harm us or others. If we're married, we deny ourselves the thrill of an intimate relationship, passionate romance, or sexual encounter with someone else—because we know that it is not good for us, for our spouse, or for the other person. Or we deny ourselves the supposed satisfaction of harming or humiliating a person who offended us. Both are simple moral behaviors (not cheating and not being violent), but it is an asceticism of sorts. Being a follower of Christ means that kind of denial.

Asceticism can also mean denying ourselves good things, not

just evil ones. If we are too attached to a thing or an action, even if those things or actions are good in themselves, then it may be healthy to distance ourselves. St. Ignatius Loyola calls these "disordered attachments." A disordered attachment can be an attachment that wasn't healthy to begin with—or it can be a perfectly fine attachment that has become too important to us. A disordered attachment prevents us from following God more closely. For instance, you want to stay abreast of the latest news and keep up with your friends on social media. But mere interest can turn into obsession, and you find yourself spending an inordinate amount of time on your phone—and you're becoming more stressed and irritable. Science has shown that these actions can become addictive: the dopamine levels in our brains released as a reward for what scientists call "successful social interactions," refined through thousands of years of evolution, are triggered when we see positive messages from other human beings (including "likes" on social media).[25] As a result, something neutral—a desire to keep informed—becomes a disordered attachment. Ignatius would ask us to let go of it, to take steps to battle the addictive behavior and in this way to deny it.

Finally, to "deny ourselves" means a kind of *death to self.* Here we let go of entire parts of ourselves that prevent us from moving closer to God.

Is there a *pattern* that is preventing you from living a freer life? Not simply a single sin or attachment but a way of life? Are you vain? Arrogant? Addicted to being right? Maybe you enjoy harboring grudges or nursing resentments. Maybe you're obsessed with financial success or your physical appearance. Maybe you focus too much on the opinions of other people. Maybe you still think of yourself as unworthy of love. Some of these patterns may need to die.

Whatever needs to die needs to be left behind. Jesus wants to invite you into new life, but first you must be willing to leave those things in the tomb. Why not let this be the moment that you let it go?

In Every Death, a Rising

But the dying is not the most important part of the Lazarus story. Everyone dies. People in first-century Bethany knew this. Because of the poor sanitary conditions and only rudimentary medicine, death was a constant companion. But rising from the dead? In Jesus's ministry this had happened only twice before, once with the daughter of Jairus, the synagogue official, and again with the son of the Widow of Nain. But neither of those was as dramatic as the Raising of Lazarus. Lazarus's rising is the point of the story.

Yet the miracle is described in the simplest, sparest terms: the two verses that begin this chapter. For, as Raymond Brown says about John's Gospel, "The marvelous is not important." What is important is that Jesus has offered the crowd a powerful sign of his ability to give life.[26]

John's description of the crowd's reaction is also nonexistent. By contrast, the Synoptic Gospels regularly describe the strong reactions to Jesus's miracles. Onlookers are usually "amazed" or "astounded." When Jesus stills the storm on the Sea of Galilee, the disciples ask, "What sort of man is this, that even the winds and the sea obey him?"[27] Sometimes witnesses to the miracles want to proclaim him king.

But in John's Gospel we hear nothing. After Lazarus emerges from the tomb, one would expect to hear, as one does in the Synoptics, "And all were amazed." Or "And they said, 'We have never seen anything like this.'" Or perhaps a variation on what the disciples said when Jesus stilled the storm at sea, "Who, then, is this, who can raise the dead?"

More important for John is whether the greatest of Jesus's signs leads people to believe. John Meier notes that in each of the signs, Jesus gives on the physical level "some sort of fuller, more joyful, or more secure life to people whose lives were in some way restricted, saddened or threatened."[28] These signs reach a "crescendo" in the Raising of Lazarus.[29]

The Raising of Lazarus, by Kristen Wheeler. The artist has depicted the current-day tomb and even included the plants that bloom in a nearby garden.
COURTESY OF THE ARTIST

John does recount the long-term reactions to the Raising of Lazarus: "Many of the Jews therefore, who had come with Mary and had seen what Jesus did, believed in him. But some of them went to the Pharisees and told them what he had done."[30]

Some believed, and some didn't. Some accepted Jesus as the Messiah and others didn't. It's hard to believe that anyone wouldn't believe in Jesus's power after seeing him call Lazarus out of the tomb.

In Richard Zimler's novel *The Gospel According to Lazarus*, the newly raised man becomes a celebrity in Bethany and a suspected miracle worker: "A number of other strangers soon come to my door," Lazarus says, "imploring me to relieve their ailments and afflictions."

In John's Gospel, Lazarus's later renown makes him dangerous to the chief priests, the temple officials appointed by Rome: "When the great crowd of the Jews learned that he [Jesus] was there, they came not only because of Jesus but also to see Lazarus, whom he had raised from the dead. So the chief priests planned to put Lazarus to death as well, since it was on account of him that many of the Jews were deserting and were believing in Jesus."[31]

The important factor for John is that the sign of the Raising of Lazarus prompts people to believe or not believe. It is what the Greeks would call a "crisis," a time for a decision. The word *krisis* comes from *krinein*, meaning "to decide." For all who saw it, Lazarus's raising would have forced the question: Do I believe in Jesus or not?

In our own time, most of you reading the story of Lazarus and most of you reading this book have probably already made your choice for Jesus. The crisis for you may be different: Do you believe that Jesus can give you new life—not in the way that he gave it to Lazarus, but in your life as you live it?

The final act in the story of Lazarus is not about death, but about life. And moving toward life is more than simply letting something die in the tomb. Or even dying to self. Because neither are things that we do. Rather, God invites us to let go in order that we might receive new life. For every death to self there is a rising. And we have to let go.

But the real work—the raising—is done by God.

It is also important to remember the cost to Jesus of doing this. As Brendan Byrne points out, Jesus had put his own life at risk by leaving a region of safety (across the Jordan) to travel to Judea to raise Lazarus, which reveals something important for all of us: "Here lies the most profound truth of the sequence: Lazarus stands in for each one of us. Each one of us is 'Lazarus': the 'friend' of Jesus, 'the one whom he loved.' For each one of us he left the 'safe country' of his existence with the Father in order, at the cost of his own life, to rescue us from death."[32]

What does this mean in practice? None of us is going to be raised from the dead as Lazarus was. But we are invited to accept not only that God *can* give us new life, not only that God *wants* to give us new life, but that God *is* giving us new life. In many ways.

"When Really You're Fine"

Sometimes new life is a matter of a new perspective. Recently I was offered a beautiful image of that.

Out of the blue I got an email from the friend of a friend. Chiara was the niece of an elderly priest who had worked for decades in Catholic parishes in Brooklyn and Queens, and whom I had never met. Now, at age seventy-three, Father Andrew was near death, having come to the end of lengthy cancer treatments. Over the years, he had read some of my books, and his niece asked if I might meet with him virtually, over the internet, since he was struggling with his prayer. She asked if I might do a guided meditation with him. I said I was happy to.

Father Andrew and Chiara appeared onscreen a few days later, the priest lying in a comfortable recliner on the first floor of his rectory, an oxygen mask strapped to his face, alongside his smiling niece and another, younger, priest, who had been mentored by Father Andrew as a youth.

Father Andrew was a kind and gentle soul whom I liked immediately. Over the next hour, I led him through a simple guided meditation, inviting him to imagine himself at his favorite place, which turned out to be a beach on the southern shore of Long Island, and envision Jesus coming to speak with him. Afterward, I told him that he could do that meditation whenever he wanted. Eight days later, his niece told me that he had died.

The day after we met, Chiara sent me a note along with this reminiscence, an example of how even the slightest shift in perspective can mean new life. She gave me permission to share it with you.

Chiara and her uncle, Father Andrew.
COURTESY OF CHIARA MONTALTO

A few weeks ago, my husband and I brought my uncle to the beach. We put him in his wheelchair and walked him up and down the boardwalk. For a while, he and I sat there looking out at the ocean. We saw these two big ocean liners that looked like they were about to collide. Uncle reminded me that they were fine, it was just our perception. We spoke about how things appear one way from afar but then as you get closer—it's totally different. Sometimes it seems like you are on a collision course, when really you're fine.

Chiara wrote me again a few weeks after her uncle died:

Maybe it's hindsight, but I believe that when we had that conversation at Rockaway Beach about the ocean liners, we both knew that they represented death, though neither of us articulated it.

From my perspective, it seemed so far away, out in the distant future, not just a month away. I guess I'll never quite know how he felt, but I do know that while he expressed some anxiety to me about death in those weeks, he also was at peace and even cracked jokes about it.

A change in perspective can bring a person new life.

Remember Who Is Calling You

Coming out of the tomb will feel strange at first. As it probably did to Lazarus.

In Zimler's *The Gospel According to Lazarus*, the raised man is dazed after his time in the tomb. Initially he can barely remember the miracle. Jesus, touchingly, asks for forgiveness for arriving late. "Too late for what?" Lazarus says to himself.

In time, his family helps restore him to full health. But it takes him a while to live fully; at first, he walks on "unsteady" legs. In two dramas, William Butler Yeats's play *Calvary* and Kahlil Gibran's *Lazarus and His Beloved*, Lazarus even prefers to stay in the tomb.

It can feel like that at first. We hear the invitation to die to self and to experience new life, and we try to let go of the past. We see things, like Father Andrew's ocean liners, from a new perspective and suddenly things seem new.

Yet we wonder how to walk into the future, how to embrace the new life that God has given us.

Initially it will feel unnatural, uncertain, unsteady, sometimes even false. Who are we to live in the new life? Who are we to say that we have been freed when we see so many people still in their tombs? (My friend Joseph McAuley said to me, "If we all knew what was to happen after we were born, we might want to stay in the womb!") It's natural for us to feel this way, to ask such questions. Yet this is where God wants us.

This may sound abstract. What might it mean in the concrete? Let's take a specific case and a general case. Both are common in the spiritual life.

Let's say that you feel an invitation to be kinder. You're not a hardened criminal or a moral monster, but you've been, at times, cruel. You wield a sharp tongue with glee. Other people even praise you for your sarcasm. Whether out of spite, vengefulness, or a desire not to let anyone take advantage of you, you're sometimes pretty mean to other people. You've always made excuses: "They deserved it." "No one should get the better of me." "It's a dog-eat-dog world." Or maybe you think you are a great wit, cutting people down to size, à la Oscar Wilde.

But at heart you have to face it: sometimes you're mean.

Then something happens—a look of hurt on someone's face, a chance conversation, a friend challenging you, a family member hurt by what you said, a therapist helping you see things in a new light, an experience on a retreat, a sudden insight in prayer—that makes you realize that you're being called to let that die. A Jesuit once described for me a biting remark he made about another Jesuit, who would often write (very good) articles about the same topic. My friend walked into a room and said, "Oh, I see that *America* magazine published your article again!" When the assembled crowd laughed, my friend saw the other Jesuit's face crumple in embarrassment. It was then that he saw he had to be kinder.

That part of you—the mean part—is not what God wants for you. You realize that being kind is an enormous part of the Christian life—of any moral life. It does not comprise a complete moral system (at some point one has to look beyond just individual kindness and into larger social questions of justice), but it is an essential part of living a moral life. Being kind, which may sound banal, now takes on greater import.

You realize that you need to stop bad-mouthing people behind their backs, spreading negative stories about them; you need to be more patient when people are rude to you; you need to lend a helping hand more to your friends and family who are in need; you need to listen more; you need to be more attentive—to be, in a word, kind. It suddenly seems like the most important thing in the world. Your heart quickens when you think of changing. You *want* to change, as my Jesuit friend told me that he did.

You trust that God wants you to let that part of you go, once and for all. It *has* to go.

But there's a problem: you're not sure how to do it. The negative trait has been so much a part of you that it almost feels like giving up a limb. You wonder: What will my friends think if I suddenly become nicer? If I lose my famous sarcasm? For that matter, what will happen if I let down the armor that I've been using to protect myself? Like Lazarus you emerge, probably blinking in the sunlight of God's love.

Or perhaps your desire to change is not focused on a particular failing but is a more universal desire, something that affects almost every aspect of life.

Perhaps you feel that it's finally time to become an adult. You've been handling things for so long the way that you did when you were a child or an adolescent. Perhaps you react to difficult things the way a child would: with impatience, petulance, or simply a desire that those things would just go away. You often respond purely out of emotion: raging at people when they contradict you, sulking when you are criticized, and being resentful when things don't go your way, much as a small child would. Maybe you're tired of your childish attitudes and behaviors. It's the way you've always lived, but you want to change. You want to become more adult.

Or perhaps you shirk responsibilities, preferring to let others do the hard work in your family, among your friends, or on the job. In Ronald Rolheiser's superb book *Sacred Fire*, which lays out a spirituality for "Christian maturity," he speaks about the responsibilities of middle age. In this phase of life, you've made choices and commitments and carry "major responsibilities." In his vivid words, "We carry the car keys, the house keys, and the debt for both."[33]

Sacred Fire brought together much of what I had been thinking as I turned fifty, when for many people life can seem an endless round of responsibilities, work, and stress, especially after we have taken on the commitment of marriage or parenthood or even priesthood. Rolheiser says that this is the time when we are called to an adult embrace of even the "boredom, the longing for a second honeymoon, mid-life crisis, misunderstanding, disillusionment and numerous other things that eat away at our fidelity like rust on iron."[34]

In those times, says Rolheiser, "real life depends on staying the course." Many years ago, when I was in a time of discernment over a course of action, my brother Jesuit Daniel Berrigan wrote a letter to me reminding me that I was a Jesuit "for the long haul" and to make decisions with that in mind. Both he and Rolheiser were getting at the same thing: the need for fidelity, keeping promises and honoring commitments that you have made. This also means a certain amount of letting go of other possibilities. Every choice, as my current spiritual director says, is a renunciation of sorts.

Father Rolheiser poses a question that a gifted counselor might pose to an adult facing the temptation to walk away from the life of an adult: "What do you really want to do here?" He notes that this question works on three levels, but it is the last one "upon which life-giving decisions most often turn: What do I think is the *wisest thing to do* here? What would *I most like to do* here? What do *I have to do* here?" All these questions are part of the adult way of life, which you now feel invited to live.

To return to the image of Lazarus, you feel the call to come out of the tomb, to live in a new way, whether it's letting go of a particular habit, like being mean, or moving into a whole new way of approaching life, like being more of an adult. You feel it's an invitation from God to emerge from the tomb—and it is.

As you first emerge, it's natural to feel unsteady. You've been in the dark for so long that the light will seem strange. The tomb feels safe and the outside feels dangerous. Death feels like life and life feels like death. But this is a lie, one way that you are kept away from God. And the voice that says "You can't do this" or "You'll never get out of here" or "This isn't real" is not coming from God.

Then you take the first tentative step out of the tomb. You try to live as if you were free of your grave cloths. You curb your tongue and find that you're still alive. You try to be kind and find that it feels good. The mean thoughts and sarcastic quips come into your mind, but you are getting better at letting them die within you. Some days, inevitably, you fail.

This is when we are called to remember that we are not simply engaged in a self-improvement project, noble as that may be. Our change is also not simply something that we realized in therapy, as important as that is too. Nor is it simply something that randomly came up in our prayer, or that we read in a book, or that a trusted friend or spiritual adviser suggested. All these things are important in themselves. But something else is going on. We are responding to God's *call*. We know that God wants us to do this, wants us to change, and wants us to succeed.

But the process can be difficult. And it is then that we must remember *who* is calling us.

In our reflections on this Gospel passage, we may have downplayed something important: Lazarus's role. Now, I won't speculate on where Lazarus was during those four days—heaven, hell, purgatory, or some other place—which is unknowable this side of the grave.[35] All we know is that, as Jesus told the disciples emphatically, he was dead.

But after being called from that mysterious place, Lazarus must make a decision: to listen to Jesus's voice, to rise from the stone bed on which he lay, and to walk out covered with his grave cloths, wondering what will await him; or to remain inside his tomb.

Lazarus is not passive: he must act. Lazarus has a choice. So do we.

This is our call, as we try to move toward the light that is offered to us. And, like us, Lazarus can only "come forth" because he knows and trusts in the person who calls him. He not only hears the words coming from the entrance to his tomb, but he recognizes the distinctive voice, and trusts the person speaking to him.

This is our call as well: to remember who is saying to us, "Come forth!"

For Your Reflection

1. What does it mean for you to "come out" of the tomb? What parts of your life might this refer to?

2. Have you ever felt that you are "not enough"? What helps you to feel that you are, as the psalm says, "wonderfully made"?

3. How does "dying to self" relate to your own life? How does "rising" relate to your life?

4. Chiara told a lovely story about a change in perspective. Remember a time when a change in perspective helped you move ahead.

5. The two examples of change used here—wanting to be kinder and wanting to be more adult—are common among people. Where are you being invited to new life?

16

Unbind Him

Believing in the Promise of New Life

Jesus said to them, "Unbind him, and let him go."

One of the most arresting depictions of the Raising of Lazarus is a large sculpture at the University of Oxford in England. It is the work of Jacob Epstein, an American artist who eventually became a British citizen (and was knighted) and who was also the son of Polish Jewish refugees.

Epstein's larger-than-life-size *Lazarus* is tightly, almost mercilessly, bound in his burial cloths, having just emerged from his tomb in Bethany. The stone sculpture has jolted and intrigued visitors since its placement in the vestibule of New College Chapel in 1948. The former Soviet premier Nikita Khrushchev, after seeing it, said it was the kind of thing that kept him up at night (or caused him nightmares, depending on the source). Epstein's supposed response: "Why don't they stick to murder and leave art to us?"[1]

What caused the Soviet premier nightmares is unknown, though it may have been the bizarre posture of the raised man. Lazarus's hands are bound tightly against his hips, though his elbows flare out. From the front, the figure seems completely covered by his wrappings. Most arrestingly of all, Lazarus's head is twisted back (or forward) at an uncomfortable, dangerous, even impossible angle,

Lazarus, by Jacob Epstein
(University of Oxford).
COURTESY OF JOSEPH SIMMONS, SJ

with his chin touching his shoulder. It looks as if Jesus has forcibly "stood up" or "raised up" someone who moments before was lying down—which may have been the intent of the sculptor. His eyes are firmly closed, though the expressive face looks awake.

Perhaps Lazarus has just heard Jesus's voice calling him to new life: the head and ears are just beginning to turn toward him, the eyes about to open, but the body, used to death, is slow to follow. Perhaps his mind knows he is raised but the rest of him has yet to be convinced. Or perhaps he is reluctant to leave the tomb behind; in fact, it's difficult to tell which way the figure is facing—toward Jesus or toward the tomb?

In Epstein's hands, Lazarus is still bound: a butterfly still encased in its cocoon.

What was he thinking as he sat up from the stone slab? What was he thinking as he was still bound tightly with his grave cloths, as in Epstein's sculpture? What was he thinking as he perceived light through the cloth that covered his eyes?

We can imagine him stunned of course, knowing that he must now slowly make his way to the entrance of the tomb. A welter of feelings would have coursed through him as his heart began to pound and blood rushed back to his limbs. But I've always thought the most powerful of these feelings would be gratitude for Jesus's friendship after perhaps doubting that he cared at all.

Jesus came for me, he would have thought. *Jesus cares for me. Jesus loves me.*

Loosen Him

In John's Gospel, even after being raised from the dead, Lazarus isn't completely free. Something else must happen. His friends and family must help him. In case that isn't clear, Jesus tells them. The Greek is simple: *Lusate auton.* "Loosen him" or "unbind him." Then Jesus says, *aphete auton hypagein.* "Let him go."

As at the removal of the stone blocking the tomb, the people who gathered with Martha and Mary are not mere bystanders. No, Jesus asks them to *participate* in the giving of new life. Brendan Byrne says the community is asked to "remove the bonds of death" from Lazarus.[2] And, as we noted in the last chapter, the community is also implicitly asked to do something else: to recognize the meaning of this great sign—that is, to believe.

Jesus has accomplished several things, summed up by Francis Moloney.[3] The one who had declared himself to be the Resurrection and the Life has "intervened" in the life of all those gathered: "He has made the action of God visible in the lives of all who have participated in this event, not only Lazarus." And the transformation of Lazarus, for the writer of John's Gospel, is not even the main point. Jesus's action reveals the *doxa tou theou*, a complicated phrase meaning the "glory of God," but it also has connotations of "belief in God." Jesus has done this in order that Martha and Mary, as well as "the Jews" who accompanied them, might believe.

But Moloney notes something else: "The greater transformation would be acceptance on the part of all who witnessed the miracle that Jesus was the Son of the Father, the Sent One of God. . . . A remarkable sign has shown the glory of God . . . but the reader has yet to discover how the miracle of the raising of Lazarus will be the means by which the Son of God will be glorified."[4]

For now, however, the crowd and the sisters are asked to do something simpler: remove the man's wrappings and set him free.

Wes Howard-Brook notes that Lazarus's belief contrasts with whatever imperfect faith the sisters had professed. Lazarus trusts in Jesus completely, as evidenced by his listening and immediately coming forth from the tomb. Now all that needs to be done is the unbinding of the "wrappings of disbelief." It is for Jesus's followers to "undo the culture of death that leaves even the living bound."[5]

Let's look at this unbinding and how it might relate to our lives today, as we conclude our meditations on the greatest of Jesus's miracles.

Let Him Go

The image of the formerly dead man's sisters and friends gingerly removing the wrappings from Lazarus's face and body is a powerful one. Martha and Mary would have placed those cloths on his lifeless body just a few days before. Imagine what must have been going through *their* minds: *Is it really him?* Can this be happening? Will we hurt him? We've never taken burial cloths *off* before! What will happen to him now?

The same kinds of questions arise when we see someone who is metaphorically dying or dead—that is, when we see people who are still locked in their own tombs. Many of us have family or friends who are struggling with serious emotional problems: anger,

Jesus calls to his friend, Lazarus, to come out of the tomb.

John 11:1-44

Gift of Life, by John August Swanson.

negativity, arrogance, as well as unhealthy addictions. How can we help "unbind" them?

We can look to Lazarus's friends for some answers. We turn our attention from Jesus, Mary, and Martha to the friends and bystanders among them, perhaps even some doubters.

Lazarus's friends and family must have been thunderstruck by what they had seen. It's hard for me not to cast my mind back to that 1977 Franco Zeffirelli film *Jesus of Nazareth* and his depiction of the Raising of Lazarus, which still gives me goose bumps. As the figure of Lazarus, tightly bound in bandages, emerges from the dark cave in the side of a cliff, many in the crowd shrink back, in terror or awe, some sinking to their knees.

A case might be made that the disciples had already heard about or even witnessed the two other raisings from the dead. But even if some of the disciples had seen the Raising of Jairus's Daughter or the Son of the Widow of Nain, this was different. In the first case, it wasn't clear to the disciples that the little girl was dead. Jesus himself said that she was only sleeping. Jesus took her by the hand and said, "*Talitha koum*." ("Little girl, arise.")[6] It's a gentle, quiet tale that takes place in the privacy of someone's home, with only three of the disciples present.

As with most of the miracle narratives in the Synoptic Gospels, the evangelist records the reaction of the parents. They were "astounded." The Greek is *exestēsan*: her parents were "standing outside themselves," from which derives the term "ecstasy." In common parlance, they were "beside themselves."

The Raising of the Widow of Nain's Son is more public, with Jesus encountering the dead man during a presumably crowded funeral procession in the open air, his mother weeping over the dead body.[7] The loss of her son would have been not only emotionally but potentially financially devastating, as the widow might have depended on her son after her husband's death. Jesus approaches the bier and says, "Young man, I say to you, rise!" And he does. The crowd's reaction is also not muted. Luke describes it in detail: "Fear seized all of them; and they glorified God, saying, 'A great prophet has risen among us!' and 'God has looked favorably on his people!' This word about him [Jesus] spread throughout Judea and all the surrounding country."

We can see a progression in these three raisings, with Lazarus being the most dramatic. In the case of Jairus's daughter, the little girl is still at home, on her bed, still clothed, just recently deceased. The son of the widow of Nain has been taken from his house and dressed in burial cloths and therefore dead for some time, but he is not yet in the tomb.

Neither of these miracles is as dramatic as the Raising of Lazarus, who has been dead for several days, bound in his burial cloths, and shut away in a cold, dark tomb. Thus, the reaction of the crowd, though not described by John, must have been more intense. They must have found it nearly impossible to believe. As some people still do today.

It can be hard to accept that people grow, people can change, and people can cast off the things that have held them in bondage, the things that have kept them in the tomb. How are we to respond to the "resurrections" of those around us?

First, even in our doubt and amazement and fear, we need to trust that people can and do change, with God's help. Not trusting means not believing in the power of God to bring new life to someone.

What does this mean concretely? When someone tells you that they want to turn over a "new leaf in life" and become more generous, more forgiving, more loving, or less addicted to unhealthy patterns, try to *believe them.* Of course there are times when we must protect ourselves from people who consistently return to their addictions, and may even use or abuse us, but here I'm speaking of a person genuinely committed to change. When someone tells you that they are planning to begin a program to move past their addictions, to start therapy to confront an emotional problem, to start spiritual direction to help them get their life back on track, *believe them.* Even though you may, like the bystanders, find it hard to believe this is possible, give them the gift of your belief not only in them, but in what God can do in them.

Help to unbind them with your belief in them and in God's action in them. In this way you can help them to live new life.

Second, understand that you won't hurt them by helping them.

When my friend Kevin collected me from the hospital after the surgery a few years ago and drove me home, I was still in pain from the operation, and so when he helped me out of bed, he did so very gingerly; I could tell that he was worried about unintentionally hurting me. Worry can be a sign of love.

Those who removed Lazarus's bandages were probably worried that they would unintentionally cause him pain. Imagine the confusion they must have felt!

When our friends have changed, we might think that accepting them as new people will somehow do them damage, because they are "fooling themselves." They'll never be able to change, and so we fear that we will "enable" them. Especially if they have tried before and failed in their efforts, friends and family may not give them a second chance. But we can also hurt people by denying them the freedom to change.

Imagine a friend who tells you that she will be spending more time with the poor. You think, "She's never done anything like this before. If I encourage her, I'll just be hurting her. Someone's got to be honest with her." Instead, you might hurt her by not allowing her to grow.

Third, help them with gentleness and love.

Lazarus's friends probably removed those bandages carefully. In Richard Beard's novel *Lazarus Is Dead*, his sisters rush to unwrap him, their hands trembling as they feel his newly warm body. Later on, Lazarus enters a ritual bath, a *mikveh*, and watches as the remaining strips of linen "soak from his body."

There is an art to helping people who have changed: being patient with them, giving them room to question, encouraging them in their changes, even sticking with them if they return to their old ways. The help must be done carefully if the person, still unsteady, is to move on.

This is the meaning of the final words in the passage: *apheta auton hypagein.* They are usually translated as "Let him go free." But *hypagein* means "go" or "go away," and while "freedom" is implied, the main intent is for Lazarus to simply "go."

Elsewhere, that same word is used to describe Jesus's movement: "As he went, the crowds pressed in on him."[8] Or to record the men with leprosy going away after their healing: "And as they went, they were made clean."[9] Or with Jesus asking the Twelve, after some have left him, "Do you also wish to go away?"[10] *Hypagein* is used in all of these instances.

In each of them, there is freedom of movement. Jesus comes and goes as he pleases, with crowds trailing. The people suffering from leprosy are freed of their illness. And the disciples are free to stay or go. So although the verse simply means "to go," there is freedom. Lazarus too is now able to go. Released. Free.

Someone Untie Him

From the standpoint of Lazarus, he needed to *allow* others to help him off with his bandages. He had to let others care for him. This is sometimes more difficult than doing things for ourselves, even with God's help. Humility requires us to say, "I can't do this on my own."

Jacob Epstein's *Lazarus* is visibly incapable of removing his own bandages. His hands are still immobile, tightly bound to his hips and legs. If he tried to take one step, he would topple. In this, he evokes compassion. Lazarus needs help.

My Jesuit brother Eric Immel told me that this passage had affected him when he was going through "the hardest" year of his life during his Jesuit training. While on retreat, he realized something: "I had convinced myself that no one wanted me—not my students, not my co-workers, not my friends, not my family. I was utterly broken and saw no way out."

In response, his retreat director suggested that he pray with the Raising of Lazarus. Eric sat in a chapel, underneath a stained-glass depiction of the narrative in John's Gospel. After meditating on the characters in the story he realized that he could only be Lazarus, and so he imagined himself in the tomb, "abandoned, alone, empty."

Then in his prayer he imagined hearing the "grinding of the stone" as it was rolled away and the muffled tones of Jesus's voice. He was being called into new life by Jesus. To move away from the old wounds and the darkness.

But there was more. Even after Jesus had called Eric to new life, something else happened. I'll let him tell the rest of the story:

> Then, the voice again, unmuffled this time. "Someone untie him."
>
> Feet shuffled forward, and then two hands gently held my face. They worked around the back of my head. The cloth across my eyes and nose loosened, and then, warm air and bright sunlight hit my face. I opened my eyes, and met the eyes of another—smiling, deep brown eyes filled with tears. The

eyes of my co-worker Shannon. She said, as she always said, "I'm glad you're here."

Another stepped forward—my student Adriana—who set my arms free, and who wrapped me up in a bear hug. Then another student, Isaac, who unwrapped my legs and then, with a smirk, bent down and tied my shoe for me. "You don't want to trip," he said. A line of people came forward—my parents, my niece and nephew, brother and sister, friends, Jesuits, other co-workers and students—they all did their part in setting me free. *We need you,* they all said in their own ways. *We're with you.*

Finally, Jesus said, "It's time to go." And then, to me, "You coming?" And so I went—where else would I go?

We have to be willing to allow others to "unbind us," to help with the process that begins with God but also includes our friends and families. We must have the humility to allow others to help us, to let us go, to let us go free.

For Your Reflection

1. Francis Moloney notes that the "greater transformation" in this story would be "acceptance on the part of all who witnessed the miracle." John's Gospel often points to faith as the longed-for response to Jesus's "signs." What "signs" in your life have moved you to believe?

2. Why do you think John neglects to describe the reaction of the crowds?

3. We looked at three ways that we can help our friends who move toward change: by realizing that change is possible, by knowing that you won't hurt them if you help them to change, and by helping them gently and lovingly. Have you ever helped a friend or loved one change in these ways?

4. Who has helped to "unbind you" and "let you go free"?

5. Who have you helped to "unbind"?

17

Come Forth!

A Conclusion

What happened to Lazarus after he was raised from the dead? It's a question I'm often asked when I bring up my interest in this story. What happened to the recipient of Jesus's greatest miracle? Did he become a living example of Jesus's saving power? Did he live a long and happy life? Did he have children who passed along the story? Was his presence in Judea a tool for evangelization for years to come? Or are films like *The Last Temptation of Christ*, based on the Kazantzakis novel, which depict him being murdered by Jesus's opponents after the miracle, more accurate?

What can we know about Lazarus's fate?

The Gospel of John is spare, telling us only two things. First, at the conclusion of the Raising of Lazarus narrative, "the Jews" were planning to kill him. Second, in the following chapter, he is present at a meal with Jesus, along with Mary and Martha. The passage is brief:

> Six days before the Passover Jesus came to Bethany, the home of
> Lazarus, whom he had raised from the dead. There they gave a
> dinner for him. Martha served, and Lazarus was one of those at the
> table with him. Mary took a pound of costly perfume made of pure

The Raising of Lazarus, by Julius Spradley of
Contemplative Iconography.
COURTESY OF THE ARTIST

nard, anointed Jesus' feet, and wiped them with her hair. The house
was filled with the fragrance of the perfume.[1]

This is only a few days after Jesus raised Lazarus. In fact, the
nard may have been what remained after the sisters had anointed
Lazarus's body.

Interestingly, John Meier in *A Marginal Jew* suggests that the
dinner deepens our appreciation of Lazarus's being raised from the
dead: "The ordinary Palestinian life to which Lazarus is restored
is graphically represented by the feast at which both he and Jesus
recline." Being raised from the dead means being brought back to
the old life in which he had participated.[2]

But what happened then? Was he assassinated? The Gospels

are silent. But this is not surprising. Like the other evangelists, the writer of John's Gospel is more concerned with Jesus, not Lazarus, even if he were the Beloved Disciple.

At the end of John's Gospel, however, Peter asks the Risen Christ, "Lord, what about him?" (referring to the "disciple whom Jesus loved"). Jesus responds, "If it is my will that he remain until I come, what is that to you? Follow me!" John continues: "So the rumor spread in the community that this disciple would not die."[3]

As I mentioned earlier, this line has been suggested as a possible link between the Beloved Disciple and Lazarus. For how could the rumor that a disciple would "not die" be applied to anyone other than Lazarus? As Ben Witherington III has noted, it makes little sense to ask that question of, for example, a fellow fisherman from Galilee.

In that case, do we know much about the death of the Beloved Disciple? If Lazarus were the BD, what do we know about how his life ended?

"The conundrum is that the disciples of the Beloved Disciple assumed that since he had died once and then been raised by Jesus, surely he would not die a second time before the return of Christ," Witherington wrote to me. "But he did."

Witherington believes that the traditions that the BD went to Ephesus with Mary "probably have some basis." As we know, Jesus entrusted Mary to the Beloved Disciple at the Crucifixion. If the traditions about Mary dying in Ephesus are true, then it is reasonable to suppose that the Beloved Disciple traveled there with her and may have died there. But Witherington admits that things are "opaque" and the evidence "piecemeal."

Francis Moloney had another answer to the question. He wrote me in an email: "There is no clear response to this question. The question of how and when the Beloved Disciple died is complicated by the fact that we do not know for sure who the BD was."

For the record, Father Moloney is skeptical about claims identifying Lazarus as the Beloved Disciple, and he believes that the BD is more an anonymous figure with which readers can identify. It is more of a literary device, he said: "The use of anonymity means, in essence, everyone can do it."

Prescinding the question of whether Lazarus was the Beloved Disciple, Moloney believes that Lazarus did indeed come to a "violent end," as he put it. He sees the comments about "the Jews" planning to kill him as written by the author after the event had happened for a community that knew this had indeed happened. "By the time the Fourth Gospel appeared," Moloney continued, "Lazarus had already been put to death as well. The narrative takes that for granted."

It's a fascinating answer to what I thought was the unanswerable question of Lazarus's fate, and I was happy when Father Moloney fleshed things out. He began with the reminder that in the New Testament, as in much literature, both ancient and contemporary, the story of the hero is being written much later than the time of the actual events. John's Gospel is written about AD 100 but tells the story of a life that was lived in the early 30s. The same is the case with the Synoptics, which were written from roughly 65 to 90.

"Things have happened to characters in the story *from a later period* known to the storyteller," Moloney wrote. "She or he is able to tell the story, *prophesying* that certain things would happen, certain of the truth of the prophecy, as the author *knows* that they have happened."

Scholars call this a *vaticinium ex eventu*: a prophecy put on the lips of a character, or a comment from the narrator (as in John 12:9–11, the passage about "the Jews" killing Lazarus), based upon the knowledge of what happened later. The clearest examples are Jesus's predictions of his own death, said Father Moloney. "Jesus would have never said what is reported in Mark 10:32–34, where he goes into some detail about his trial."

He continued: "I am confident that Jesus spoke of his death but did not 'foretell' his trials and the passion in all its details. His original prophecy (in terms of the Son of Man) has grown in the

Christian storytelling traditions in the light of *what actually happened at a later time*, thus producing Mark 10:32–34."

All this leads to Father Moloney's scholarly conclusion about Lazarus's fate: "I am suggesting that the same literary practice is present in John 12:9–11. Jesus's enemies decide that both Jesus and Lazarus had to die because of the amazement and wonder generated by the spectacular miracle of the Raising of Lazarus."

Why does John's Gospel report this?

"The most likely answer," Moloney said, "is that John's audience knew that Lazarus had been slain by Jesus's enemies. If not, then John's narrative comment is wrong, and the 'truth' of the Gospel can be questioned. . . . I do not suggest that this is 'knock-down proof' that Lazarus was killed by Jesus's enemies (as in *The Last Temptation of Christ*), but it points strongly in that direction."

So we don't know for sure. We don't have "knock-down proof," and the evidence is "opaque." And the death of Lazarus is not mentioned in John's Gospel or in any of the three Synoptics.

Amy-Jill Levine wonders, however, if the author of John's Gospel wrote this passage to reinforce his point that "the Jews" are evil. "Had 'the Jews' really killed him," AJ wrote, "why not note it?" She continued: "We choose how to read, and this choice includes how much we want to vilify 'the Jews' and how much we think John wants to vilify them."

The Facts and the Legends

In an email exchange, Ben Witherington wondered whether there were signs of Lazarus's legacy even in Luke's Gospel. Luke notes that after the Resurrection, Jesus led the disciples back to Bethany, in Judea, from which point he ascended to heaven. "Now of course," wrote Witherington, "Bethany is at the bottom of the slope called the Mount of Olives. I wondered if perhaps Jesus did this to join up the Galilean disciples with the Judean ones led by the Beloved Disciple and his family."

That prompted what he called a "further aha." He recalled chapters 14 through 17 in the Gospel of John, where Jesus repeatedly says that he must return to the Father—return, that is, to heaven so that he can send the Holy Spirit to the disciples.

Witherington asked: "Is the reason that Luke and the Fourth Gospel are the only ones that really mention the Ascension because of this finish in Bethany, the home of the Beloved Disciple and his family? Or is it in order to have his mother Mary incorporated into the fellowship with all these disciples, both Galilean and Judean, because the Beloved Disciple had taken her back to his house in Bethany?" Still later in Acts 1:14 we find Mary and at least some of her family together with the disciples in the Upper Room awaiting Pentecost.

Did Jesus return to Bethany, the home of Lazarus, to unite the Judean and Galilean disciples and pay tribute to the Beloved Disciple? Was it to "incorporate" Mary, now in the Beloved Disciple's care, into the body of the disciples, the group that now constitutes the early church? Witherington's "aha" points out possible connections between Bethany, the Beloved Disciple, Lazarus, and Mary.

It's another tantalizing theory. But since the Gospels are silent on the matter, we'll never know for certain what happened to Lazarus.

As a result of the uncertainty, multiple legends grew around what happened to Lazarus after being raised from the dead. If he were the Beloved Disciple, he would have been present at the Crucifixion. And his being raised from the dead was one of the factors, at least in John's Gospel, that led to his death. William Barclay notes that even Palm Sunday, which marks Jesus's triumphant entry into Jerusalem, may have a connection with Lazarus. It might be argued that, without the miracle in nearby Bethany, the adulation he receives from the crowds is "inexplicable."[4] Then again, the crowds wanted to make Jesus king all the way back in John 6.

But what happens to Lazarus after the Crucifixion and Resurrection? In an Eastern tradition, Lazarus is supposed to have fled from his home in Judea, fearful of plots against his life. He ends up in Cyprus, where he is appointed by Saints Paul and Barnabas as the first bishop of Kition, the present-day city of Larnaca. There he is supposed to have died for a second time. According to tradition, his tomb was lost and then rediscovered in AD 890 bearing the inscription, "Lazarus, four days dead, friend of Jesus."

His remains were transferred to Constantinople (present-day Istanbul) by the Byzantine emperor Leo VI. (These remains were reportedly looted in the thirteenth century by Frankish soldiers and taken to Marseille.) To compensate the people of Larnaca for the transfer of these precious relics, Leo built the imposing Church of St. Lazarus, or Agios Lazaros, over the saint's tomb, which still stands. Today, according to Richard Beard, the ceremonial chairs reserved for bishops, near the main altar of every church in Larnaca, bear the image not of Jesus but of Lazarus.[5]

One travel guide for Larnaca describes some of the local traditions surrounding Lazarus. After being raised from the dead, he developed the reputation for being "something of a curmudgeon" who never smiled, on account of the horrors he had seen during his time with the dead. Also, he is responsible for creating the salt lakes around which the town is now built, after cursing a local vineyard owner for not providing him with wine. He is supposed to have lived for thirty years before his (second) death.[6]

In 1972, during a renovation of the Church of St. Lazarus in Larnaca, some human remains were discovered in a marble sarcophagus located under the altar. The authorities announced them to be relics of Lazarus. In 2012, the church gave a portion of the relics to a delegation of the Russian Orthodox Church led by Patriarch Kirill of Moscow and All Russia, then on a four-day visit to Cyprus. Later, the relics were sent to a convent in Moscow, where they are venerated today. According to the Orthodox scholar Sister Vassa Larin, however, the monastery was probably named not after Lazarus of Bethany but after the founder of the monastery, the Venerable Ephrosin of Pskov, who was named Eleazar before becoming a monk.

Church of St. Lazarus, Larnaca, Cyprus.
WIKICOMMONS

As we've mentioned, in many Orthodox churches today, Lazarus Saturday is celebrated on the day before Palm Sunday. On that day, by tradition, hermits would leave their hermitages in the wilderness to return to the monastery for Holy Week services. And the sweetened pastries called *lazarakia*, or "Little Lazaruses," may have originated in Cyprus. In some parts of Greece "Lazarine carols" are sung on that day.

In the West, the tradition was quite different. Lazarus, along with his sisters, was supposedly cast into a boat without oars and a rudder and ended up in Marseille. His relics followed a circuitous route until they arrived at Autun, where today the great Cathedral of St.-Lazare stands. In Marseille, then, the Eastern and Western traditions about St. Lazarus meet up, with varying degrees of historicity.

The conclusion of New Testament scholars like Father Moloney and others conflicts with cultural traditions about Lazarus in the East and West, which also conflict with one another. Lazarus's historical fate remains unclear.

Lazarus's Fate in Art

This lack of secure evidence has given poets, novelists, and screen-writers free rein to imagine what happened to Lazarus after he was raised from the dead.

Nikos Kazantzakis's *The Last Temptation of Christ* describes the resurrected man in vivid terms, all of which bespeak death. After being raised, he stank terribly, and for some days afterward his sisters cleaned him of the small earthworms that still clung to him from the grave. Grass was tangled in his hair and beard. Neighbors would visit him to ask about the afterlife, which he would answer with a laconic yes or no. Later on, light bothered him; his arms, legs, and stomach were swollen; his face was bloated and exuded a liquid that made the burial shroud stick to his skin (Lazarus had never removed the shroud, despite Jesus saying, "Unbind him").

The novel follows the hints of the New Testament that Lazarus eventually was murdered. So does Martin Scorsese's film. On the day of the Last Supper, Lazarus meets Barabbas, the brigand who would later be freed on Good Friday instead of Jesus. Barabbas asks Lazarus which is better, death or life? "Six of one, half dozen of the other," says Lazarus blandly. Then Barabbas grabs him by the throat and is horrified that his fingers go in and out of the flesh, which is "like air," and draw no blood. Before tearing his scalp off and wrenching his arms from his body, Barabbas shouts in terror, "Are you a ghost?" It's a gruesome scene.

In the film, Lazarus is murdered by Saul, before he becomes Paul. The film preserves the novel's strange interchange:

Saul: How do you feel?
Lazarus: I like the light.
Saul: What was it like? Which is better: death or life?
Lazarus: I was a little surprised . . . wasn't that much difference.

Saul then asks for Lazarus's hand and stabs him.

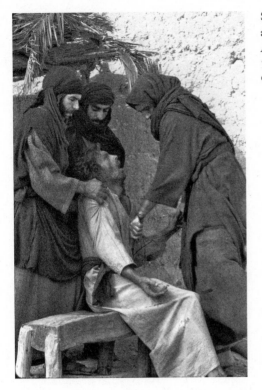

Saul (Harry Dean Stanton) assassinates Lazarus (Tomas Arana) in Martin Scorsese's *The Last Temptation of Christ.*
COURTESY OF UNIVERSAL STUDIOS

Barabbas and Lazarus have another fictional encounter in Pär Lagerkvist's novel *Barabbas*, later made into a movie, in 1961, starring Anthony Quinn. In this retelling the disciples bring the newly raised man to Barabbas as a way of enabling Barabbas to believe. Lazarus is described as having a face that "looks like a desert," sallow, parched, desolate; he passes his food at the table with "dry, yellow fingers." Jesus's disciples regularly send people to Bethany to meet with Lazarus, to be converted, and many are. This was Lazarus's way of repaying the "great debt" of having been brought back to life. But despite many entreaties, Lazarus does not speak of death. Even when, as in Kazantzakis's novel, Barabbas asks him directly.

"I have experienced nothing," says Lazarus. "I have merely been dead. And death is nothing." The character may be alluding to a line from the Book of Qoheleth (or Ecclesiastes), "The dead know nothing."[7]

In Richard Zimler's *The Gospel According to Lazarus*, the raised man is an eyewitness to the crucifixion of Jesus, which makes sense. His raising would have been only a few days before Jesus's death and so it stands to reason that Lazarus would have witnessed the Passion and Death of his friend. In fact, the description of the Crucifixion in this novel, told from the point of view of Lazarus, may be the most powerful imagining of that scene that I have ever read, since it is written from the point of view of someone Jesus loved—indeed, of *hon phileis*.

In the novel, written as a letter to Lazarus's grandson, the two men have known each another since boyhood. As a young man, Lazarus had once saved Jesus from drowning during an accident. Now he must watch his friend die:

> Yeshua's head has fallen forward, his chin against his chest, and his breathing is unsure. I imagine him in darkness, his soul gazing up, then down, no longer knowing which way leads towards life and which towards death. Blood is seeping from his right heel, which has just been nailed to the side of his upright, and the executioner, who kneels by Yeshua's left foot, has just raised his hammer again.
>
> At the first crack of bone, I hear a scream louder than any I have ever heard before, but it is not from Yeshua.
>
> "Stop!" I shriek again, and I keep crying it over and over.[8]

In Zimler's book, Lazarus escapes murder by Jesus's opponents, but hunted, he must flee. His combative sister Martha (here portrayed as a termagant) has betrayed both Jesus and Lazarus and their sister Mary. So he leaves Bethany with his children and ends up plying his trade as a mosaicist on the island of Rhodes. There he writes his testimony to his grandson.

And in Bill Cain's recent *The Diary of Jesus Christ*, an imagined memoir, Jesus asks Lazarus to attend to him at his own death, and even to call out Jesus's name at the tomb.

Come to Believe

We would all love to know what happened to Lazarus. And if we could speak to him, we would be filled with questions: Why did your sisters describe you to Jesus as "he whom you love"? Were you his best friend? Did you know him as a boy? Are you the Beloved Disciple? Were you angry when Jesus failed to appear before you died? Did he ever explain why he did that? Or, as the fictional Saul asks Lazarus in Martin Scorsese's movie, "What was it like?"

But on this side of heaven, we will probably never know answers to such questions. Nor will we know how he died, the second time.

For the believer in Jesus as Lord, however, less important than where Lazarus's life ended (Bethany or Marseille or Ephesus) or how he died (killed by Jesus's opponents, stabbed by Saul, beheaded under Diocletian, died peacefully after time with Mary) was the world-changing gift of life he received from Jesus. On that day at Bethany, he was freed from the bonds of death, allowed to "go free."

But not just for himself. Lazarus's freedom was a gift given to the entire community.

Jesus freed Lazarus from the bonds of death. He restored him to life, to his sisters, and to his friends. He did this for his beloved friend, perhaps even his Beloved Disciple. But it was not simply a gift for Lazarus. It was a gift for all those around him, a sign, a *semeion*, to reveal the identity of Jesus to the assembled crowds, to help them "come to believe."

This may make the story of Lazarus seem like something meaningful only to those in the crowd that day in Bethany, with little connection to our own lives. I hope this book has shown that this is not the case. The message of the Raising of Lazarus is as relevant to pilgrims in twenty-first-century Al Eizariya as it was to Jesus's disciples in first-century Bethany. It is as meaningful to a young executive in New York City today as it was to a peasant farmer from Galilee in the time of Christ.

Like Lazarus, the message of that story is revivified every time

Entrance to the Tomb of
Lazarus. Here you can see
the narrow entranceway
to the inner tomb through
which pilgrims must crawl.
COURTESY OF YAMID
CASTIBLANCO, SJ

someone reads or hears it. Lazarus at the entrance to his tomb stands
as an invitation to all of us who feel that our lives are over, who feel
that there is no hope, who think that things are dead. Lazarus, too,
says, "Come forth!"

Come Forth!

All of us come before God unfree in some way. All of us have things
that we need to let die to follow God more freely, to love more deeply,
and to become the people God desires us to be. And God has an
intense desire to free us, to offer us new life.

How can we know this? Freedom is the constant desire of
God for humanity throughout both the Old and New Testaments,

throughout what theologians call salvation history. In the Old Testament, God leads the people of Israel out of slavery into freedom, continually willing their freedom, always asking them to choose freedom. "I have set before you life and death, blessings and curses. Choose life so that you and your descendants may live."[9] And in the New Testament the constant movement of Jesus is freeing people: from sin, from illness, from isolation, from despair, and from darkness.

In fact, the first words out of Jesus's mouth as he announces the beginning of his public ministry in the synagogue of his hometown Nazareth are about freedom. Before his fellow townspeople, he utters his programmatic message about his ministry. "The Spirit of the Lord is upon me," he says in the synagogue at Nazareth. "He has sent me to proclaim release to the captives and recovery of sight to the blind, to let the oppressed go free."[10]

Freedom rings through Jesus's public ministry like a bell. And he excoriates those who oppose this opening freedom that leads to the flourishing of human beings. When Jesus heals a woman who has been physically "bent over" for eighteen years, he doesn't say, "You are healed," but "You are set free from your ailment." The word used is *apolelysai*, from the same Greek root that Jesus uses in his words to Lazarus: "*Lusate auton.*" Be loosed, be untied, be freed.

Jesus's desire to free people runs through his public ministry until it reaches its ultimate climax in his untying Lazarus from the bonds of death. And at Jesus's Resurrection the Father would free the Son from his own bonds of death. We cannot doubt God's desire to free us from our burdens, our tombs, our grave cloths, to give us new life.

The Gospel story of the Raising of Lazarus initially may have seemed far removed from your experience. But I hope now you can see how it invites you to freedom, and how the new life that was given to Lazarus is being offered to you.

God will call to us in those words every day of our lives, until we hear him say on the final day, when we will make the journey from darkness into eternal light: *Come forth!*

For Your Reflection

1. At the beginning of the book, I asked, "Who is Lazarus for you?" Now that we have journeyed together through his story, along with Martha and Mary and Jesus, who is Lazarus for you?
2. What has to "die" in the tomb for you to live?
3. What enables you to hear God's voice calling you to new life?
4. Who has helped you move into the new ways that God has in store for you?
5. How can you help others out of their tombs?

"Come Forth!," by William Hart McNichols.
COURTESY OF THE ARTIST

Acknowledgments

As I was writing *Jesus: A Pilgrimage*, the then-editor of *America*, Drew Christiansen, SJ, who was also scholar of Jewish-Christian relations, told me that I had to go to the Holy Land. I demurred, thinking that a trip would ruin my pristine mental images of the Holy Land. Drew continued to push, saying that I couldn't write about Jesus without having visited where he lived. He was right, and since then I've been back several times on pilgrimages—and each time I have visited Al Eizariya. So the first note of thanks is to Drew, for encouraging me all those years ago. Sadly, he died as this book was being written.

Next, I thank all the New Testament scholars mentioned in this book whose work has helped me understand more deeply the story of Lazarus. For me, there are few things more exciting than coming upon an insight that unlocks a Bible story in a new way. Several corresponded with me and answered questions about Lazarus during the writing of this book. I thank in particular Amy-Jill Levine; Ben Witherington III; Brendan Byrne, SJ; Francis Moloney, SDB; and Michael Peppard. Each of them also took the time to review the final manuscript and made many helpful corrections, suggestions, and additions, some of which are repeated verbatim in the book.

I also thank my Jesuit community at America House in New York

City, who accompanied me as this book was being written, largely during the COVID pandemic between 2020 and 2023. During those long dark months, we cooked for one another, cleaned the house with one another, celebrated Mass together, and tried to keep one another reasonably sane. While we were doing this and mourning those Jesuits who had died and praying for all those other millions of deaths and even more illnesses, I was thinking about Jesus raising Lazarus from the dead after Lazarus's own illness and his sisters' intense grief.

Thanks to the many pilgrims who have joined me and my fellow Jesuits and colleagues at America Media on several pilgrimages to the Holy Land and who have carefully made their way down the steps into Lazarus's tomb every year and shared their spiritual experiences with me afterward. Thanks to Scott Scherer of Catholic Travel Centre for arranging for some amazing photos of Al Eizariya, the Church of St. Lazarus, and Lazarus's tomb; as well as two Jesuits, Yamid Castiblanco, SJ, and Daniel Cuesta, SJ, who took photos in Al Eizariya; and Joseph Simmons, SJ, who took photos of the Jacob Epstein sculpture in Oxford.

Thanks also to the artists who created original works of art for this book: the Rev. William Hart McNichols, Kristen Wheeler, and Julian Spradley, as well as to the artists, or their estates or representatives, who gave permission to reproduce their work: Ruben Ferreira, Kelly Latimore, Bodhan Piasecki, John August Swanson, and the Rev. John Giuliani.

Thanks to Donald Cutler, my longtime literary agent, who passed away as I was writing this book. Don was my agent for many years, and, having been an Episcopal priest for a time, he was always attentive to the theological matters in my books. He helped me enormously both professionally and personally, and I miss him a great deal. My new agent, Roger Freet, was greatly helpful in carrying this new book to completion.

Thanks to my longtime and favorite editor Vinita Wright, who always makes my books immeasurably clearer, tighter—better. Thanks to Heidi Hill for her indefatigable and truly remarkable fact-checking and to Joseph McAuley at America Media for helping to input so many of the changes into the increasing numbers of manuscripts.

Thanks also to the team at HarperOne for their support over the years, and with this book in particular: Mickey Maudlin, Courtney Nobile, Chantal Tom, Katy Hamilton, Laina Adler, Adrian Morgan, Lisa Zuniga, Terri Leonard, Jessie Dolch, Natalie Blachere, Yvonne Chan, Tanya Fox, Nancy Singer, Stephen Brayda, Ann Edwards, and Makenna Holford.

Finally, and most of all, thanks to God, who makes all things possible.

Notes

Chapter 1: Al Eizariya

1. In the Temple Scroll that was found among the ancient manuscripts (often called the Dead Sea Scrolls) discovered at Qumran, an archaeological site discovered in Israel in the twentieth century, three villages three thousand cubits east of the Jerusalem Temple are mentioned. (The Dead Sea Scrolls date roughly from the third century BC to the first century AD.) In his book *The Beloved Disciple: Whose Witness Validates the Gospel of John?* (Valley Forge, PA: Trinity Press International, 1995), James Charlesworth quotes from this Temple Scroll (11QTemple 46.16–18): "And you shall make three places towards the east of the city [Jerusalem], separate from one another, into which the lepers shall come" (185). See also B. J. Capper, "The Essene Religious Order of Ancient Judaea and the Origins of Johannine Christianity," *Qumran Chronicle* 22, nos. 1–4 (2014): 39–71.
2. Jerome Murphy-O'Connor, *The Holy Land: An Oxford Archaeological Guide* (Oxford: Oxford Univ. Press, 2008), 152.
3. *Egeria: Diary of a Pilgrimage* (Mahwah, NJ: Paulist Press, 1970), 102.
4. Quoted in Linda Seidel, *Legends in Limestone: Lazarus, Gislebertus, and the Cathedral at Autun* (Chicago: Univ. of Chicago Press, 1999), 44.
5. C. H. Dodd, *The Interpretation of the Fourth Gospel* (Cambridge: Cambridge Univ. Press, 1953), 363.

Chapter 2: A Certain Man

1. William Butler Yeats, *Calvary*, Digireads.com Publishing, 2011, 10.
2. Moving from science fiction to science, when damaged particle detectors—for example, at CERN, the European Organization for Nuclear Research—are supercooled, they can regain their previous effectiveness. Scientists call this the "Lazarus effect."

3. The Greek word used, *tis*, is probably better translated as "someone" rather than "certain man"; so, "Now someone was ill . . ."

4. Mark 5:1–18.

5. The idea that Jesus may not have known their names raises the question of Jesus's two "natures," human and divine, as well as his human and divine consciousness. Christian belief (which I share) is that Jesus is fully human and fully divine. The theological conundrum, however, is this: As a human being with a human consciousness, Jesus can know only what he learns (including someone's name). As someone with a divine consciousness, he would have known everything (including the names of those he healed). We'll treat the question of Jesus's natures and his consciousness in chapter 9.

6. Amy-Jill Levine graciously answered many of my questions about Lazarus, Martha and Mary, and the Jewish milieu of the time, often communicating via email. In instances when I don't include a note for her comments, I'm quoting from those more informal communications.

7. John P. Meier, *A Marginal Jew: Rethinking the Historical Jesus*, vol. 2, *Mentor, Message, and Miracles* (New York: Doubleday, 1994), 882.

8. Raymond E. Brown, *An Introduction to the Gospel of John*, ed. Francis J. Moloney (New Haven: Yale Univ. Press, 2003), 215.

9. Mary ("Miriam" in Hebrew, "Mariam" in Greek), for example, is the name of the sister of Moses and can also mean "drop of the sea," "bitter," "rebellious," or "beloved." The name may also be related to Mariamne, King Herod the Great's Hasmonean wife. Martha ("Martha" in Greek as well) is from the Aramaic "Marta," meaning "the lady" or "mistress," as in the mistress of the house. And, as we have seen, Lazarus means "God has helped."

10. Meier, *Marginal Jew*, 774.

11. Meier, *Marginal Jew*, 774.

12. Meier, *Marginal Jew*, 774.

13. Brendan Byrne, *Lazarus: A Contemporary Reading of John 11:1–46* (Collegeville, MN: Liturgical Press, 1990), 69–83.

14. Byrne, *Lazarus*, 70.

15. Meier, *Marginal Jew*, 805.

16. Byrne, *Lazarus*, 73.

17. I apologize to those who find the term "lepros" offensive. Simon is referred to in the Gospels as *Simōn ho lepros*. At the time, the word could refer to someone who had one of a variety of skin ailments.

18. Luke 10:41–42.

19. Byrne, *Lazarus*, 74.

20. Luke 16:19–31.

21. Byrne, *Lazarus*, 76.

22. Meier, *Marginal Jew*, 825.

23. Byrne, *Lazarus*, 81.

24. Meier, *Marginal Jew*, 830.

25. Luke 7:11–17.

26. Mark 5:21–43; Matt. 9:18–26; Luke 8:40–56.

27. Mark 5:41.

28. Mark 7:31–37.

29. Other examples: Jesus's words on the cross, *"Eloi, Eloi, lama [sabachtani]"* (interestingly, a mix of Aramaic and Hebrew); Jesus's use of the name "Mariam," and Mary Magdalene's response, *"Rabbouni,"* on Easter Sunday, as well as Jesus's calling the Father "Abba."

30. Matt. 11:3.

31. Matt. 11:4–6; cf. Luke 7:22–23.

32. In 1 Kings 17:17–24, Elijah raises a widow's son; in 2 Kings 4:18–37, Elisha raises the Shunammite's son; and in 2 Kings 13:21, a dead man is revived when his body is thrown into a grave with Elisha's bones.

33. Meier, *Marginal Jew*, 831.

34. Byrne, *Lazarus*, 81.

35. Meier, *Marginal Jew*, 831.

36. Daniel J. Harrington, *Meeting St. John Today: Understanding the Man, His Mission, and His Message* (Chicago: Loyola Press, 2011), 9.

37. Meier, *Marginal Jew*, 773.

38. Meier, *Marginal Jew*, 837.

Chapter 3: He Whom You Love

1. Ken Shulman, "A Tintoretto Reappears in Rural Pennsylvania," *New York Times*, July 23, 2000, section 2, p. 29; Franco Mormando, "Lazarus Raised Again: A Tintoretto Masterpiece Is Found at a Jesuit Residence in Pennsylvania," *America*, February 13, 1999.

2. Mormando, "Lazarus Raised Again," 11–13.

3. Gerhard Lohfink, *Jesus of Nazareth: What He Wanted, Who He Was* (Collegeville, MN: Liturgical Press, 2015), 92.

4. Bargil Pixner, *With Jesus in Jerusalem: His First and Last Days in Judea* (Israel: Corazin Publishing, 1992), 56.

5. Lohfink, *Jesus of Nazareth*, 92.

6. St. Augustine, *Tractates on the Gospel of John* 29.

7. Brendan Byrne, *Come to the Light: Reflections on the Gospel of John* (Collegeville, MN: Liturgical Press, 2021), 66.

8. Max Lucado, *You Are Never Alone* (Nashville, TN: Thomas Nelson, 2020), 83.

9. Luke 10:40.

10. Lohfink, *Jesus of Nazareth*, 67.

11. For more on Jesus's sense of humor and the residues of this in the Gospels, see my book *Between Heaven and Mirth: Why Joy, Humor, and Laughter Are at the Heart of the Spiritual Life* (New York: HarperOne, 2011).

12. John 15:15.

13. Bill Cain, *The Diary of Jesus Christ* (Maryknoll, NY: Orbis Books, 2021), 161–62.

14. Today the ruins of Sepphoris reveal a prosperous town of perhaps thirty thousand people, with wide, paved streets; a royal fortress; an amphitheater that could seat four thousand people; and even the ruins of a "mosaic store," where various patterns were displayed on the floor for avid customers.

15. The term *tetrarch*, applied to Herod Antipas, comes from the Latin word meaning "ruler of a quarter." After the death of King Herod the Great in 4 BC, his kingdom was divided four ways among his sons, Herod Archelaus, Herod Antipas, and Philip, and briefly his sister Salome.

16. Richard Zimler, *The Gospel According to Lazarus* (London: Peter Owen Publishers, 2019), 114–15.

17. Zimler, *The Gospel According to Lazarus*, 115.

18. Colm Tóibín, *The Testament of Mary* (New York: Scribner, 2012), 21.

19. Raymond E. Brown, *An Introduction to the Gospel of John*, ed. Francis J. Moloney (New Haven: Yale Univ. Press), 195.

20. Raymond E. Brown, *The Gospel According to John I–XIII*, Anchor Bible Series 29 (New York: Doubleday, 1981), xciv–xcviii.

21. Martin Hengel, *The Johannine Question* (London: SCM, 1990), 124.

22. Ben Witherington was gracious enough to communicate with me through emails and conversations. In instances where I provide no note, I am quoting from one of those emails or conversations.

23. Mark 10:38.

24. In that same email, Witherington explained these arguments against
    John, the son of Zebedee, as the source of the Fourth Gospel: "There is
    a *P. Oxy* papyrus [*Papyri Oxyrhynchus*, a group of ancient manuscripts]
    that indicates that John Zebedee, like his brother, was martyred early
    on and could not have produced this Gospel late in the first century
    [the usual date attributed to it]. And, besides, Jesus predicted the
    martyrdom of the Zebedees: they were to receive a 'baptism' like his
    (Mk. 10:35–45)."

25. John 19:25–27.

26. James H. Charlesworth, *The Beloved Disciple: Whose Witness Validates
    the Gospel of John?* (Valley Forge, PA: Trinity Press, 1995), 189.

27. Byrne, *Come to the Light*, 66.

28. Quotations from Ben Witherington about the Beloved Disciple are
    taken from a presentation he made to the Society of Biblical Literature,
    "The Historical Figure of the Beloved Disciple in the Fourth Gospel,"
    later published as "What's in a Name? Rethinking the Historical Figure
    of the Beloved Disciple in the Fourth Gospel," in *John, Jesus, and
    History*, vol. 2, *Aspects of Historicity in the Fourth Gospel*, ed. Paul N.
    Anderson, Felix Just, and Tom Thatcher (Atlanta: Society of Biblical
    Literature, 2009), 203–12. Witherington takes up these same questions
    in his fascinating book *What Have They Done with Jesus? Beyond
    Strange Theories and Bad History—Why We Can Trust the Bible* (New
    York: HarperOne, 2006).

29. John 18:15.

30. Amy-Jill Levine, however, doubts this connection, pointing out that
    Caiaphas was not a Pharisee and the Pharisees were not close to the
    priesthood.

31. John 20:3–4.

32. John 20:8.

33. Mark W. G. Stibbe, *John as Storyteller: Narrative Criticism and the
    Fourth Gospel* (Cambridge: Cambridge Univ. Press, 1994), 80.

34. John P. Meier, *A Marginal Jew: Rethinking the Historical Jesus*, vol. 2,
    Mentor, Message, and Miracles (New York: Doubleday, 1994), 839.

35. James H. Charlesworth, quoting W. H. Brownlee in *The Beloved
    Disciple: Whose Witness Validates the Gospel of John?* (Valley Forge, PA:
    Trinity Press International), 190.

36. Luke 1:26–38.

37. Luke 1:36.

38. John 19:27.

39. Charlesworth, *Beloved Disciple.* Charlesworth is summarizing the scholarship here of J.-M. Léonard in "Notule sur l'Évangile de Jean: le disciple que Jésus aimait et Marie," *Études Théologiques et Religieuses* 58 (1993): 355–57.

40. John 21:22.

41. John 21:23.

42. Stibbe, *John as Storyteller,* 80.

43. In his book *John as Storyteller,* Stibbe also includes a lengthy analysis of why he believes that the Beloved Disciple is not John, the son of Zebedee (pp. 77–80).

44. Brown, *Gospel According to John I–XII,* xcv.

45. Brown, *Gospel According to John I–XII,* xcv.

46. Isa. 43:19.

47. Henri J. M. Nouwen, *Life of the Beloved: Spiritual Living in a Secular World* (New York: Crossroad, 1992), 31–32.

48. Henri J. M. Nouwen, *You Are the Beloved: Daily Meditations for Spiritual Living* (New York: Convergent, 2017), 4.

49. A spiritual director is a professionally trained person who helps another person see where God is active in their prayer and daily life. During a retreat the same person might be called a "retreat director."

50. Henri J. M. Nouwen, *Beyond the Mirror: Reflections on Death and Life* (New York: Crossroad, 2001), 55.

51. Luke 10:17. Some early manuscripts have seventy disciples, not seventy-two.

52. Rom. 16:7; 1 Cor. 15:7.

53. Helpful in understanding this is Jonathan Potter, "Apostles vs. Disciples," Bible Odyssey, https://www.bibleodyssey.org:443/tools /ask-a-scholar/apostles-vs-disciples.

54. Luke 10:37.

55. Sandra Schneiders, *Written That You May Believe: Encountering Jesus in the Fourth Gospel* (New York: Crossroad, 2003), 188–96.

56. John 13:15–17. My italics.

Chapter 4: Jesus Loved Martha and Her Sister

1. Luke 10:38–42.

2. Elizabeth Schrader, "Was Martha of Bethany Added to the Fourth Gospel in the Second Century?" *Harvard Theological Review* 110, no. 32 (2017): 360–92.

3. Eric Ferreri, "Mary or Martha? A Duke Scholar's Research Finds Mary Magdalene Downplayed by New Testament Scribes," *Duke Today*, June 18, 2019, https://today.duke.edu/2019/06/mary-or-martha-duke -scholars-research-finds-mary-magdalene-downplayed-new-testament -scribes.

4. Schrader, "Was Martha of Bethany Added?"

5. For a longer introduction to the examination of conscience (its aims, background, and methods) see my books *The Jesuit Guide to (Almost) Everything: A Spirituality for Real Life* (San Francisco: HarperOne, 2010) and *Learning to Pray: A Guide for Everyone* (San Francisco: HarperOne, 2021).

6. George Ganss, ed., *The Spiritual Exercises of St. Ignatius Loyola* (Chicago: Loyola Press, 1992), 121, no. 315.

7. Luke 10:40.

8. Matt. 8:23–27; Mark 4:35–41; and Luke 8:22–25.

9. Mark 4:38.

10. Matt. 8:25.

11. Matt. 16:22.

12. Mark 10:37; Matt. 20:21.

13. Job 10:1.

14. William A. Barry, *A Friendship like No Other: Experiencing God's Amazing Embrace* (Chicago: Loyola Press, 2008), 133.

15. I speak more about this in my book *Learning to Pray*.

16. William A. Barry, "'I Have a Dream,' Says God, 'Join Me,'" unpublished manuscript, 16.

17. Luke 10:38.

18. David Marcombe, *Leper Knights: The Order of St. Lazarus of Jerusalem in England, c. 1150–1544* (Suffolk: Boydell Press, 2004), xviii.

19. Marcombe, *Leper Knights*, 15.

20. The Military and Hospitaller Order of Saint Lazarus of Jerusalem, http://ordersaintlazarususa.com/.

21. John 12:1–8.

22. Mark 14:3–9.

23. Elisabeth Schüssler Fiorenza, *In Memory of Her: A Feminist Theological Reconstruction of Christian Origins* (New York: Crossroads, 1994).

24. Matt. 26:6–13.

25. Luke 7:37–38.

26. Luke 7:48.

27. Sandra Schneiders, *Written That You May Believe: Encountering Jesus in the Fourth Gospel* (New York: Crossroad, 2003), 106–10.

28. Acts 6:1–6.

29. Schneiders, 100–1.

Chapter 5: Two Days Longer

1. Richard Zimler, *The Gospel According to Lazarus* (London: Peter Owen Publishers, 2019), 26.

2. Philip Schaff, ed., *Nicene and Post-Nicene Fathers*, vol. 14, *St. John Chrysostom: Homilies on the Gospel of St. John and the Epistle to the Hebrews* (New York: Cosmo Classics, 2007), 227.

3. Raymond E. Brown, *The Gospel According to John I–XIII*, Anchor Bible Series 29 (New York: Doubleday, 1981), 431.

4. Peter Chrysologus, Sermon 63, PL 52, 375–77.

5. Francis J. Moloney, *The Gospel of John*, Sacra Pagina 4 (Collegeville, MN: Liturgical Press, 1998), 326.

6. John 2:4. For those who doubt the sharpness of his answer, it's important to note that the words that a demon uses when shouting at Jesus (*ti hēmin kai soi*: literally, "What to us and to you?") in Luke 4 are the same words Jesus uses with his mother at the Wedding Feast at Cana (*ti emoi kai soi*). Admittedly, we don't know the tone (or the original Aramaic), but they are not the gentlest of words. Francis Moloney writes: "There have been many attempts to soften this retort, but whatever one makes of it, it is not the type of response one would expect from a son to a mother. . . . Some element of harshness cannot be eliminated from these words" (*The Gospel of John*, Sacra Pagina 4 [Collegeville, MN: Liturgical Press, 1998], 67, 71).

   Raymond Brown writes: "In the OT [Old Testament], the Hebrew expression has two shades of meaning (a) when one party is unjustly bothering another, the injured party may say 'What to me and to you?' i.e. What have I done to you that you should do this to me? What subject of discord is there between us? (Judges xi 12; II Chronicles xxxv 21; II Kings xvii 18); (b) when someone is asked to get involved in a matter which he feels is no business of his, he may say to the petitioner 'What to me and to you?' i.e. That is your business; how am I involved? (II Kings iii 13; Hosea 14:8). Thus there is always some refusal of an inopportune involvement, and a divergence between the views of the two persons concerned; yet (*a*) implies hostility while (*b*) implies simple disengagement. Both shades appear in NT usage; (*a*) appears when the demons reply to Jesus (Mark i:24; v:7); seemingly (*b*) appears here. It is interesting, however, that some Greek Fathers interpret John ii 4 in sense (*a*) and think it a rebuke to Mary" (*The Gospel According to John I–XII*, Anchor Bible series 29 [Garden City: New York, 1966], 99).

7. Francis J. Moloney, "'Can Everyone Be Wrong?' A Reading of John 11:1–12:8," *New Testament Studies* 49, no. 4 (2003): 505–27, 511.

8. Colm Tóibín, *The Testament of Mary* (New York: Scribner, 2012), 24.

9. John P. Meier, *A Marginal Jew: Rethinking the Historical Jesus*, vol. 2, *Mentor, Message, and Miracles* (New York: Doubleday, 1994), 799. Meier also points out that the number of "signs" in John is fluid, depending on which New Testament scholar is counting them. Some make much of seven distinct signs, but Meier suggests that the evangelist's "blasé attitude" toward the exact number of signs may make one wonder whether the number seven was all that important to the writer of the Fourth Gospel.

10. We need to be cautious here, as elsewhere in John, with negative images of "the Jews" in terms of the "money changers" (see chapter 6 for more on "the Jews"). As Amy-Jill Levine said to me, "The point of the Temple incident is not economic, or exploitation of the poor. The Synoptic concern is a 'den of thieves,' where sinners feel safe. John's concern, which involves anyone buying or selling, is that all of Jerusalem should be holy." And of course most Christian churches today, including Catholic ones, take up collections during Mass and promote fundraising drives for parishes and dioceses and so on.

11. Stanley Marrow, *The Gospel of John: A Reading* (Mahwah, NJ: Paulist Press, 1995), 181.

12. Raymond Brown, *An Introduction to the Gospel of John*, ed. Francis J. Moloney (New Haven: Yale Univ. Press, 2003), 102. Brown offers a complex and subtle analysis of the connections between the Synoptics and John in his chapter 3.

13. Mark 4:3–9.

14. John 17:21–24.

15. Mark 7:27; 3:21.

16. Alexander Schmemann, "Saturday of Lazarus," schmemann.org/byhim/lazarussaturday.html.

17. Elizabeth Johnson, *Creation and the Cross: The Mercy of God for a Planet in Peril* (Maryknoll, NY: Orbis Books, 2018), 183.

18. 2 Cor. 12:10.

19. "The Romero Prayer," Archbishop Romero Trust, http://www.romerotrust.org.uk/romero-prayer.

Chapter 6: Let Us Go to Judea Again

1. After World War II, Pope Pius XII, in response to criticism (and in the wake of the Holocaust), said that the Latin *perfidus* meant "unbelieving" or "faithless," not "treacherous" or "dangerous." But all the possible translations were awful. In 1959 Pope John XXIII ordered the word removed from the Good Friday liturgy.

2. "Declaration on the Relation of the Church to Non-Christian Religions, *Nostra Aetate*, Proclaimed by His Holiness Pope Paul VI on October 28, 1965," https://www.vatican.va/archive/hist_councils/ii_vatican _council/documents/vat-ii_decl_19651028_nostra-aetate_en.html.

3. "Prayer of the Holy Father at the Western Wall," Jubilee Pilgrimage of His Holiness John Paul II to the Holy Land (March 20–26, 2000), https://www.vatican.va/content/john-paul-ii/en/travels/2000 /documents/hf_jp-ii_spe_20000326_jerusalem-prayer.html.

4. It is also important to note what had been done positively in that arena: Pope Pius XI declared anti-Semitism a sin in his 1937 encyclical *Mit brennender Sorge* and ordered it read from all the Catholic pulpits in Germany. It was the first time that Nazi racist policies were publicly condemned, incurring Nazi fury at the pope and the Catholic Church.

5. John 4:9.

6. Raymond Brown, *An Introduction to the Gospel of John*, ed. Francis J. Moloney (New Haven: Yale Univ. Press, 2003), 157.

7. In her book *The Pharisees*, co-edited with Joseph Sievers (Grand Rapids, MI: Eerdmans, 2021), Levine makes the point that the Gospels began the process of lumping all these groups together, which culminates in John, where we find the undifferentiated "the Jews."

8. On the Pharisees, see Sievers and Levine, *Pharisees*. The volume includes a contribution by Pope Francis, in which he cautions against using the term "Pharisees" as a stereotypical negative exemplar.

9. Brown, *Introduction to the Gospel of John*, 171.

10. Another Jewish scholar, Adele Reinhartz, a former president of the Society of Biblical Literature, addresses this question in her book *Cast Out of the Covenant: Jews and Anti-Judaism in the Gospel of John* (Lanham, MD: Lexington Books/Fortress Academic, 2018).

11. Brown, *Introduction to the Gospel of John*, 172.

12. Raymond Brown writes: "In order to alert hearers/readers to John's peculiar understanding and that he is not thinking of all those who in the first century were Jews by birth, in commenting on hostile passages I have written 'the Jews' with quotation marks. I would maintain strongly that although the designation 'the Jews' should not be eliminated if one wishes to understand John's mentality, it should be carefully explained" (*Introduction to the Gospel of John*, 167).

13. John P. Meier, *A Marginal Jew: Rethinking the Historical Jesus*, vol. 2, *Mentor, Message, and Miracles* (New York: Doubleday, 1994), 807, 864.

14. Brown, *Introduction to the Gospel of John*, 168.

Chapter 7: So That You May Believe

1. Matt. 7:7–8.

2. Luke 11:11–13.

3. Paul J. McCarren, *A Simple Guide to John* (Lanham, MD: Rowman & Littlefield, 2013), 90.

4. Luke 9:60; Luke 17:6; Matt. 13:44.

5. Mark 8:27–29.

6. See Brendan Byrne, *Life Abounding: A Recording of John's Gospel* (Collegeville, MN: Liturgical Press, 2014), 187.

7. John 9:4–5.

8. John Dear, *Lazarus, Come Forth! How Jesus Confronts the Culture of Death and Invites Us into a New Life of Peace* (Maryknoll, NY: Orbis Books, 2011), 42.

9. John P. Meier, *A Marginal Jew: Rethinking the Historical Jesus*, vol. 2, *Mentor, Message, and Miracles* (New York: Doubleday, 1994), 844.

10. St. Paul uses this in 1 Thess. 5, in what may be the earliest New Testament text.

11. Byrne, *Life Abounding*, 187.

12. C. H. Dodd, *The Interpretation of the Fourth Gospel* (Cambridge: Cambridge Univ. Press, 1953), 367.

13. Mark 4:11–12.

14. Matt. 13:13.

15. John C. Haughey, *Housing Heaven's Fire: The Challenge of Holiness* (Chicago: Loyola Press, 2002), 85.

16. Luke 2:52.

17. Jer. 18:4.

18. Jer. 29:11.

19. Elizabeth Johnson, *Consider Jesus: Waves of Renewal in Christology* (New York: Continuum Books, 1992), 42.

Chapter 8: If You Had Been Here

1. John Dear, *Lazarus, Come Forth! How Jesus Confronts the Culture of Death and Invites Us into a New Life of Peace* (Maryknoll, NY: Orbis Books, 2011), 59.

2. Daniel J. Harrington, *Meeting St. John Today: Understanding the Man, His Mission, and His Message* (Chicago: Loyola Press, 2011), 55. Also, *Accompanying Them with Singing: The Christian Funeral* (Louisville: Westminster John Knox, 2009), by Thomas G. Long, is a fascinating book that discusses funeral practices in Jesus's time.

3. Brendan Byrne, *Come to the Light: Reflections on the Gospel of John* (Collegeville, MN: Liturgical Press: 2021), 67.

4. Stanley Marrow, *The Gospel of John: A Reading* (Mahwah, NJ: Paulist Press, 1993), 186.

5. *Homilies of St. John Chrysostom*, Homily 62; John 11:21.

6. John P. Meier, *A Marginal Jew: Rethinking the Historical Jesus*, vol. 2, *Mentor, Message, and Miracles* (New York: Doubleday, 1994), 810.

7. I discuss the practice of "Ignatian contemplation" in *The Jesuit Guide to (Almost) Everything: A Spirituality for Real Life* (San Francisco: HarperOne, 2010) and, in more detail, in *Learning to Pray: A Guide for Everyone* (San Francisco: HarperOne, 2021).

8. Luke 5:4.

9. Mark 4:38.

Chapter 9: You Are the Messiah, the Son of God

1. Don Denny, "The Last Judgment Tympanum at Autun: Its Sources and Meaning," *Speculum* 57, no. 3 (1982): 532–47.

2. The story of the Cathedral of St. Lazarus in Autun is told brilliantly in

Linda Seidel's book *Legends in Limestone: Lazarus, Gislebertus, and the Cathedral at Autun* (Chicago: Univ. of Chicago Press, 1999), 7.

3. Marian Bleeke, "The Eve Fragment from Autun and the Emotionalism of Pilgrimage," in *Crying in the Middle Ages: Tears of History*, ed. Elina Gertsman (New York: Routledge, 2013), 27–28.

4. Neil Stratford, quoted in Seidel's *Legends in Limestone*, 43.

5. Francis J. Moloney, *Signs and Shadows: Reading John 5–12* (Minneapolis: Fortress, 1966), 161.

6. John P. Meier, *A Marginal Jew: Rethinking the Historical Jesus*, vol. 2, *Mentor, Message, and Miracles* (New York: Doubleday, 1994), 811.

7. John Dear, *Lazarus, Come Forth! How Jesus Confronts the Culture of Death and Invites Us into a New Life of Peace* (Maryknoll, NY: Orbis Books, 2011), 3–4.

8. Wes Howard-Brook, *John's Gospel and the Renewal of the Church* (Maryknoll, NY: Orbis Books, 1997), 77.

9. Brendan Byrne, *Come to the Light: Reflections on the Gospel of John* (Collegeville, MN: Liturgical Press, 2021), 68.

10. John 8:57–58.

11. Exod. 3:14.

12. John 10:30.

13. Mark 8:27–30; Matt. 16:13–20; Luke 9:18–20.

14. Ben Witherington offered a fascinating take on the reason for that specific location: "One of the places I love to take people is Caesarea Philippi, and the proper question to be asked is why in the world did Jesus take his disciples all the way there to raise the question of his identity? If you go there, you discover this was originally the Greek city of Panyas or Banyas, and the cave of Pan was there in the cliff, from which flowed a stream. More importantly, there in the cliff wall were niches with statues of pagan deities, all of whom were seen as 'sons of God' in some sense. And, most recently, in Jesus's own time, there was a temple of Augustus with the beginnings of the imperial cult, where the emperor himself was worshipped as a god. So why in the world would Jesus go there to reveal his identity? Well, he could point to the statues and the temple and say, 'These are the parodies of which I am the reality.'

"But there is another interesting aspect to this site. The cave was seen as an entrance way into the underworld, Hades. If Jesus indeed said 'On this rock I will build my assembly/community and the gates of Hades will not prevail against it,' what he is talking about is not Gehenna or hell, he is talking about the land of the dead. In other words, it's a promise that his community founded on rock will never die out. We could debate what or who the rock is, but my point is that the setting of this dramatic confessional scene where Jesus's identity is made clear, and Peter's and the other disciples' commission is also made clear, is crucial to understanding this passage. A text without a context is just a pretext for whatever we want it to mean, and this story has a dramatic pagan context."

15. Matt. 8:27.

16. Aquinas's view, however, does not appear in more contemporary church documents like the work of the International Theological Commission in their rich meditation on the topic, *The Consciousness of Christ Concerning Himself and His Mission*, published in 1985.

17. N. T. Wright, "The Biblical Formation of a Doctrine of Christ," in *Who Do You Say That I Am? Christology and the Church* (Grand Rapids: Eerdmans, 1999), 47–68, esp. 64–65.

18. Luke 2:19.

19. F. J. Sheed, *To Know Christ Jesus* (New York: Sheed & Ward, 1962), 127.

20. Mark 5:25–34.

21. Krister Stendahl, "The Apostle Paul and the Introspective Self-Consciousness of the West," *Harvard Theological Review* 5, no. 4 (1963).

22. Elizabeth Johnson, *Consider Jesus: Waves of Renewal in Christology* (New York: Continuum Books, 1992), 42.

23. Some of this discussion appears in a shorter form in my book *Jesus: A Pilgrimage* (San Francisco: HarperOne, 2014).

24. John 1:40–41.

25. Ellis Winward and Michael Soule write in *The Limits of Mortality* (Ecco Press; Hopewell, NJ, 1993) that a human being can survive at most thirty days without food and water and be conscious for no more than twenty-five.

26. William Barclay, *The Gospel of Matthew, The New Daily Study Bible* (Louisville: Westminster John Knox, 2001), 76. "Its source must be Jesus himself."

27. Johannes Baptist Metz, *Poverty of Spirit* (Mahwah, NJ: Paulist Press, 1998), 3.

28. John 2:1–12.

29. See chapter 9, note 14.

30. Mark 9:31; cf. Matt. 17:22–23.

31. Luke 9:22.

32. Mark 15:34; Matt. 27:46.

33. Johnson, *Consider Jesus*, 42.

34. Matt. 8:27.

35. Matt. 16:16.

36. Raymond Brown, *An Introduction to the Gospel of John*, ed. Francis J. Moloney (New Haven: Yale Univ. Press, 2003), 160.

37. John 20:31.

38. Amy-Jill Levine, *The Misunderstood Jew: The Church and the Scandal of the Jewish Jesus* (San Francisco: HarperOne, 2006), 127.

39. Levine, *The Misunderstood Jew*, 127.

40. John 17:1.

41. Matt. 3:13–17; Mark 1:9–11; Luke 3:21–22.

42. Mark 14:36.

43. Gal. 4:6.

44. Some have translated "Abba" as "Daddy," although many contemporary scholars dispute that translation. Georg Schelbert, of the University of Fribourg, critiqued the reading of "Daddy" in a 1981 essay and then later in a 2011 book-length treatment titled *ABBA Vater* (in German). He claims that this translation is in "error" and "unwarranted." He writes: "In the Aramaic language of the time of Jesus, there was absolutely no other word [than Abba] available if Jesus wished to speak of or address God as father" (my translation). Top scholars still disagree on this. Amy-Jill Levine notes that Joachim Jeremias, the eminent biblical scholar who originally proposed "Daddy" in the 1970s, later recanted his views, so "we've known for decades" that, as the biblical scholar James Barr wrote in an article in the *Journal of Theological Studies*, "Abba isn't 'Daddy.'" On the other hand, Ben Witherington says, "It's false to say that Jews had no other way to address God than Abba. Of course they had 'Ab,' and 'Abi,' which we find in the Old Testament. Furthermore, Abba was a term of intimacy used by children of their father, and disciples of their teacher. So it had a mundane sense as well. While 'Abba' is not slang for 'Daddy,' in the mouth of a child it does mean 'Father dearest,' and there were other ways to address both a human father and God."

45. Exod. 4:22.

46. Luke 3:23–38.

47. 2 Sam. 7:14–17.

48. Mark 12:18.

49. Levine, *The Misunderstood Jew*, 58.

50. Brendan Byrne, *Lazarus: A Contemporary Reading of John 11:1–46* (Collegeville, MN: Liturgical Press, 1991), 50.

51. Byrne, *Lazarus*, 52.

52. Byrne, *Lazarus*, 52.

53. John 6:51.

54. John 14:2.

55. Rom. 8:38–39.

56. Luke 4:16–30; Matt. 13:54–58; Mark 6:1–6.

57. To be clear, I meant that the words came into my mind very clearly during prayer, not that I heard them audibly.

Chapter 10: When She Heard It

1. Wes Howard-Brook, *John's Gospel and the Renewal of the Church* (Maryknoll, NY: Orbis Books, 1997), 80–81.

2. Ps. 27:14.

3. John 20:19.

4. C. H. Dodd, *The Parables of the Kingdom* (New York: Charles Scribner's Sons, 1961), 5.

5. "My yoke is easy" may also be drawing on his carpentry background. At the time, only the most talented *tektōn* would be able to make a yoke that was "easy," or would fit to the team of oxen.

6. Mark 4:26–29.

7. Mark 4:27.

8. Matt. 13:24. In fact, the Greek is plural: the kingdom/reign of heavens. As Amy-Jill Levine and Marc Zvi Brettler explain in their book *The Bible With and Without Jesus: How Jews and Christians Read the Same Stories Differently* (San Francisco: HarperOne, 2020), for ancient Jews and for Jews of New Testament times, there were, surprising as it may seem to us, "multiple heavens" (81).

9. Matt. 13:29–30.

10. Matt. 13:37–39.

11. The connection between Congressman John Lewis and this parable came from a homily by Joseph Parkes, SJ.

12. Katharine Q. Seelye, "John Lewis, Towering Figure of Civil Rights Era, Dies at 80," *New York Times*, July 17, 2020, https://www.nytimes .com/2020/07/17/us/john-lewis-dead.html.

13. Associated Press, "Civil Rights Veteran Is Honored in Selma," *New York Times*, March 9, 1998, https://www.nytimes.com/1998/03/09/us /civil-rights-veteran-is-honored-in-selma.html.

14. John Lewis, "Forgiving George Wallace," September 16, 1998, *New York Times*, https://archive.nytimes.com/www.nytimes.com/library /opinion/lewis/091698lewi.html.

15. William Yardley, "Elwin Wilson, Who Apologized for Racist Acts, Dies at 76," *New York Times*, April 1, 2013, https://www.nytimes .com/2013/04/02/us/elwin-wilson-who-apologized-for-racist-acts -dies-at-76.html.

Chapter 11: She Knelt at His Feet

1. Francis J. Moloney, "Can Everyone Be Wrong? A Reading of John 11:1–12:8," *New Testament Studies* 49, no. 4 (2003): 505–27.

2. Francis J. Moloney, *The Gospel of John*, Sacra Pagina 4 (Collegeville, MN: Liturgical Press, 1998), 219.

3. Moloney's examples: "Nathanael replied, 'Rabbi, you are the Son of God! You are the King of Israel!" (John 1:49); "When the people saw the sign that he had done, they began to say, 'This is indeed the prophet who is to come into the world'" (John 6:14). Both Nathanael, who bases his confession on Jesus's seeming to know what Nathanael had just been doing—sitting under a fig tree—and the "people," who simply respond to his miracle, are set forth as people with incomplete understanding. Moloney wonders whether we are to see Martha in this light as well. On the other hand, what more should they have been able to understand, given the information that they had? Can anyone in John understand unless Jesus allows them to?

4. Francis J. Moloney, *Signs and Shadows: Reading John 5–12* (Minneapolis: Fortress, 1996), 165.

Chapter 12: See How He Loved Him

1. Paul McCarren, *A Simple Guide to John* (Lanham, MD: Rowman & Littlefield, 2013), 93.

2. St. John Chrysostom, *Homilies on the Gospel of John*, Homily 62.

3. The Greek *dokein* means "to seem" or "to appear."

4. John 1:29–39.

5. John 1:29.

6. Wes Howard-Brook, *John's Gospel and the Renewal of the Church* (Maryknoll, NY: Orbis Books, 1997), 255.

7. The noun *dakryōn* appears in Heb. 5:7, "significantly," as Francis Moloney notes, in the passage on Jesus's "cries and tears."

8. Brendan Byrne, *Lazarus: A Contemporary Reading of John 11:1–46* (Collegeville, MN: Liturgical Press, 1991), 59.

9. William Barclay, *The New Daily Study Bible*, vol. 2, *The Gospel of John* (Louisville: Westminster John Knox, 2001), 113: "In ordinary classical Greek the usual usage of *ebrimisthai* is of a horse snorting."

10. Raymond Brown, *The Gospel According to John I–XII*, Anchor Bible series 29 (New York: Doubleday, 1966), 425.

11. Francis J. Moloney, *Signs and Shadows: Reading John 5–12* (Minneapolis: Fortress, 1996), 167.

12. Moloney, *Signs and Shadows*, 167; Byrne, *Lazarus*, 58.

13. John Dear, *Lazarus, Come Forth! How Jesus Confronts the Culture of Death and Invites Us into a New Life of Peace* (Maryknoll, NY: Orbis Books, 2011), 71.

14. John P. Meier, *A Marginal Jew: Rethinking the Historical Jesus*, vol. 2, *Mentor, Message, and Miracles* (New York: Doubleday, 1994), 815.

15. John 12:27.

16. John 13:21.

17. Moloney, *Signs and Shadows*, 167.

18. Brown, *Gospel According to John*, 426.

19. Byrne, *Lazarus*, 59.

20. Brendan Byrne, *Come to the Light: Reflections on the Gospel of John* (Collegeville, MN: Liturgical Press, 2021), 69.

21. Luke 12:25.

22. Brown, *Gospel According to John*, 426.

Chapter 13: Take Away the Stone

1. Brendan Byrne, *Lazarus: A Contemporary Reading of John 11:1–46* (Collegeville, MN: Liturgical Press, 1991), 61.

2. See Urban C. von Wahlde, "Biblical Views: A Rolling Stone That Was Hard to Roll," *Biblical Archaeology Review* 41, no. 2 (2015).

3. John 5:1–8.

4. William Barclay, *The New Daily Study Bible*, vol. 2, *The Gospel of John* (Louisville: Westminster John Knox, 2001), 210.

5. Francis J. Moloney, *The Gospel of John*, Sacra Pagina 4 (Collegeville, MN: Liturgical Press, 1998), 171–72.

6. Jodi Magness, *Stone and Dung, Oil and Spit: Jewish Daily Life in the Time of Jesus* (Grand Rapids: Eerdmans, 2011), 146–60.

7. Byrne, *Lazarus*, 61.

8. Richard Beard (*Lazarus Is Dead: A Novel* [New York: Europa Editions, 2012], 60) quotes one medieval "mystery play" from 1451 where the line is rendered: "He stynkygh ryght fowle long tyme or this."

9. Beard, *Lazarus Is Dead*, 60.

10. Beard, *Lazarus Is Dead*, 60.

11. Raymond E. Brown, *The Gospel According to John I–XII: A New Translation with Introduction and Commentary*, Anchor Yale Bible 29 (New York: Doubleday, 1966), 426.

12. John Dear, *Lazarus, Come Forth! How Jesus Confronts the Culture of Death and Invites Us into a New Life of Peace* (Maryknoll, NY: Orbis Books, 2011).

13. Beard, *Lazarus Is Dead*, 121.

14. Francis J. Moloney, *Signs and Shadows: Reading John 5–12* (Minneapolis: Fortress, 1996), 170.

15. Luke 10:40.

16. For more about relics, see James Martin, ed., *Awake My Soul: Contemporary Catholics on Traditional Devotions* (Chicago: Loyola Press, 2004).

17. Luke 1:26–38.

18. Luke 1:36.

19. 1 Cor. 13:12.

20. St. Augustine, *Homilies on the Gospel of John* (Hyde Park, NY: New City Press, 2009), 121.

21. Joanna Weaver, *Lazarus Awakening: Finding Your Place in the Heart of God* (New York: Waterbrook Press, 2012), 85–100.

Chapter 14: Father, I Thank You

1. Luke 5:16; John 14:13.

2. Mark 6:47–48.

3. Luke 11:1.

4. Daniel J. Harrington, *Jesus and Prayer: What the New Testament Teaches Us* (Frederick, MD: Word Among Us Press, 2009), 49.

5. Brendan Byrne, *Lazarus: A Contemporary Reading of John 11:1–46* (Collegeville, MN: Liturgical Press, 1991), 63.

6. Matt. 11:25–27.

7. Harrington, *Jesus and Prayer*, 47.

8. John 10:30.

9. Stanley Marrow, *The Gospel of John: A Reading* (Mahwah, NJ: Paulist Press, 1993), 195.

10. Karl Rahner, "The Prayer of Need," ch. 5 in *The Need and the Blessing of Prayer*, trans. Bruce W. Gillette (Collegeville, MN: Liturgical Press, 1997), 56. In an interview with *America* in 1979, the great theologian said that he felt his book on prayer was "for me at least just as important as more scholarly matters—even though it was 'only' a devotional book" ("Living into the Mystery: Karl Rahner's Reflections at 75," *America*, March 10, 1979, 177–80).

11. Mark 14:36.

12. Luke 22:42.

Chapter 15: Lazarus, Come Out!

1. Alexander Schmemann, *The Christian Way*, http://www.schmemann.org/byhim/lazarussaturday.html.

2. Magness is looking at practices of the Qumran community or sect, and she wonders if the presence of so many rock-cut tombs among the wealthy in Jerusalem "suggest[s] that they may not have considered this type of enclosed space as equivalent to a corpse-impure house or tent." Still, the Jewish rules about the impurity of the corpse and the Qumran practices suggest a general taboo around gravesites. *Stone and Dung, Oil and Spit: Jewish Daily Life in the Time of Jesus* (Grand Rapids: Eerdmans, 2011), 161.

3. Mark 15:37.

4. John 5:25.

5. "Behold, I am standing by thee. I am thy Lord; thou art the work of My hands. Why has thou not known Me, because in the beginning I Myself formed Adam from the earth and gave him breath? Open thy mouth thyself in order that I may give thee breath." "The Resurrection of

Lazarus," homily attributed to St. Athanasius, trans. Joseph Buchanan Bernardin, *American Journal of Semitic Languages and Literatures* 57, no. 3 (1940): 262–90.

6. Brendan Byrne, *Come to the Light: Reflections on the Gospel of John* (Collegeville, MN: Liturgical Press, 2021), 65.

7. Byrne, *Come to the Light*, 70.

8. Raymond Brown, *The Gospel According to John I–XII*, Anchor Bible series 29 (New York: Doubleday, 1966), 427.

9. Francis J. Moloney (*The Gospel of John*, Sacra Pagina 4 [Collegeville, MN: Liturgical Press, 1998]) writes, "There is no need to raise the problem of how a person so bound would be able to walk, as do [Hoskyns and Bultmann]. . . . They suggest that we have a 'miracle within a miracle' (Hoskyns)" (342).

10. Colm Tóibín, *The Testament of Mary* (New York: Scribner, 2012), 26.

11. Mark Gevisser, *The Pink Line: Journeys Across the World's Queer Frontiers* (New York: Picador, 2021), 65–66.

12. Stephanie Langston, "Bedford County Parents Grieve Son Bullied Before Suicide," WKRN.com, last updated December 3, 2021, https://www.wkrn.com/news/local-news/bedford-county-parents -grieve-son-bullied-before-suicide/.

13. Exod. 20:4.

14. "Father G: Thought of the Day," YouTube: Homeboy Industries, April 17, 2013, https://youtu.be/dbSoMOkVe8s.

15. Ps. 139:13.

16. Ps. 139:14.

17. Ps. 8:4–5.

18. Matt. 22:39.

19. *Summa Theologica*, II–II, q. 25, a. 4. St. Thomas also writes, "The love with which a man loves himself is the form and root of friendship. For if we have friendship with others, it is because we do unto them as we do unto ourselves, hence we read in Ethic. ix, 4,8, that 'the origin of friendly relations with others lies in our relations to ourselves'" (Matt. 22:39).

20. George Ganss, ed., *The Spiritual Exercises of St. Ignatius Loyola* (Chicago: Loyola Press, 1992), no. 236.

21. Mark 8:34; Matt. 16:24; Luke 9:23.

22. Daniel J. Harrington, *The Gospel of Matthew*, Sacra Pagina 1 (Collegeville, MN: Liturgical Press, 1991), 151.

23. *The New Jerome Biblical Commentary*, The Gospel According to Matthew, Benedict T. Viviano, OP, 660.

24. Luke 22:42. Ben Witherington in an email again pointed out the difference between Jesus's temptations and ours, reminding us that even though his temptations intersect with ours, as they do during his time in the Judean desert, they are nonetheless unique: "As for the temptation at Gethsemane, what sort of person is tempted to avoid saving humanity by dying on a cross? The cup referred to is surely the one mentioned in the Old Testament—the cup of God's wrath poured out on sin. Again, the temptation to avoid the cross is not in this case a normal temptation."

25. The documentary, *The Social Dilemma* (2020), addresses this phenomenon at length.

26. Raymond Brown, *Gospel According to John I–XII*, 437.

27. Matt. 8:27.

28. John P. Meier, *A Marginal Jew: Rethinking the Historical Jesus*, vol. 2, *Mentor, Message, and Miracles* (New York: Doubleday, 1994), 799.

29. Meier, *A Marginal Jew*, 798.

30. John 11:45–46.

31. John 12:9–11.

32. Byrne, *Come to the Light*, 71.

33. Ronald Rolheiser, *Sacred Fire: A Vision for a Deeper Human and Christian Maturity* (New York: Image Books, 2014), 76.

34. Rolheiser, *Sacred Fire*, 108–9.

35. Many writers have speculated on where Lazarus was in this time. In his book *You Are Never Alone*, Max Lucado writes, "Lazarus did not want to go back to earth. Of that I'm certain. But when Jesus commands, his disciples obey. Of that Lazarus was certain. So his spirit descended from the heavens and down through the skies until he reached the Bethany Burial Garden. He reentered and reanimated his body. He stood up and lumbered toward the mouth of the tomb." Max Lucado, *You Are Never Alone* (Nashville, TN: Thomas Nelson, 2020), 88.

Chapter 16: Unbind Him

1. *Oxford Essential Quotations*, 5th ed., Oxford Reference, published online in 2017, https://www.oxfordreference.com/view/10.1093/acref/9780191843730.001.0001/q-oro-ed5-00012237?rskey=b0kVUs&result=1241.

2. Brendan Byrne, *Lazarus: A Contemporary Reading of John 11:1–46* (Collegeville, MN: Liturgical Press, 1991), 65.

3. Francis J. Moloney, *The Gospel of John*, Sacra Pagina 4 (Collegeville, MN: Liturgical Press, 1998), 333.

4. Francis J. Moloney, *Signs and Shadows: Reading John 5–12* (Minneapolis: Fortress, 1996), 173.

5. Wes Howard-Brook, *John's Gospel and the Renewal of the Church* (Maryknoll, NY: Orbis Books, 1997), 84.

6. Luke 8:40–42, 49–56.

7. Luke 7:11–17.

8. Luke 8:42.

9. Luke 17:14.

10. John 6:67.

Chapter 17: Come Forth!

1. John 12:1–3.

2. John P. Meier, *A Marginal Jew: Rethinking the Historical Jesus*, vol. 2, *Mentor, Message, and Miracles* (New York: Doubleday, 1994), 776. Meier also notes that the same restoration to "ordinary life" happens with the son of the widow of Nain and the daughter of Jairus: "The return to ordinary life is intimated in various ways in each story of raising the dead."

3. John 21:21–23.

4. William Barclay, *The New Daily Study Bible*, vol. 2, *The Gospel of John* (Louisville: Westminster John Knox, 2001), 117.

5. Richard Beard, *Lazarus Is Dead: A Novel* (New York: Europa Editions, 2012), 224.

6. Jos Simon, *The Rough Guide to Cyprus* (London: APA Publications, 2016), 52. The people of Marseille and Autun may quibble with this final line in a sidebar on Agios Lazaros: "From Constantinople the Crusaders took the remains to Marseille, where they promptly disappeared never to be seen again."

7. Qoh. 9:5.

8. Richard Zimler, *The Gospel According to Lazarus* (London: Peter Owen Publishers, 2019), 337.

9. Deut. 30:19.

10. Luke 4:18–19.

For Further Exploration

In my research, writing, and prayer, I drew upon all these books in various ways and am grateful to all the authors. Rather than listing them as a bibliography I hope to give you a sense of each book so that you might explore the story of Lazarus further.

Anderson, Paul N., Felix Just, and Tom Thatcher, eds. *John, Jesus and History*, vol. 2, *Aspects of Historicity in the Fourth Gospel*. Atlanta: Society of Biblical Literature, 2009.

> This collection of fascinating papers by a group of international scholars, convened by the Society of Biblical Literature, looks at the historicity of John's Gospel. Three excellent essays explore material related to Lazarus: Richard Bauckham's "The Bethany Family in John 11–12: History or Fiction"; Ben Witherington III's "What's in a Name? Rethinking the Historical Figure of the Beloved Disciple in the Fourth Gospel," a landmark essay that focuses on Lazarus as the BD; and Derek M. H. Tovey's "On Not Unbinding the Lazarus Story: The Nexus of History and Theology in John 11: 1–44."

Andreyev, Leonid. "Lazarus," in *Selected Short Fiction of Leonid Andreyev*. Middletown, DE: Rusalka Books, 2020.

> In this short story Lazarus is less a figure to be celebrated than a figure of death. As in many fictional treatments of Lazarus, he ends up meeting the Roman emperor in this dark tale, written in 1906.

Augustine. "Tractate 49," *Tractates on the Gospel of John.*

> Saint Augustine's homily on the Raising of Lazarus is in keeping with some patristic literature focused on the effect of sin and includes some touching observations about Mary, Martha, and Lazarus.

Barclay, William. *The New Daily Study Bible,* vol. 2, *The Gospel of John.* Louisville: Westminster John Knox, 2001.

> William Barclay was a beloved New Testament scholar who wrote in a clear and vivid style, frequently offering real-life examples to illuminate his ideas. Grounded in careful scholarship, his take on Lazarus is especially helpful for homilists and preachers.

Beard, Richard. *Lazarus Is Dead: A Novel.* New York: Europa Editions, 2012.

> This lovely short novel toggles between an imagined story of Lazarus's death and raising and comments throughout on historical evidence as well as depictions of Lazarus in art.

Berry, George Ricker. *The Interlinear Literal Translation of the Greek New Testament.* Grand Rapids: Zondervan, 1974.

> As the title notes, this is a word-by-word and line-by-line translation of the Greek New Testament into English. You can find many similar resources online, for example, at BibleHub.com.

Brown, Raymond E. *The Gospel According to John I–XII: A New Translation with Introduction and Commentary.* Anchor Yale Bible 29. New York: Doubleday, 1966.

> Raymond Brown, SS, a Catholic priest, was one of the twentieth-century's great New Testament scholars, and this is his magisterial exegesis of the Gospel of John. This book, part of the Anchor Bible Commentary series, is one of the most thorough exegetical treatments of the narratives, done in Father Brown's careful style.

Brown, Raymond E. *An Introduction to the Gospel of John,* ed. Francis J. Moloney. New Haven, CT: Yale Univ. Press, 2003.

> Completed after his death by another renowned Johannine scholar, Francis J. Moloney, Father Brown's revision of an introduction to his

landmark Anchor Bible Commentary series (above) is a wonderfully accessible introduction to many themes in the Fourth Gospel.

Byrne, Brendan. *Lazarus: A Contemporary Reading of John 11:1–46.* Collegeville, MN: Liturgical Press, 1991.

> This may be the best short treatment by a New Testament scholar on Lazarus. Father Byrne looks at the story line by line and in great depth. He treats both the text (as a scholar) and the underlying meaning (as a believer). Father Byrne's monograph is a treasure for Lazarus lovers, and I learned something new on almost every page. Byrne's more recent book, *Come to the Light: Reflections on the Gospel of John* (Collegeville, MN: Liturgical Press, 2021), a series of meditations on the Fourth Gospel, also has a succinct, personal, and very powerful chapter on the Raising of Lazarus.

Cain, Bill. *The Diary of Jesus Christ.* Maryknoll, NY: Orbis Books, 2021.

> A lively, incisive, and at times even playful fictional memoir of the Son of God by a talented screenwriter (and brother Jesuit). In his chapter "A Cure for Death," Jesus writes his memories of the raising of his friend, whose family "controlled a big part of the building trade." Touchingly, he asks Lazarus to call to him at his own death.

Chancey, Mark A. *Greco-Roman Culture and the Galilee of Jesus.* Cambridge: Cambridge Univ. Press, 2005.

> A scholarly look at the combination of Hellenistic (Greek) and Roman cultures alive in Galilee at the time of Jesus. Helpful for understanding Jesus's public ministry as well as the overall milieu in which he and many of the disciples lived.

Charlesworth, James H. *The Beloved Disciple: Whose Witness Validates the Gospel of John?* Valley Forge, PA: Trinity Press International, 1995.

> A model of careful scholarship, this book examines the possible candidates for the Beloved Disciple and includes a good (and far-reaching, in terms of time and place) summary of the various scholarly arguments for and against one or another person. Charlesworth sets forth arguments both in favor of and against Lazarus. In the end, he believes that it is not Lazarus but the Apostle Thomas who has the greater claim.

Crossan, John Dominic. *The Historical Jesus: The Life of a Mediterranean Jewish Peasant*. San Francisco: HarperSanFrancisco, 1991.

> One of the great contemporary works of scholarship on the "Historical Jesus" (looking at what we can know about Jesus from purely historical sources, rather than from the perspective of faith), by a professor of biblical studies. Crossan was a member of a group of scholars called the Jesus Seminar, which, in the 1990s, revived interest in what is often called the "search for the Historical Jesus."

Crossan, John Dominic, and Jonathan L. Reed. *Excavating Jesus: Beneath the Stones, Behind the Text*. New York: HarperCollins, 2001.

> A scholar of the Historical Jesus (Crossan) and a professor of New Testament studies and archaeologist (Reed) team up to look at archaeological finds that shed light on the life of Jesus of Nazareth and daily life in Galilee and Judea.

Dear, John. *Lazarus Come Forth! How Jesus Confronts the Culture of Death and Invites Us into a New Life of Peace*. Maryknoll, NY: Orbis Books, 2011.

> An often-brilliant book by a Catholic priest and peace activist that looks at how Jesus not only confronts death but an entire culture and worldview of death, in the process challenging our ignorance and denial of a militaristic and war-loving world. I read John's book toward the end of my writing and research, but still found new insights, after having read countless books on Lazarus.

Dodd, C. H. *The Interpretation of the Fourth Gospel*. Cambridge: Cambridge Univ. Press, 1953.

> Dodd was one of the most well-known biblical scholars of the mid-twentieth century and had a knack for writing in a clear, accessible style. His book on John's Gospel uses the Greek liberally (but, sadly, with no transliteration) and is a model of careful scholarship.

Gibran, Kahlil. *Lazarus and His Beloved*. New York: New York Graphic Society, 1973.

> In the only play written by Gibran, a Lebanese poet and philosopher, Lazarus, in dialogue with his sisters, regrets being raised from the dead, preferring to be with God in death.

Harrington, Daniel J. *Meeting St. John Today: Understanding the Man, His Mission, and His Message*. Chicago: Loyola Press, 2011.

An excellent short overview of John's Gospel by an eminent Jesuit New Testament scholar and my professor of New Testament in graduate school.

Howard-Brook, Wes. *Becoming Children of God: John's Gospel and Radical Discipleship*. Maryknoll, NY: Orbis Books, 1994.

One of the most provocative and original books around on John's Gospel, written by a legal scholar, theologian, and social-justice advocate. Howard-Brook focuses on the response necessitated in the real world by what John's Gospel elaborates and offers original insights on the Fourth Gospel (and Martha, Mary, and Lazarus) that I found nowhere else.

Howard-Brook, Wes. *John's Gospel and the Renewal of the Church*. Maryknoll, NY: Orbis Books, 1997.

A close reading of John's Gospel, with an emphasis on the demands for social justice and the "conversion" of the church. Frequently brilliant.

Johnson, Elizabeth A. *Consider Jesus: Waves of Renewal in Christology*. New York: Continuum Books, 1992.

A superb short book on Christology, that is, how we understand who Jesus was (and is). Her section on Jesus's self-consciousness is especially good—and clear. Probably the best short introduction to contemporary Christology around.

Kazantzakis, Nikos. *The Last Temptation of Christ*. New York: Simon & Schuster, 1960.

In one of the most well-known novelizations of the Gospels (later made into a riveting film by Martin Scorsese), Kazantzakis offers a vivid (but brief) portrayal of the Raising of Lazarus as well as his (fictional) death at the hand of Barabbas.

Lagerkvist, Pär. *Barabbas*. New York: Vintage, 1951.

Later made into a film starring Anthony Quinn, this novel follows the life of the man released by the crowd on Good Friday in Jesus's stead. His encounter with Lazarus is an encounter with someone who still carries death with him.

Levine, Amy-Jill. *The Misunderstood Jew: The Church and the Scandal of the Jewish Jesus*. San Francisco: HarperOne, 2006.

> A brilliant, even essential, book in which a New Testament scholar highlights the many lazy stereotypes unthinkingly passed down from generation to generation about Judaism in Jesus's time. Levine expertly situates Jesus in the life and times in which he lived and shows how the Judaism of the time was far more complex (and compassionate) than most contemporary Christians believe.

Lohfink, Gerhard. *Jesus of Nazareth: What He Wanted, Who He Was*. Collegeville, MN: Liturgical Press, 2015.

> When Lohfink's beautiful book on Jesus was first published, the eminent New Testament scholar Daniel J. Harrington, SJ, called it "the best Jesus book I know." No wonder: it is beautifully written and always insightful. His comments on Jesus's "resident disciples," who didn't follow Jesus along the road, is helpful in understanding the roles of Mary, Martha, and Lazarus. Still, Lohfink is clear in calling Lazarus a "friend," not a "disciple."

Magness, Jodi. *Stone and Dung, Oil and Spit: Jewish Daily Life in the Time of Jesus*. Grand Rapids: Eerdmans, 2011.

> This fascinating book by an expert in early Judaism looks at archaeology and ancient literature to help us understand daily life in Galilee and Judea. Her chapter "Tombs and Burial Customs" is especially useful when exploring the story of Lazarus.

Marcombe, David. *Leper Knights: The Order of St. Lazarus of Jerusalem in England, c. 1150–1544*. Woodbridge: Boydell Press, 2003.

> Though focused on the military and charitable religious order's activities in England, Marcombe's exhaustive history does a good job of untangling the obscure history of this utterly fascinating group dedicated to Lazarus. Beginning with the earliest days of the order, Marcombe details the origins of a religious community, still extant, that began in Jerusalem in the twelfth century and early on included both the healthy and "lepers."

Marrow, Stanley B. *The Gospel of John: A Reading*. Mahwah, NJ: Paulist Press, 1993.

Father Marrow taught John's Gospel to generations of students (and me) in graduate theology studies at the old Weston Jesuit School of Theology (now the Boston College School of Theology and Ministry). His passage-by-passage examination of John's Gospel offers both exegesis and pastoral insights.

McCarren, Paul J. *A Simple Guide to John*. Lanham, MD: Sheed & Ward, 2013.

Part of the Simple Guide to the Gospels series, this compact book offers an accessible introduction to John's Gospel, passage by passage.

Meier, John P. *A Marginal Jew: Rethinking the Historical Jesus*, vol. 2, *Mentor, Message, and Miracles*. New York: Doubleday, 1994.

Meier's colossal series *A Marginal Jew* is the *sine qua non* of studies on the "Historical Jesus" (what we can know about the life and times of Jesus of Nazareth, versus more theological considerations). His analysis of the Lazarus story carefully examines each of the elements for its historicity, and he also posits a hypothetical reconstruction of the original "primitive" story that was later edited by the writer of John's Gospel.

Moloney, Francis J. *The Gospel of John*. Sacra Pagina 4. Collegeville, MN: Liturgical Press, 1998.

The Sacra Pagina series is probably the best New Testament commentary around. Each volume, edited by Daniel J. Harrington, SJ, offers careful scholarship, thoughtful insights, and expert historical analysis of the book in question passage by passage. (It covers each book in the New Testament.) This book is no exception—a boon for anyone interested in learning more about the Fourth Gospel. Father Moloney is especially good at responding to the various schools of thought on John's Gospel, including the Lazarus narrative.

Moloney, Francis J. *Signs and Shadows: Reading John 5–12*. Minneapolis: Fortress, 1996.

A close reading of these chapters from John's Gospel, in a somewhat less academic presentation than the Sacra Pagina series (above).

O'Neill, Eugene. "Lazarus Laughed," in *Nine Plays*. New York: Modern Library, 1959.

This highly allegorical drama features a raised Lazarus as an apostle for laughing at death (literally: he laughs a good deal in this rather strange play).

Pixner, Bargil. *With Jesus Through Galilee According to the Fifth Gospel* and *With Jesus in Jerusalem: His First and Last Days in Judea*. Israel: Corazin Publishing, 1992.

Both lavishly illustrated books, by a Benedictine monk who had lived in Jerusalem for twenty-five years and was prior of Dormition Abbey in the Old City, offer insights about the Holy Land and Jesus's public ministry that I've not run across in any other book. Father Pixner's deep knowledge of the area, including Bethany, shines through in both books.

Sanders, E. P. *Judaism: Practice and Belief, 63 BCE–66 CE*. New York: Continuum Books, 1992.

A scholarly overview of Jewish religious practice in the time of Jesus. The chapter "Hopes for the Future" is a fine examination of Jewish beliefs on the afterlife.

Schneiders, Sandra M. *Written That You May Believe: Encountering Jesus in the Fourth Gospel*. New York: Crossroad, 2003.

Schneiders's book on the Gospel of John includes the fascinating insight that Jesus came to establish a community of equals. Solid research and a feminist perspective help inform this accessible and inviting commentary.

Seidel, Linda. *Legends in Limestone: Lazarus, Gislebertus, and the Cathedral of Autun*. Chicago: Univ. of Chicago Press, 1999.

A thorough overview of the cathedral in Autun, France, named after St. Lazarus and known mainly for its stunning tympanum of the Last Judgment. Seidel, an art historian, traces the traditions associated with Lazarus's relics and the connection between the tomb in Bethany and the architecture of the reliquary tomb in Autun.

Stibbe, Mark W. G. *John as Storyteller: Narrative Criticism and the Fourth Gospel*. Cambridge: Cambridge Univ. Press, 1992.

This difficult-to-categorize book is both a traditional exegesis of John's Gospel and a look at it as a literary whole. His section on Lazarus as the

Beloved Disciple is especially strong and clear. As befits a book on literary style, it is also beautifully written.

Tóibín, Colm. *The Testament of Mary.* New York: Scribner, 2012.

A fictional memoir by a brilliant novelist. Jesus's mother's reminiscences include a finely wrought narrative of the Raising of Lazarus. Strangely, Jesus's own resurrection is presented as a dream, which makes one wonder: If Lazarus can be raised, why not Jesus?

Weaver, Joanna. *Lazarus Awakening: Finding Your Place in the Heart of God.* New York: WaterBrook Press, 2011.

Written by a popular Christian author, this charming and effective spirituality book offers many helpful insights into the story and draws connections between Lazarus's story and our own. Weaver's passages on the various "stones" in our lives is especially good.

Witherington, Ben, III. *What Have They Done with Jesus? Beyond Strange Theories and Bad History—Why We Can Trust the Bible.* San Francisco: HarperOne, 2006.

This fascinating book, written by a world-renowned New Testament scholar, looks at the historicity of various aspects of Jesus's life and the lives of his disciples. It is presented in a clear and lucid style and includes an entire section that fleshes out Witherington's theory of why Lazarus is the mysterious Beloved Disciple in John's Gospel.

Yeats, William Butler. *Calvary.* Digireads.com, 2011.

In this short play, the Irish-born poet uses the style of Japanese Noh drama to construct a drama of mainly dialogue, in which Lazarus bitterly regrets his being brought back to life.

Zimler, Richard. *The Gospel According to Lazarus.* London: Peter Owen Publishers, 2019.

This tremendously effective novel brings to life all the important real-life characters in the story—Jesus, Lazarus, Mary, and Martha—as well as other fictional ones. At times I was stunned at how successful this novel is in conjuring up the world of first-century Judea.